FAMILY

Susan Hill was born in Scarborough, Yorkshire, in 1942. She was educated at grammar schools there and in Coventry and studied at King's College, London. Her works include *Gentleman and Ladies*, *A Change for the Better*, *I'm the King of the Castle* (Somerset Maugham Prize), *The Albatross and other stories* (John Llewelyn Rhys Memorial Prize), *Strange Meeting*, *The Bird of Night* (Whitbread Award), *A Bit of Singing and Dancing*, *In the Springtime of the Year*, *The Woman in Black* and *Lanterns Across the Snow*, as well as the illustrated *Shakespeare Country* and *The Spirit of the Cotswolds*. She has also written books for children, *One Night at a Time*, *Mother's Magic* and *Can It Be True?* (Smarties Prize), and an autobiographical book, *The Magic Apple Tree*. In addition she has edited the Penguin Classics edition of Thomas Hardy's *The Distracted Preacher and Other Tales* and is a regular broadcaster and book reviewer for various journals and newspapers.

Susan Hill is married to the Shakespeare scholar Stanley Wells. They have two daughters and live in the Oxfordshire countryside.

Susan Hill

Family

PENGUIN BOOKS

PENGUIN BOOKS

Published by the Penguin Group
27 Wrights Lane, London W8 5TZ, England
Viking Penguin Inc., 40 West 23rd Street, New York, New York 10010, USA
Penguin Books Australia Ltd, Ringwood, Victoria, Australia
Penguin Books Canada Ltd, 2801 John Street, Markham, Ontario, Canada L3R 1B4
Penguin Books (NZ) Ltd, 182–190 Wairau Road, Auckland 10, New Zealand

Penguin Books Ltd, Registered Offices: Harmondsworth, Middlesex, England

First published by Michael Joseph 1989
Published in Penguin Books 1990
1 3 5 7 9 10 8 6 4 2

Copyright © Susan Hill, 1989
All rights reserved

Made and printed in Great Britain by
Cox & Wyman Ltd, Reading, Berks.

Except in the United States of America,
this book is sold subject to the condition
that it shall not, by way of trade or otherwise,
be lent, re-sold, hired out, or otherwise circulated
without the publisher's prior consent in any form of
binding or cover other than that in which it is
published and without a similar condition
including this condition being imposed
on the subsequent purchaser

Imogen Susanna Wells

27 May – 30 June 1984

'a lily of a day'

Contents

Author's Note

At her birth in 1984, Imogen was admitted to what was then known as the Special Care Baby Unit (SCBU) of the John Radcliffe Hospital in Oxford, and this is the name still used in some hospitals and familiar to many people. But the name preferred by the medical profession is now Special Care Nursery which is the term I have used throughout this book.

Acknowledgements

The extract on page 25 is taken from *The Pursuit of Love* by Nancy Mitford and is reprinted by permission of the Peters Fraser and Dunlop Group Ltd.

The quotations on page 137 are from *Pregnancy* by Gordon Bourne and are reprinted by permission of Cassell plc. *Pregnancy* is also available in a Pan paperback.

Foreword

When I began to plan this book, I thought that it was going to be simply the story of Imogen, my second child, who was born three months prematurely and died at the age of five weeks; but the moment I began to think about it in depth, and then to write, I discovered that it was about a great many other things that formed the background to her life and death.

Principally, then, this is the story of the obsessive determination to succeed in having another child: in writing about that, I had to investigate the reasons for it. My search took me, slightly to my own surprise, back to my own birth and early childhood.

This is an entirely personal story. I am writing mainly about myself and my family and speaking only for us. I am unqualified to do anything else.

I began the book because other women urged me to do so, and continued with it in the hope that it might prove of interest and help to them: to women in the throes of trying to have a child, women battling with infertility problems, women enduring miscarriage and its aftermath, women who have suffered the stillbirth of an infant, a premature birth, or neonatal death; women who have had any of the thousand-and-one complications, mishaps and miseries that are commonplace in our maternity hospitals every day (even though so very many others do, of course, sail through pregnancy and childbirth without any problems at all).

Such women are vulnerable, afraid, depressed, bewildered,

tired and isolated: they need moral support, loving care, friendship, reassurance and tactful handling – I know. They also need the encouragement of others who have been in the same or a similar boat, who have survived and come through; they need the message of hope that, however awful the disasters that may have struck them, however many the setbacks, things so often do go right in the end (though of course it would be quite wrong to suggest that they always do).

The book draws no general conclusions and makes no comparisons. The details of any treatment and advice I received will be recognised by other women as being common practice in most maternity hospitals and Special Care Nurseries today, but nevertheless these should not be taken as anything other than descriptions of what happened in *my own particular case*.

I was a private patient entirely from choice, in order to be assured of consultant care, for reasons which I explain in the course of the book, and to have the comfort of a single room. (In the event, because of the problems that arose during my pregnancy with Imogen, I would have been looked after by a consultant and given a room of my own in any case.)

Imogen was not a private patient because there are no such things in the Special Care Nurseries of National Health Service hospitals, and the treatment and care she and I received would have been exactly the same for a National Health Service maternity patient and her baby in the circumstances. Nothing extra was done for us, we did not 'buy' any special privileges, we jumped no queues, received no preferential treatment in any department.

Imogen's story is at the heart of the book, and it is to the constant and loving memory of her that it is dedicated.

But it is also dedicated in great gratitude to many other people, to all those without whose love, care, skill and support we would none of us have come through, and to all the women who wrote or talked to me about their own experiences and, in telling their stories, helped both themselves and me.

I owe to my own mother, as well as to Matron Evans of

Scarborough, a debt which I can never now repay. To have seen my daughters would have been their best reward.

Many people among the doctors, nurses and ancillary medical staff who cared for us ought to be personally thanked, but must be included in a general tribute, and this especially embraces those at the John Radcliffe Maternity Hospital in Oxford. From no one there did I ever receive an impatient, thoughtless or brusque word, but was treated throughout with unfailing concern, friendliness and efficiency. To a woman in a vulnerable state of mind and body, that meant everything.

To everyone in the Neonatal Unit at the John Radcliffe, during Imogen's life there, my gratitude is still inexpressible. They cared for her as if she were their own.

The consultant in charge of the unit, Dr Andrew Wilkinson, was absent in the United States at that time; nevertheless, he has taken a close personal interest in the Imogen Wells Fund, of which he is a Trustee, and in this book. While I have been writing it, he has been more than generous with his time, advice and assistance, all in the course of a heavy work schedule. He read the book in typescript and made valuable corrections and comments, and I am especially grateful to him for his help.

He also introduced me to Dr Patricia Hamilton at St George's Hospital, London, and I owe thanks to her and members of her team for allowing me to spend a day in their unit; this proved most helpful in putting my own experience of having a premature baby into general perspective, and gave me impartial and up-to-date information and advice.

To Mark Charnock, doctor and friend, my family and I owe more than gratitude, for his professional care and unfailing encouragement over the course of many weary months; and our debt extends to his wife Margaret for the uncomplaining cheerfulness with which she endured her husband's absences from home on our behalf.

Many woman friends and their families shared in the experiences recounted in this book, and gave us both practical help and loving support – especially Judy Bogdanor, Ann Campbell, Pam Edmonds-Seal, Pat Gardner, Louisa Lane Fox, Polly Mitchell, and Joan Tranter and her staff at

Greycotes School, Oxford. The personal experiences of other woman friends were an inspiration to me, especially those of Angela Howard-Johnson, Gillian Morriss Kay and Emily Petherbridge.

Anne Robinson has not only typed the book perfectly from my near-illegible handwriting, she has helped me to keep going through the writing of it and bravely re-lived her own painful past experiences as she has worked.

For the rest and greatest part, my debt is to my family.

Clemency came to crown a sad story with joy at the last, but Jessica illumined much of its course with her own bright presence, as well as sharing in both the grief and the gladness.

For my husband's abiding love and steadfast strength there really are no adequate words of gratitude but perhaps, after all, none are necessary.

An end and a beginning

September. Towards the end of the afternoon of a day poised between late summer and early autumn.

I sat in the garden beneath the magic apple tree.

Below me, on the other side of the low stone wall, the countryside fell away, the meadows sloping down to the stream and the line of willow trees that stand beside it, and then rising gently up again, to the far, high slope of the other side of the village.

Here, there are still unploughed pastures, copses and spinneys and woods of broadleaved trees and, braiding the fields, undisturbed hedgerows. The leaves had not yet begun to turn – or had they? I looked, and everywhere was the dark, even green of late August, but looked again, and there, surely, was the first flash of yellow.

The corn had long since ripened and been harvested, the combines had droned through all the day and in the last of the light, the wagons had toiled up the lane past our cottage gate, laden high as the roof with the bales of straw.

Now, looking down on to Otmoor, I could see the earth, dark as mahogany again, freshly turned over and ready for the sowing of winter wheat, for when fields are farmed intensively for corn, the poor earth works hard for its living, it has little time to rest and recuperate between crops – like a woman who goes with scarcely a pause, from baby to baby.

Ah . . .

In the garden, the sweet-pea frame and the bean wigwam

stood tall, and there were still a few last flowers to be cut, some beans still hung down like green sword blades, waiting, if we did not pick them in time, to be caught and pinched by the first of the frosts. On the other side of the garden, the hollyhocks, tall too, like gangling girls dressed in washed-out cotton dresses, and the sunflowers, and the michaelmas daisies, just beginning.

The apple trees were laden, branches bent over like the backs of very old women, under the weight of their fruit. And berries everywhere, in the garden and beyond the garden, all along the hedgerows, berries and fruits, blood red, damson dark, blackberries, sloes, rowans, elder. In the farthest corner, one of my favourite plants of all, Honesty – its Latin name, a true description, *Lunaria annua*, for the seed pods are papery pale and translucent, exactly like small full moons.

There was still some warmth left in the last of the sun, but the air, when the breeze stirred it and shifted the branches of the apple tree, smelled unmistakably of autumn, slightly damp, earthy, mushroomy. And then, curling into my nostrils, came the smoke of someone's bonfire from across the valley – wood smoke, pungent, nostalgic, slightly melancholy.

On the wall the cats sat, newly emerged from the day's sleep on cushions, under beds, beginning to wash and think about darkness and the prowling, hunting night ahead. But the dog lay, nose on crossed paws, not asleep, just content and companionable.

Soon the rest of the family would be home. There would be a stirring; activity, conversation, a different mood.

But for now, I sat on in the late sunlight, entirely settled, entirely content, heartbeat slow, breathing still. I remember the moment, the hour, the day, with extraordinary vividness because all of a sudden, everything seemed to be intensely clear, brilliant, heightened, and I was *aware*, in a great rush of awareness, of knowing, seeing, feeling, understanding: aware of myself, of where I was, now, here, and how I had arrived here, aware of time seeming to stand still and the world ceasing to turn, and of the past and the present and the future coming together, telescoping into one another and fusing, so that there was no difference or distinction between them. It was, I suppose, simply a moment of vision.

Beside me, in the white wicker crib under the apple tree boughs, my infant daughter, my third child, lay quietly sleeping, the fingers of one hand curled up towards her face, her hair dark, dark on the white mattress. Clemency Isabella Grace.

Then the last four years and a whole chain of other events reaching way way further back into my own past came together. I saw them in one total, complete picture, re-experienced them, knew them for what they were and completely grasped their simple meaning. It was extraordinary, and perhaps like we are told the moment of death will be, or as people have described their experiences at those moments when they have thought they were on the point of death.

Except that that unreeling of a whole lifetime, so they say, only lasts for a split second but my vision of everything that had brought me to this moment, here in my September garden, stayed with me, and even opened out so that I had ample time to examine it in detail, and reflect upon it.

So I sat on and reached out my hand to touch my sleeping child, and remembered, lovingly, gladly, vividly, wonderingly. Gratefully remembered. I retraced the steps of a journey. It ended here.

But where, where did it begin?

Part I

Part of the Past

Chapter 1

With a small girl on a beach, perhaps. Although, of course, in one sense the story must go back further than that: beyond my own childhood lay that of my mother, and then of hers, and this is a story about mothers and daughters, and all of them have played a part.

But those are details I can never trace. I can only remember my own childhood, and see how important certain things in it must have been in forming the person I was to become, and helping to direct the course of the journey I was to take.

And most important of all, perhaps, were those Saturday and Sunday afternoons which always began with our walk along the beach.

Those memories are always of winter, never of summer. In summer, we set out from home and took a different route to my godmother's house, through the streets and quiet residential avenues, with an occasional detour to enjoy the cliff-top parks and gardens. For my mother greatly disapproved of the beaches of our town in the summer season; she was snobbish about the charabanc loads of day-trippers and incurably anxious on my account about crowds and germs – polio from bathing, septicaemia from bare feet cut on broken glass, food poisoning from ice-creams. She disliked all the things that held such forbidden glamour for me, the pleasure-grounds and the fun fair, the winkle stalls, the rock shops, the ghost train, the fish and chips, the rows and rows and rows of deckchairs.

But when the visitors had departed and the peace of winter

came again, we returned, to walk to my godmother's via the beach, and best of all, if the tide was out, across the whole stretch of the sand itself. I was always far behind my mother, partly because she walked so fast, with quick, short, determined strides although she was only very small – barely five feet in height. I could never keep up with her.

But more, I wanted to dawdle, to be as 'by myself' as I could, to enjoy the glory of it all. Children generally accept where they happen to find themselves living without much question, and I suppose it has only been in later life, miles away from Yorkshire and the sea, that I have fully appreciated all the joys of living there, and recognised my own childhood luck.

But when I was out of doors, on the beach during those winter weekend afternoons, I know that I was totally happy, and that I never failed to look up and all around me with wonder and delight. Scarborough, that Regency spa town built upon the cliffs above the great North Sea, has a breathtakingly beautiful setting, and I can still feel my own pleasure in running, running, across the wet, hard, flat sand, with the wide sky all above and around, towards that expanse of sea, remember the feel of the wind as it stung my face, and the rawk of the seagulls, how I loved the light and the space, and the smell of the air, the taste of the salt on my lips when I licked them.

After that came the pleasure of hurrying away, as the wind blew up the grey banks of cloud, before the rain and the dark and the storm came, hurrying behind my brisk mother, up the steep winding paths of the cliff towards the esplanade above, and on to the glowing, sweet-smelling haven of my god-mother's kitchen.

Whenever I dream of my childhood, I am either alone on that winter beach, or there in my godmother's kitchen where the loaves of new-baked bread stood in a row on the table beneath the wooden rack of drying nappies, and the kettle sang on the black range.

They are dreams so rich and glorious that I don't think I ever wake without knowing a moment of the purest disappointment and grief for the loss of that past, for I was as happy in that house as I have ever been in my life.

To begin with, I was born there, and years afterwards I was to

12

learn from my mother a great deal about that time, for she reminisced endlessly and in detail so that I could picture her, knew so much about her experiences and what she thought and felt. Though sometimes, in re-telling her part of this story, I have had to try and put myself in her shoes and *imagine* how it was.

In 1941, the world was at war; my father was away in the Royal Air Force and my mother was on her own in a strange new town, expecting her first child.

She had come to Scarborough, as she had done so many significant things in her life, on a sudden whim. Years before, she had left her own family home because she was determined to have a career, be independent, and because she had been quite unable to live with her own mother and sister. Like most of her generation, she had left school at the age of fourteen, but although not well-educated by today's standards she was intelligent and well-read, and also extremely talented as a seamstress and dress-designer. She had gone into the fashion trade and learned the business from the bottom, 'picking up the pins'. She was headstrong, knew exactly what she wanted, worked prodigiously hard.

By the time the war came, her career had taken her to Edinburgh and there, in her early thirties, she had met what I now realise was the one love of her life. He was an officer in the Polish army, stationed in Great Britain, and my mother would have given up everything she had worked for in her own life, her own country, to marry him. But because he was a serviceman, permission had to be sought from his superiors before he could marry anyone, let alone a foreigner. It was refused, and Stefan was posted straight back to Poland. My mother never saw or heard from him again.

Bitter, angry and desperately unhappy, she made a characteristically abrupt and reckless decision. She would go out at once and look for a husband, and she would marry the first man she could persuade to ask her, no matter whether she cared for, or even liked him, or not.

So, in April 1941, she met and married my father who was stationed briefly in Scotland. By the following month, she was pregnant; that autumn he was posted away. Perhaps in a state of shock at what she had done, and no longer wanting or having any reason to remain in the city which held so many memories for her, my mother cast about for a place to go. She wanted to rest, to take stock of the sudden changes in her life, have a holiday, be alone.

Scarborough. She had never been there, but someone had told her how beautiful it was, and she felt that the sea air would do her good. Her marriage may have been a sudden and strange one, but she wanted to do the best she could for her child. Besides, Scarborough in Yorkshire was a quiet resort, a safer place to be in war-time than any city.

She could, of course, have gone back to her own family, in an equally quiet county, Lancashire, but she would never do that: she had made her decision, burned her boats, and she was nothing if not proud. (The first her family learned of my father's existence was in a letter written a month after the wedding.)

No, she would go to Scarborough mainly because it had no associations for her, find a place to stay, and be alone with her pregnancy. Whether I could have taken myself off like that, in similar circumstances, I don't know, but I am delighted that she did because my birthplace, my home town, was such a rare and remarkable one, and was to make a profound impact upon me as I grew up. I have always believed very strongly in the influences of places upon people, and how those places help to make them what they are.

The moment my mother arrived in Scarborough, she loved it – the bracing air, the sea, the magnificent views, the elegant Regency buildings and the society of the town. She booked herself into a small hotel on the South Cliff but, quickly realising how happy and settled she felt in the place, decided to rent a small furnished flat and stay as long as she felt like it. (In the end, that was sixteen years, and she did not leave from choice.)

She was extremely fit which was as well, since in those days, women were not given the meticulous, month-by-month ante-natal care that had become routine by the time I had my own children. In the 1940s, you found out that you were pregnant (and confirmation of that could take a long time: there were no speedy morning-after home test kits then), registered with your doctor, and booked a place for your confinement, unless you were planning to have the baby at home. If all was well at that first consultation, you probably didn't see anyone again until the birth.

But my mother was thirty-five, then as now considered on the old side to have a first baby – and she had been brought up with a great respect, almost amounting to awe, for doctors. She not only registered with a good one in the town, but asked to be referred to a consultant obstetrician. It was he who recommended that she book a bed in the private nursing home he attended. (There was no National Health Service in 1941: all medical treatment had to be paid for, and confinement in a general hospital was reserved for seriously ill and high-risk mothers.) At her age, and living alone, my mother was not considered a good candidate for a home delivery.

And so, one September morning, she walked from her flat, along the beach and up the cliff path, through the gardens, towards a tall Edwardian house set at the top of a rise and with a view of the grey North Sea.

The board at the gate read Dybdale Nursing Home. The brass plate over the bell on the front door was engraved – Miss G. Evans, SRN Matron. My mother rang and was shown into a small hall that smelled of beeswax furniture polish and disinfectant. There were flowers in a copper bowl on the table and small ornaments, and pictures on the wall – one of an English cottage garden, all crown imperials and gillyflowers; the other, a reproduction of Jesus, the Light of the World, that captivating, sentimental picture by Holman Hunt, so loved by the pre-war generations. From upstairs came the cry of a baby; from downstairs, the rattle of teacups. A bell rang, voices called.

As my mother stepped into the hall and stood waiting to be ushered into the Matron's room, she felt, I think for the first time in years, that she was at home. The house was welcoming, the atmosphere was friendly. So this would be all right then. Here she would be more than happy to have her baby. She would be safe, comfortable, cared for. She had visited enough sick aunts and elderly neighbours in other nursing homes in the past to know that they were by no means all like this, that many felt cold and forbidding, unfriendly, not places in which you would ever want to linger. This one was very different.

And then the maid in the blue apron reappeared. Matron would see her now. She was led down to the basement to meet for the first time the woman who was to prove so very important a person in the next few years of her life, and the first of mine.

She was called Matron by her staff and patients, Miss Evans by people outside, but I can only ever think of her by the name I learned to call her from the beginning – Aunty Matron.

She was a very small Welshwoman, with blue eyes, a sharp, slightly red-veined face, a pointed nose, and grey hair that was cut straight and short but somehow still managed to frizz out on both sides from under her starched white cap. She had been trained in the old, hard and strict school of nursing, at St Thomas's Hospital in London, before the First World War.

By the time my mother arrived in her sitting-room that day, Miss Evans was well on in her sixties, and she had as much energy as anyone of half that age – energy and efficiency, a briskness that concealed great warmth, and iron-strong Christian principles. She did not merely lead her staff, she worked with them, alongside them. In the years I knew her, I saw her do every job in the place, emptying the slops, kneading the bread, carrying tea trays, turning bedridden elderly patients, pacing the floor with crying babies. She asked nothing of anyone that she did not do herself. She acted as midwife, accompanied the consultants on their rounds, called the priest, laid out the dead.

And it was entirely typical of her that she should have seen my mother on that first morning, not in an office, which was what my mother had expected, but in her own sitting-room.

It is a room I remember so well from my early childhood that when I close my eyes, I am back there, sitting on the over-stuffed pale blue moquette sofa, admiring the antimacassar embroidered with a picture of a lady in a crinoline and large bonnet. A small room, with small tables covered in ornaments, brass, china, glass, presents from grateful patients.

In winter, a coal fire always burned brightly in the grate, and

16

at any time of the year at all, there might well be a little wooden crib, with a baby tightly rolled in white swaddling sheets, sleeping on the canvas slung between its struts. For any baby that was fretful or fractious, or about which she was mildly worried, Aunty Matron kept close to her, in her own room beside the fire and even beside her own bed. As often as not, when I went to visit on those Saturday and Sunday afternoons, she had a baby somewhere about her person, tucked neat and tight under her arm while she went about some other business.

The babies born in the Dybdale Nursing Home were loved babies. They spent their time there as part of a family that extended from the room of their own mother, down into the nursery and the kitchen and Aunty Matron's own sitting-room. When there were a lot of them, their cribs used to cluster in the dining-room where the doctor would often be eating a meal after a late round or a long delivery.

My earliest memories are of that place and of the astonishing, loved and loving woman who became my godmother. And of babies. Babies howling, babies brought down red and slimy from birth, to be washed in a bowl of warm water on the kitchen table: babies in rows of cribs, sleeping fast, babies being suckled, babies being carried up the steep stairs from the basement to their mothers, two tucked under each of my godmother's arms. It was there that I first knew the smells of babies. When I was five or six years old, I used to go quietly by myself into the nursery, or my godmother's room and stand looking down at them in wonder, taking in every detail about them, the way the pulse throbbed close to the fragile-looking skin on the top of their heads, the down on their cheeks, the way they seemed so curled up within themselves, still part of some other secret world. I liked to listen to their snuffling, and watch them as they stirred and shifted and raised their eyelids and wrinkled their brows in sleep, simply to stand there, with the bright fire glowing, and be with them. It was the beginning of a passionate involvement with and close physical feeling for very small babies which became submerged in adolescence and early womanhood so that I forgot that it was there until it surfaced again with such overwhelming force, many years later.

It was from Matron Evans, from her midwives and nurses,

but as much as anything simply from being about the maternity home, that I absorbed a great deal of information about babies, and in particular about the process of childbirth. I was never actually told, as many children have to be, how they grew inside their mothers and then were born – the facts of life were all around me and no one made any attempt to hide them, though they were, it has to be said, partial and rather biased facts. For this was an almost exclusively female world. The doctor was called in only when things became too difficult, dangerous or protracted for my godmother and the other midwives to cope with – and although she never took unnecessary risks, it was a matter of pride with Matron Evans that this was rarely. Fathers played a wholly attendant and decorative supporting role in the business. They appeared, perhaps, at the beginning when bringing their wives into the nursing home, and then were banished to perform their traditional ritual of floor-pacing elsewhere until informed of the good news some time later. After that, during the lying-in period – a long one, up to two weeks, then – they merely brought flowers and sat beside beds and peered briefly into cribs for the strictly limited visiting hours. As this was wartime, many fathers never appeared at all, so the mothers were visited by more women, their own mothers and sisters, and the female atmosphere of the place was scarcely disturbed.

The result of this, and of my own absentee father, combined with the reticence of the times about sex, meant that I had a curiously lopsided view of the business of babies, knowing far more than most children ever learn about some aspects of it, and absolutely nothing about the rest. At the age of six, I could have told you almost anything you wanted to know about how babies were born, in considerable obstetric detail. Indeed, I was once summoned before the Sister Superior of my convent school for doing just that.

One of my class mates had a new baby brother and was regaling us, in the dark privacy of the cloakroom, behind the coats, about how her parents had acquired him. They had, she said, gone to the hospital some months before and chosen a baby from a lot of little seed packets – exactly like those you had in the garden shed in springtime. The hospital had then grown the baby in a special crib, and when he was ripe to be picked, as it were, they had gone back to fetch him. I can still remember the scorn with which I listened to this preposterous tale, and my own anxious wish to put everyone right by giving them the true version of events. I did so, in clear and exact detail – though I have to say that I was completely disbelieved, my story being voted far more fantastic and unlikely than the original version. And although I had been speaking in a stage whisper, one of those ever-present, entirely silent nuns had been gliding by and had stopped to overhear. The consequences were most unpleasant and the lecture I received about chastity, and impurity of thought and word, and corruption of innocence, was fearsome. Its aim was to crush and humiliate, as well as to prompt remorse and repentance. In fact, it had a completely different effect. I was angry, and I was indignant, and I made that much quite clear for I knew, I *knew* what was the truth, and I could not understand why this nun did not – or, if indeed she *did*, why she maintained such a curious attitude to it.

A horrified letter was written to my mother who, to her everlasting credit, marched down to school, and confronted the Sister Superior with a scathing attack on their unrealistic and out-dated attitudes. I had been brought up to know the simple truth, and although I had never been egged on to gossip about it, neither had I been told that there was anything to be concealed: the birth of babies was a normal, natural process, my mother maintained, and what was more, it was God-given. She admonished me gently to keep quiet on the subject if ever it arose among my friends again, but she refused to make me feel guilty and ashamed, or to chastise me in any way.

She behaved, I think, with admirable sense. Yet, upon the rest of the subject of babies she maintained an absolute and prudish silence. In the absence of my father, and of men from that close, nursing-home world, I remained for years in total ignorance of how those babies got where they did, until well into adolescence when I made it my business to find out from books, and by asking questions of the mothers of certain friends. It was certainly something I could never have discussed with my own mother, or even mentioned, though I gathered from a few very dark remarks, dropped or overheard, that she regarded the whole topic of sex with disgust and loathing.

Otherwise, on the subject of babies and of pregnancy and childbirth, both of others but, most particularly, her own, she was totally, exhaustively frank and open – far too much so.

From my hours spent at Dybdale, I gleaned an awful lot of knowledge about childbirth. I spent a great deal of time there in those early years. I sat at the great scrubbed deal table in the kitchen, drawing and crayoning, and listening, listening, and no one ever thought to lower their voices or suppress the facts. I overheard conversations about how 'the head's showing' and 'number 17's only an inch dilated', and 'if this goes on much longer, number 5's going to need forceps', and 'you'd better go up to 4, she's starting to push'.

I knew that many women spent hours and hours and hours in labour, that it was painful and exhausting, and that they screamed. I knew that the business involved blood and slime and tears: that doctors had to be sent for in the middle of the night, and gas administered to put the women to sleep. I knew that some mothers died, and so did their babies, and that this distressed Aunty Matron most particularly, because she prided herself on the safety of her home, and her own skills in delivery; but more than anything, she cared. She cared for the women, and their childbirth and their babies, and any suffering beyond what she regarded as 'the norm' she would do anything to avoid or alleviate. And all death in childbirth was a tragedy and evidence of her own personal failure. She could seem hard and brisk with those mothers she regarded as malingerers, making an unnecessary fuss and ringing the bell in panic at every twinge of a contraction, but in the face of real fear, real suffering, she was inexhaustibly gentle and encouraging and compassionate, and mothers came back to her again and again, to be delivered of baby after baby, and could never speak too highly of her.

And chief among those was my own mother, whose life Matron Evans saved and whose favourite baby I became, though my mother never returned to repeat her experiences of childbirth, in the Dybdale Nursing Home or any other, and who could ever have blamed her?

20

There must, surely, have been plenty of perfectly easy, straightforward labours and deliveries in that house during the years I was so often there. Those must have been the ones about which nobody said very much because there was no need, they were uneventful, routine. What I heard news of, what I remember so vividly, were the dramas and the tragedies. But, of course, childbirth forty and more years ago *was* in general far more dangerous and difficult than it is now, and the available pain relief was so much less pleasant and effective. No epidural anaesthetics then.

Although maternity homes like the one run so impeccably by my godmother were as hygienic as possible, and the standard of nursing care was high, women still ran the risk of dying from the appalling puerperal fever, from thromboses caused by the long period of immobility after delivery that was still thought necessary, and from septicaemia. Surgeons and midwives were by no means unskilled, yet the injuries inflicted permanently to the female pelvic floor from pro-longed labour, and awkward forceps deliveries, were common and horrible, and often caused a subsequent lifetime of misery – not to mention dread of any future childbearing.

Add to everything that I learned from my godmother, the tales my mother told me about my own birth and, really, it is a wonder I ever allowed myself to risk having a baby at all. Many women become obsessive about re-living their opera-tions – it's an old music hall joke. But I doubt if very many of my generation, and subsequent ones, enjoy telling and re-telling the horrendous, gruesome stories of their awful experi-ences in the delivery room that I was so often to hear. It is partly, I think, that childbirth is simply not as bad as it used to be – although it is certainly not always the blissful, fulfilling experience many modern propagandists would have us believe. But, in general, things have improved out of all recognition, and they continue to improve. Modern obstetrics has plenty of good tricks up its sleeve, too, and anaesthetics are getting safer and more effective and, best of all, more widely available with each year that passes.

I do not really blame my poor mother, not any more. The older I grow, and the more I think about the things she told me, the more I understand what an appalling time she had, how much she suffered, in ways that were probably quite unavoidable at the time but which would never have been allowed to occur today.

Nobody taught women much about the process of child-birth in the 1940s, there were no preparation classes for happy groups of fat ladies, no relaxation, deep-breathing or psycho-prophylaxis, no National Childbirth Trust. But above all, there was precious little *information*. There were obstetric and general medical textbooks for doctors and nurses, but the woman in the street could not get hold of those and would have been more hindered than helped by them if she had. Perhaps there were one or two discreet pamphlets obtainable in plain brown envelopes from distant addresses, or veiled and unhelpful articles in a few general books about family health, but the idea that women could go along to library or bookshop and consult the hundred and one explicit popular introductions to, and descriptions of, pregnancy and childbirth that are now available on the open shelves would have been unthinkable.

So, in spite of being no fool, and being interested in her condition, in spite of having a surgeon for her own godfather, and a growing friendship with the Matron who was to look after her in her confinement, my mother sailed through nine months of pregnancy and into labour in almost total, and perhaps quite happy, ignorance of what was going on, and what was to come.

The flat she was living in was on the other side of the town from the maternity home but she liked walking, and felt it kept her fit through her pregnancy. She began to drop in to have coffee, and deepen her friendship with the staff at Dybdale; and she went not into Matron's sitting-room, but into the kitchen. Most people did.

Here she sat and soon began to do this or that job, because no one ever stayed there for long with idle hands; they would be given bread to slice and butter, or trays to set – or a baby to cradle and wind and get off to sleep.

My mother had never had anything to do with babies in her life. Now, she began to learn. And, as I grew up and went to the nursing home several times a week, I learned too, learned old-fashioned ways of folding and pinning napkins and swaddling, but it was the loving that I learned best of all, the holding, rocking, soothing. Babies were entirely familiar physical objects to me by the time I was four years old.

That winter in Scarborough was a long and bitter one, even by the standards of an area of Britain well inured to harsh weather. Snow came early, and it stayed from before Christmas until the end of March; and there were the winds, too, north easterlies that cut through you like a knife, gales howling around the chimney pots and beating at the windows night after night; and always the sea, churning and heaving, or else in a rage, boiling over the Marine Drive, crashing up the cliffs and snarling back, in a foam and a lather. And then there was the war. In 1942, things were looking bleak, rationing and general material deprivation were taking their toll, anxiety, both national and personal, was a constant drain on energy and health.

Years later when I was depressed and miserable, in the midst of trying to have a second baby, I often thought of my mother in those days; it never failed to give me an injection of hope and courage. Could I have coped so well, in the middle of a war and a winter, pregnant for the first time, with an absent husband with whom I was not, in any case, particularly happy; cut off, in every sense, from my family, in a strange place? I doubt it.

But by all accounts, my mother sailed through those days of snow and ice, air-raid warnings and bad news, supported by her friends at the nursing home, and physically feeling extremely well. She always told me proudly how fit she had been when she was carrying me, how much energy she had, even in the last weeks. There were no problems at all.

It was the calm before the storm. But perhaps her general good health did stand her in good stead, and helped to pull her through when she all but died in labour, and twice afterwards.

Nowadays she would never have been allowed to go so long overdue and in view of her small stature – five feet nothing – she would have had 'Caesarian section?' on her notes from the beginning; and if she *had* been allowed a 'trial of labour' first, would have been taken into hospital to be induced at term.

As it was, she felt her first contraction in the middle of the night of 3 February. She collected her suitcase, walked through snowdrifts to the telephone kiosk to ring for a taxi and was admitted to the nursing home well before dawn.

I was not finally born until late in the night of 5 February, more than thirty-six hours later.

They say that we all have memories of our own births buried deep, deep in the subconscious; psychiatrists and other workers in the field of the human personality have claimed that the experience affects us profoundly and forever. If the birth has been a particularly difficult or traumatic one, if there have been many hours of ineffectual contractions, if the baby has been distressed with its breathing and become stuck and been helped out with forceps, or on the other hand been born too quickly and arrived in a state of shock, then the scars of all this, the fear and panic and sense of strangeness and isolation are said never to heal and cause psychological problems in later life. It sounds likely enough. When I think, in the cold light of day, about the experience of a difficult birth for a small baby, I know in my heart that it must be incredibly distressing and frightening, and even painful, and surely is *bound* to leave a mark.

But I have, of course, no conscious memory of my own birth, and if any problems and fears in my life can be traced back to those hours, I cannot trace them myself. No, the effect of my birth upon me was of a different kind, and altogether conscious.

All that I know of it is hearsay. I was raised on stories of the horror of my mother's labour and delivery, heard her tell and re-tell the tale to endless other women, neighbours, friends, family, doctors, nurses – and to me. It would be easy enough to blame her. But perhaps she did not know that I was listening, let alone how avidly, or how well I understood. Besides, I'm quite certain that she needed to pour it out so often, it was her only way of dealing with it, externalising it, she had to try to get rid of the fear and pain and shock. And I daresay there was an element of enjoyment too, she relished recounting all the gory, agonising details – people do.

There is a wonderfully funny passage in that to me funniest of all novels, Nancy Mitford's *The Pursuit of Love*, in which the girls of the Radlett family gather in the airing cupboard to exchange secret titbits of information they have gleaned about all the business of growing up.

Last holidays, our great obsession had been childbirth, on which entrancing subject we were informed remarkably late, having supposed for a long time that the mother's stomach swelled up for nine months and then burst open like a ripe pumpkin, shooting out the infant. When the real truth dawned upon us, it seemed rather an anticlimax, until Linda produced, from some novel and read out loud in ghoulish tones, the description of a woman in labour.

'Her breath comes in great gulps – sweat pours down her brow – like water – screams as of a tortured animal rend the air – and can this face, twisted with agony, be that of my darling Rhona – can this torture-chamber really be our bedroom, this rack our marriage bed. "Doctor, doctor," I cried, "do something." I rushed out into the night . . .' and so on.

We were rather disturbed by this, realizing that too probably we in our turn would have to endure these fearful agonies. Aunt Sadie, who had only just finished having her seven children, when appealed to was not very reassuring. 'Yes,' she said vaguely, 'it is the worst pain in the world. But the funny thing is, you always forget, in between, what it's like. Each time, when it began, I felt like saying, "Oh, now I remember, stop it, stop it." And of course by then it was nine months too late to stop it.'

I have laughed over it many times. But the truth is that a very great many women of my generation, and of many before it, spent years of misery and dread as a result of overhearing, or being regaled with, horror stories about childbirth. You may forget, or dismiss, what you hear a snatch of, in a bus, or a queue, or read in a book, like the Radlett girls, but what you hear your own mother telling you and others, solemnly and perhaps warningly, you do not forget. It goes down deep, and it lies, lurking like some dreadful animal, waiting to pounce.

25

I grew up to love babies, and to feel at my most secure and happy in the maternity home where I was born. But I also grew up in considerable fear of childbirth. It cast a shadow forwards over everything, it coloured my attitude to adolescence, and to young men, and caused me to retreat into myself, and into books, and the life of the imagination: for real life might mean friendship, courtship, marriage, sex – and when I came too close to those possibilities for comfort, I retreated.

Those fears, and my mother's horror stories, took a great deal of getting rid of.

I would not dream of minimising what she went through though. A protracted labour, hours and hours of contractions which got her nowhere; no epidural anaesthesia or even pethidine for her, only a small amount of gas and air for pain relief in the later stages. Finally, the consultant was called and she had a deep forceps delivery, her pelvic floor collapsed, and she had extensive perineal tearing which had to be repaired under general anaesthetic. She went into shock, and had to be resuscitated, and the day after the birth, septicaemia set in following an infection of the wound. She did not finally leave the nursing home until five weeks later.

She could still walk only with discomfort, she had physical problems for the rest of her life as a result of all the damage she had suffered, and she was told that if she ever had another child, it would kill her.

I think about that part of the past, my own and my mother's, very often. When I was having my own children, I often dreamed of it; I used to walk those cliff paths beside the North Sea, and along the terraces to the maternity home, to sit in my godmother's sitting-room in front of her fire, or in the kitchen beside the range where, during all those long days and nights when my own mother lay so ill, she nursed me in the rocking chair, fed me and changed me herself, and soothed and loved and caressed me, as if I were hers. Thinking back, I could hear the ringing of the bells and see the little red numbers swinging, hear the clatter of the trays and the wail of the babies; could smell the bread and the steaming washing, was lulled by the singing of the kettle on the range. Perfect, contented dreams. And I would wake and lie, wondering, remembering, praying, crossing my fingers. I am quite sure that those times, that place and the memory of it all, those early years when I was so close to the birth and sleep, the crying and smell of little babies, affected me profoundly and affected my attitude to everything to do with having children – bearing, loving, and losing them.

If I'd had only my mother's gruesome stories to go on, I doubt whether I would ever have been able to face the prospect of having children myself.

Fortunately, I did not. Gradually as I grew older, acquaintance with the experiences of friends began to soften the idea of childbirth somewhat for me. Some years later, when I was living in my first flat in the Midlands, I had my first encounter with birth and new babies since my childhood in Scarborough. I called on a neighbour one afternoon with a parcel that had been mis-delivered. She heaved herself to the door, in the last stages of pregnancy, a huge, ripe, round-faced girl and, to me, astonishingly cheerful. I asked her when her baby was due. 'Last Thursday,' she said, 'and it won't budge!'

When I went back home, I couldn't get her out of my mind; she was about to face that appalling agony and danger, and she seemed so chirpy, so unconcerned. I brooded on her innocence, the shock she would have.

Late that night, there was an urgent ringing at my door bell – it was her husband. Would I please call the midwife, Kath was in labour, it looked like 'any minute', and the phone box on the corner was out of order.

I sat up in my window in a dressing-gown, saw the headlamps of the midwife's car, watched the lights in the bedroom of the flat opposite, imagined the awfulness of it, felt full of dread for Kathleen. At that time, in the mid-sixties, home births were still the rule, there were very few hospital beds. In my time living in that small road, a dozen or so young neighbours gave birth at home to their babies, first, second or subsequent, with only the midwife in attendance. As I had the only telephone in the street, they mostly came to me to use it and I heard about everything that went on, felt all the tension, anxiety and fear when things went wrong, and the doctor or even the ambulance had to be called in a hurry. It all convinced me that, medically speaking at least, home was not the place to have a baby – the risks were too high.

Kathleen was all right though. Early the next morning, I slipped across to find out how things were going, expecting – because I believed that all women laboured for days and nights on end – to be told there was no news, and, I suppose, to hear the terrible screams. 'Come in. Come on in. It's a boy. They're fine. She had him at three o'clock!'

And there was Kathleen, sitting up in the big bed in the little room, her hair over her shoulders, face pink, eyes bright – Kathleen, who had had a baby only a few hours before, and who was looking wonderful, so well, so happy.

'I'm fine. Great. Nothing to it. Do you want to hold him?'

She lifted him from his cot and gave him to me and as I took him, the past came flooding back on a wave of warm, sweet baby-smell. I looked down at his fragile head with its fringe of blond hair, his eyelids faintly mauve, his hand curled up close to his cheek. I wanted to take him away with me.

After that, I spent quite a lot of time with women who were pregnant, women who had just had babies, listening to their stories, asking questions, finding things out. And gradually, the worst of my fears became allayed, my mother's experiences were put into a better perspective. I was still afraid of childbirth though.

During my twenties, I was a curious mess of emotions and convictions about myself and adulthood. I did not for one moment believe I would ever marry, or have children – and my certainty that I had not been dealt those cards made me claim vociferously that nor did I want them, I had other, more important business in hand. I would be a solitary, and a writer. But I was nevertheless sure that if ever I did have a baby, my experiences of childbirth would inevitably be as awful as my mother's had been. Other people might be proving all around me that it could be a happy, straightforward and uncomplicated business, but I was a fatalist, I knew I would never be so lucky.

But below the surface, deep, deep below, I knew that

whatever I might say, and in spite of what it might take, what I did want, one day, was a baby, was lots of babies, babies like all the ones I had so loved, felt so close to, in my godmother's nursing home. I didn't look far ahead into their later lives, never saw them as children. Only babies.

And if I was fatalistic, sure that my mother's woes would become mine, I certainly allowed history to begin to repeat itself when I got married at the same, comparatively late age as she, and found myself due to give birth to my first child when I, too, was thirty-five.

Chapter 2

But of course nothing that happened after April 1975 happened only to me – it happened to us.

Just a few of the things that I had been doing, and which had helped to make me the person I was on the day of my marriage, are relevant to the rest of the story. The moment you try to isolate certain particular events in your life, to highlight them and separate them from everything else, you realise that you can't and then you begin to understand how everything forms a chain, a pattern in which every element relates to and is dependent for its significance on every other.

I could not make complete sense of my own passionate obsession for having babies without going back to my mother's experiences, and my own birth and early childhood; and although much of what I had been, and was, when I got married, suddenly seemed irrelevant, and has continued to seem so, parts of the past threw long shadows forward. I cannot ignore or disown it all. I have said that I decided to be a writer and to be solitary, but I was never really anything else. I had been a writer since the beginning, and being alone, both literally but more especially within myself, was part and parcel of that. Many only children live for a time in an inner world of their own creating, the objects of the imagination, invented people and places and fantasies, are important to them. Many children express themselves verbally through stories and poems, or else they paint pictures or play music.

When does a child who writes become a writer? When does

an only child who invents her own playmates become the person for whom the life of the imagination, the inner world which she peoples herself, assumes greater importance than the real world? I don't know. I only know that I was never *not* a writer, never *not* creating imaginary worlds and peopling them.

And to do that with any seriousness and commitment, you have to be alone within yourself. You also have to spend a good deal of time actually being physically alone – writing is a solitary business. But a lot of writers manage to combine the essential *inner* solitariness quite successfully and happily with being companionable, having friends and a family. For a long time, I could not. I had friends, of course, very many, but I lived alone, I was distant from my parents and I did not have – on one level very much did not want – easy, close relationships. I was not a gregarious or social person, hated large gatherings, parties, jollifications. I still do.

For a few years, after I came down from the University of London, I had various part-time jobs, reviewed books, drifted, was serving my apprenticeship as a writer. I was rather unhappy, somehow bursting with the passionate need to write, and not yet having found my own voice. It was frustrating and my personal life was frustrating, and tense, at the same time. I had a long-lasting, emotional and tormented relationship with one extraordinary and very difficult man with whom I was as much in love as it is possible to be. That story does not have a place here, but it deserves to be mentioned because it was a major factor in my general misery and confusion.

But during this time, quite suddenly, a door opened, something fell into place – it's hard to know exactly how to put it – and I began to write as I had always known somehow that I could. Between 1968 and 1974 – when I look back, I am astonished at how short a time it actually was – I wrote six novels, two collections of short stories and half a dozen full-length radio plays.

I worked with great intensity; before I had finished one book, there was always an idea for the next, bubbling up from below. The only way I could cope was to isolate myself even more. I was then living in a pretty house in a small close in the Regency riverside town of Leamington Spa. (I had moved with my parents to the Midlands from Yorkshire when I was sixteen, but when I left university I did not want to return to live at home. And one of the great advantages of the freelance, solitary writer's life is that one can live anywhere at all.)

I was happy in Leamington, its atmosphere suited me, the charm of its Regency stuccoed terraces and Victorian Italianate villas was very appealing, and it reminded me a little of Scarborough, that other beautiful spa town.

But the sea was far from the heart of England, and often and often it was the sea that I longed for. Also, when I was at home, the telephone rang, neighbours and friends called. I could never settle down to work very seriously. So I took to going away, for a month or two at a time, first to a rented cottage in the depths of the Dorset countryside – Hardy country, lanes and woods and open barrows. I loved the novels of Thomas Hardy, and had felt closely influenced by the places in which they were set for some years. But there was another, stronger influence on my imaginative life and writing, that of the composer Benjamin Britten, and it was in search of the source of his music, and hoping that I would find inspiration in those places he had made his own, that I travelled to his little seaside town of Aldeburgh, in Suffolk.

For four years, from January to March, I rented a house there, overlooking – almost in – the sea. There I wrote book after book, walked for miles along the beach and across the beautiful open marshes under that astonishingly wide, wide sky, living a curious life of the imagination and of solitary confinement. I would begin a novel when I got there, and finish it eight weeks or so later – and then go back home exhausted, to recover. During the rest of the year, I wrote radio plays and stories, in shorter bursts of creativity.

I suppose I was a little like an Olympic athlete, at the peak of my fitness and powers. I was heady with the delight of having such creative energy, so many ideas, and I received plenty of rewards. I ought to have been happy and fulfilled – and part of me certainly was – but personally, emotionally, I was not, and still buried somewhere deep down must have been the urge which any woman has, to have a stable and permanent relationship with one partner – to be married and have children. I didn't acknowledge the urge publicly though – I suppose I dared not.

Perhaps that was why my thirtieth birthday, in 1972, came as such a shock. No birthday since has made much impact upon me, but being thirty was like being dealt a blow in the face. Professionally I was on the crest of a tremendous wave, but the price I paid emotionally was very high. I stamped up and down the shingle beach for hour after hour that winter, boiling with all manner of inner frustrations and confusions.

Then, in March, life dealt me a body-blow. David, to whom by now, after eight years, I was growing much closer so that we were both all but ready to commit ourselves to marriage, died suddenly of a heart attack while out walking with a friend in the Gloucestershire countryside.

I packed up the Aldeburgh house, and the manuscript of the novel I had just completed, and a close friend came to drive me home – I could not safely have done so myself.

The day after that I began the slide down into a dark, dark place, a terrible limbo in which I spent three years. The story of that time has no place here either, though the death of David – and that of my mother two years later, a sad, painful, frightened death from cancer – taught me my first lessons in loss, and grief and guilt and, in the end too, about resurrection. They were to remain with me.

The very last book of that creative period of my life came at the end of it all. I went back to my house by the sea for one final visit, to write a novel called *In the Springtime of the Year* which exorcised the ghost of David, set down all I had felt of love and loss, and marked both an end and a beginning – the end of six years of my best writing of fiction, the beginning of a personal healing.

When I emerged from that book, and packed it off to my publisher and returned home to Leamington, I felt empty and drained – and strangely restless. After a week or so in my house, I knew that what I needed was a real change, to mark the end of the chapter I felt sure I had reached – though of

33

course nothing is ever so neat as I have made that sound. At the time, I only thought I ought to do *something* to make a break with the last few unhappy years. So what else but move house?

I had lived in Leamington for seven years, but a lot of my original neighbours with whom I had got on so well had begun to move away, and the town itself was changing, too. Many of those old ladies who lingered on, like the heroine of John Betjeman's poem, relics of the past grandeur of Royal Leamington Spa, were dying at last, and the large, handsome but neglected houses to which they had been clinging went up for sale and, in many cases, were demolished, to be replaced by blocks of flats. A smart middle-class town was becoming a cosmopolitan Midlands community, with light industry spreading out all around it, traffic increasing, population expanding rapidly. I didn't disapprove, but simply felt that I no longer belonged there.

From every point of view, it was time to go.

I had first visited Stratford-upon-Avon as a stage-struck girl of sixteen in 1958, the year I moved with my parents from seaside Yorkshire to the industrial Midlands. I had dreamed about the place, looked it up on a map to see how far away it was from where we would be living – no more than twenty miles, and had gone there on the top deck of the bus as soon as I could.

Sometimes, places you have had fantasies about, built up in your imagination, are a disappointment, the reality does not match up to the dream, but Stratford was all I had hoped for, a pretty little low-built riverside town, with the central area still laid out in the way it had been when Shakespeare lived there. I loved Waterside, the view up-river to the church whose spire rose slender as a wand above the trees, the white swans gracefully, loftily sailing, the boats, the theatre itself, the chance of glimpsing one of the actors walk up the street to buy a newspaper – everything.

I had become less theatre-mad as the years went by, but I had gone on liking Stratford and during my years seven miles away in Leamington Spa, I had acquired a number of friends who lived there, and they had introduced me to others so that

34

I suddenly realised that my social scene, such as it was, had been shifting.

I wanted to leave Leamington, I had no ties elsewhere – so, where else to move to but Stratford-upon-Avon? I heard from friends about a small Victorian terraced house that was to be sold privately in the part of the town I liked best – Old Town, a few criss-cross streets that lie in front of Holy Trinity Church, a stone's throw from the river and a short walk to the theatre.

Peter, the owner, invited me to lunch and showed me round. What had once been a little front room and a little back room had been knocked into one; at the back, a window overlooked a small terrace and a walled garden full of flowering shrubs and climbing roses, with the most wonderful lilac tree near to the house. There were York-stone flags leading from the hall, a staircase up to three small bedrooms, and a bathroom. I loved it – the street, the area, and most of all, the house, it felt right, happy. When it comes to a house, I have always gone entirely on the feel of it, I've known the moment I've stepped inside whether it's right, whether I'd be happy living there or not; practical matters have always taken second place. This approach has led to my living in some houses which have been in many ways quite inconvenient and unsuitable but in which I have always felt entirely contented, settled and comfortable.

So I knew, by the time I sat down to lunch in the kitchen at West Street, that this was where I wanted to live. Peter was concerned at my eagerness, anxious that I should take my time to think things over. Before the cheese was on the table, I said, 'I want to buy this house from you.'

Fine, yes, he said, he was delighted, but –

'But – what's wrong? I'm sure I can raise the money – I love this house. Why is there a "but"?' I was horrified that I might lose it.

'But – I feel I must be honest with you. It *is* for sale, I've told you my price and I'll stick to that. It's only that someone else has seen it and I think he's interested.'

Someone else? *Who* else? Lead me to him and I'd stab him, I'd wring his neck. I'd . . . *Who* else?

'Actually, I think you may have met him. He lives up the road in a flat in the Shakespeare Institute – it belongs to the University of Birmingham and he's the Fellow in Charge there. He's called Stanley Wells.'

Stanley Wells? Yes, I remembered Stanley Wells. A few years previously I'd made an abortive start at doing a higher degree in Shakespeare Studies at the University of Birmingham. It was a flirtation with the scholarly life that lasted a term and a half and then I'd abandoned it to write a novel, but I remembered attending one class given by Dr Wells – though not very much about him.

And then, a week or two previously, I'd been invited to a party at the house of the Headmaster of King Edward VI Grammar School in Stratford, and there was introduced to Stanley Wells again – the name had been familiar but I didn't recognise him at all. He was wearing a smart black velvet dinner jacket, and he'd grown a beard which improved his looks no end. I'd exchanged a few words with him, spoken about my brief interlude as one of his students.

At the end of the party, I had stayed on to have a last cup of coffee when the rest of the guests had gone. It had been a good party but quite a large one and I had known very few people there, so I was still in some confusion about who was who. Since I was going to come and live in the town, I wanted to be able to put a name to any vaguely familiar people I might have as neighbours, or bump into in the street.

'And which one', I said in due course, 'was Mrs Wells? I don't think I met her.'

'You didn't,' said my host, 'because there isn't one.'

At the time, I thought nothing of it – or did I? Yes, I think I probably did. I think I had done more than be politely aware of Stanley Wells. I remember having a vague feeling of interest and pleasure when I heard that he was a bachelor. But I went home to Leamington from the party that night and thought no more about him.

Only now, here he was, interested in buying my house.

The evening of the day I had seen it and known for certain that this was where I desperately wanted to live, I looked up Stanley Wells's telephone number and rang him in a state of panic and rage – neither of which, of course, was remotely justified since he, after all, had seen the house before me and had every right to bid for it.

I'm not sure what I'd expected him to say – many another person would have sent me away with a flea in my ear. Not Stanley. He is not, as I was to have proved to me often and often, that sort of man: the moment he heard of my interest in the West Street house, he gave up all claim to it. Yes, he had seen and rather liked it; yes, it would suit him, but his plans were so vague, he wasn't sure if he would ever really move out of his flat; he had only made the most general enquiries about raising a mortgage and, of course, if I were seriously wanting it, I must have it, he wouldn't take his interest any further.

With the wind well and truly taken out of my sails, I put down the telephone, full of gratitude, full of excitement at the fact that now the field was clear and I really could buy the house, and thinking really what a very nice man Dr Wells must be.

Then I rang Peter, and told him I would be putting my offer in writing.

'Ah – but what about Stanley?'

I told him.

'That', said Peter, 'is typical. He really is the *nicest* man.'

It was November 1974. Peter himelf was only moving a few doors up the street, but his house was having a great many alterations and wouldn't be ready for him to move into until the following March or April. Nevertheless, we signed the contract for my purchase of his old one, and I settled down to wait in Leamington Spa. Except that I was restless there, it didn't feel like home any more, and I spent a lot of time driving over to Stratford to pester Peter about the progress of the house, and get to know the town and all my new friends better. In the street, a couple of times, I bumped into Stanley Wells – we had a brief chat, no more. I wished it *had* been more. I began to think about him rather a lot.

Looking back, I realise that I had actually decided that I would marry him more or less at the beginning, probably at that moment when I discovered he did not have a wife already. That sounds cold and calculating but it wasn't. And turn the sexes the other way round and no one would think it at all objectionable – plenty of men set their sights on marrying a woman almost the first time they meet.

As I emerged from the years of David and the slough of despond into which I had sunk after his death, I knew for certain that I needed to be married. When I met Stanley, I knew I wanted it to be to him. And he, too, was at the point in his life when he felt very much the same. For two people to meet in exactly the right place, at exactly the right time in their lives, and agree about it, still seems to me the most astonishingly good fortune, and I have never really got over its happening to me.

We met in November, knew just after Christmas that we wanted to be married, and announced our engagement on my birthday in February. I was thirty-three. Suddenly, a whole new life for the new person I felt myself becoming opened up before me.

We had a crazy, happy wedding. I finally moved into the West Street house – which of course we had each wanted and were now *both* going to have – in mid-April, and we were planning to be married at the end of May, in the Guild Chapel which stands beside and belongs to the Grammar School Shakespeare almost certainly went to. Stanley was a school governor, and in view of that and the Shakespearean connections, it seemed particularly appropriate; but the Guild Chapel is not licensed for weddings – the very few that ever take place there do so by special licence from the Archbishop of Canterbury, applications for which have to be made in plenty of time. We had, we thought, given ourselves that and I settled down to organise everything there is to be organised for a wedding. Rather a lot, I discovered. Getting married is hard work – and we were arranging everything ourselves without the benefit of parents. Stanley's elderly mother lived with his sister in Canada, I now only had my father.

Moving house is exhausting. We were both over-strained, still getting used to our new situation – having someone else in your life when you have been independent for forty-four and thirty-three years respectively is hard work, too.

I don't think we realised the weight of our mutual stress

load until Stanley went down with a bad bout of flu, and I fainted at someone's dinner party.

One evening, when we were both still recovering, Stanley came round to the new house. He was pale and he'd lost weight. I felt the same. We looked at one another.

'Let's get married next week,' Stanley said.

It seemed the best thing anyone had ever suggested. In a surge of euphoria which made us feel mildly drunk, we unscrambled our plans for the big wedding at the end of May – printed invitations, bridesmaids and all – and made new ones for a very private ceremony the following week. Stanley went charging off to see the Rector, who consulted his diary and said, 'I can only manage two days – Monday morning or Wednesday afternoon at five.'

The Wednesday was 23 April, Shakespeare's birthday. A good omen, Stanley thought, so we settled on it.

It was the most beautiful afternoon of a wonderfully warm spring, and Stratford was pink and white with blossom and magnolia, a tree I have always loved.

The whole thing was topsy-turvy. I wore the cream suit I had bought for going away in, and as we decided to turn our planned wedding reception at the end of May into a general celebratory party, I thought I could wear my long dress then. That morning, while I went to the florists to pick up my bouquet, Stanley drove in a panic to the university in Birmingham, to which the Archbishop's office had misdirected the special licence – without which, in his hand, the Rector could not legally marry us.

Clutching it, and after downing a large gin and tonic, the bridegroom brought his car round to pick me up. It was all most irregular, and it didn't matter a bit. With my father and four close friends, we went just before five into the small, cool, beautiful Guild Chapel. Less than ten minutes later we were married. We went out into the golden spring sunshine to drink champagne among the sixteenth-century buildings and be photographed among the magnolia blossom, along with the Grammar School cat.

Two days later our photograph appeared on the front of the local newspaper. The headline read: 'Novelist weds in Stratford.'

Novelist? For a moment, I wondered who they meant. I knew I had told my publisher I would be starting a new book soon, but in truth I wasn't feeling like a writer, a novelist, at all. I wasn't sure I ever wanted to write another word, my mind was on quite other things.

In the early months of our marriage, having a baby was certainly not something I consciously wanted to do – indeed, I took every precaution not to become pregnant. Whether the desire was at the back of my mind, I honestly am not sure, but I suspect that it must have been.

I certainly knew that I wanted to catch up on all the things I had missed – to catch up, I suppose, on *life* – and I knew too that I no longer had any desire to put all my creative energies and emotions into writing novels, though I very much wanted to go on being a writer, in the workaday sense, doing reviews and articles.

Before we were married, when I was first getting to know him, I had assumed that Stanley would not have any desires for a family. He was in his forties, settled into bachelor ways, an academic with fairly serious tastes – though by no means a solemn man.

I was fairly surprised then, when I mentioned to some close friends of his that obviously babies wouldn't be likely to feature in our future life, that they exclaimed that the one thing they had always been certain of about Stanley was that he loved children and would make a marvellous father.

'Does he *know* any children?' I asked.

'Oh, dozens – his godchild, nephews and nieces, visiting children – haven't you noticed all the toys he's got tucked away in corners of his study?'

I had a prowl round the next time I was there and found several old-fashioned wooden toys, a painted soldier, a cup-and-ball game. Well, well.

A few evenings later, when we were sitting by the fire after supper, I broached the subject tentatively.

'I take it,' I remember saying, 'that you wouldn't want to have children.' Rather a stiff way of putting it, but I was very unsure of my ground.

'Oh, yes,' he said, surprising me again, 'yes, I think I should like some children. I mean – not a *great* many, perhaps two or three?'

I stored this away at the back of my mind somewhere, needing to get used to the idea. The stories my mother had told me about childbirth began to come back to me over the first few weeks of marriage, adding to the general uncertainty I felt about the whole subject. For the time being, I knew that I simply wanted to relax and enjoy being married, saying Mrs Wells when giving my name, having someone coming home in the evening to share everything with – all the usual pleasures of being newly married. Although for both of us it was taking a bit of adjustment, we were extremely happy.

So when did I start looking into prams? When did whatever maternal urges that were in my subconscious begin to surface, to nag at me, so that I could not go for more than a day or two without thinking about it all? It was not much more than a year after we were married.

It's a common pattern, and most of my friends have conformed to it as their desires for children took firm shape. I used to read magazines with titles like *Mother and Baby* and *Parents* in the rack at W.H. Smith, under cover of magazines I could confess to being interested in, about the countryside or house furnishing and decorating! In the library, too, I surreptitiously went to the shelves and got down pregnancy and childbirth and childcare volumes and sat in a dark corner of the local history section, avidly reading them but not quite daring to borrow them to take home.

I began to talk about babies, to ask questions of friends with children, to imagine, to wonder. And to steer my mind away from recollections of my mother's endless birth stories. I was working my way towards motherhood yet resisting it too, nervous and uncertain, very much in two minds. When I raised the subject with Stanley, he was vaguely off-putting, which made me disproportionately upset.

We spent three weeks in France at the end of the long hot summer of 1976, in a house overlooking the most beautiful valley, not far from Cahors. We'd had a busy year, and it was a memorable holiday, full of good food and wine, sunshine and sleep. I felt strange, poised between two worlds, and not at all restless for things to change. But when we got back home to a greener, wetter England and the beginning of autumn, the desire to have a baby suddenly crystallised, and began to dominate my thoughts.

I went to the doctor, secretly, and asked if he saw any reason, at my age, why I shouldn't try and have a child. None at all, he said, carry on. Any special preparations I should make, to get myself into the peak of fitness? Today, thinking about how pre-conceptual preparation has altered, perhaps he would have answered differently. Women are advised to take particular care of their diet, even have courses of vitamins and minerals, stop the contraceptive pill for at least three months before conceiving – all sorts of careful advice is given. But our delightfully laid-back and very wise and experienced GP laughed, and told me to stop fretting and just go ahead and conceive whenever we felt like it, with the caution that because I was in my thirties, I shouldn't expect to succeed in a hurry. 'Give it six months or so.'

I went home in a state of high excitement. 'I've been to see the doctor,' I announced, practically on the doorstep. 'He says we can have a baby any time we like – straight away!'

'Oh!'

I'm quite used, now, to my husband's apparently abrupt way of sometimes saying simply 'Oh' in response to some hobby-horse or news or gossip or proposal of mine, and it hardly disconcerts me at all. It usually means he isn't going to commit himself to any fuller or more positive response until he's had a lot more time to mull it over. He is a wise and cautious man, not given to abrupt decisions or instant reactions, generally far too sensible to let himself be swept away on the tide of my sudden enthusiasms.

But on this particular day, and when I was still not always able to interpret him correctly, I was put out and upset by his apparent lack of interest and delight to match my own. I wanted a baby, I wanted one now, at once, so why didn't he?

After a time, he calmed me down. 'Now, let's talk it over carefully – it's a big decision, there are a lot of considerations.'

I couldn't see that there were, did not really understand

what we had to talk about. I was in the first grip of that single-minded, passionate need to have a baby which was so to dominate our lives some years later. Anyone who has ever experienced it will confirm that it is one of the most compelling, most powerful, all-consuming emotions possible.

Whatever Stanley's reservations were, now that the prospect of having children was a real, perhaps even imminent one, he did not voice them. What he was thinking to himself, I don't know – I rarely do. He realised how much I was beginning to want a child, and he was respectful of that desire. A few years previously, a secretary of his had suffered considerably through her desperate need to have a baby and had caused him some anxiety at her condition. He did not want me to become neurotic about it – better let me have one.

Besides, whereas I had dismissed – scarcely even taken in the meaning of – what our realistic doctor had said about older women taking longer to conceive, Stanley accepted and believed him. There would probably be plenty of time for us both to become thoroughly acclimatised to the idea of having a child – it might be a year before we managed to conceive.

A month later, I was pregnant.

Part II

Jessica

Chapter 3

But I'd never expected otherwise. Oh yes, I had *heard* what was said, about the time it takes to conceive increasing with age, but I'd never believed it would be relevant to me. Why? Blind optimism, I suppose, and a touch of that universal arrogance which gives rise to the certainty that 'it', whatever 'it' may be, couldn't happen to me. In this case, 'it' was infertility of one sort or another, difficulty in conceiving. I know this feeling I had was a common one. I've since read many an account by couples who have had fertility problems and, virtually every time, they express shock, real astonishment that this should be happening to *them*. 'Why us?' they ask. 'Surely, those things only happen to other people.' I've come to believe that this sort of blithe confidence is natural to human beings, that it is not a consequence of stupidity or ignorance, simply because we all experience it. In our heads, as a result of observation and information, we know that of course 'it' – a road accident, a heart attack, cancer or infertility – *could* happen to us. We may be well informed about the statistical chances, but we are still surprised when life deals us some particular blow.

I had assumed, in my heart of hearts, that I would conceive quickly, more or less as soon as I decided I wanted to, and I did. 'It' hadn't happened to me.

I went to see our doctor when I was about half a day overdue, hugging a urine specimen in a medicine bottle – about a pint, I remember, because I'd no idea how much they

47

needed. (In 1976, there were no pregnancy home-testing kits available.)

Dr Coigley looked at me over the top of those curious half-spectacles doctors all seem to wear. 'I can't do anything with that,' he said with wry amusement, 'it's much too early. You'll have to wait another couple of weeks – then come back with an early morning urine sample. Ask at the reception desk and they'll give you a special container.'

The disappointment must have been clear on my face because as I got to the door, he called me back with a grin: 'But you probably are,' he said.

I raced back, the (small) glass phial for my specimen safe in my bag, and burst into Stanley's room at the Shakespeare Institute. He was in the middle of a telephone call to an academic colleague but when he saw me hopping from one foot to another cut the conversation short as soon as he politely could.

'He says I probably am!'

'Are what?'

'Pregnant, of course!'

'Oh. But how does he know?'

'He just does.'

'Well, did he examine you? Did he take a test? What *do* they do? How can he be sure?'

My ever-cautious husband, wanting facts and information, not speculation and excitement. I could have sloshed him but, of course, he brought me down to earth, and perhaps that was right – he didn't want me to raise my own hopes and see them disappointed; he always counselled me against over-optimism, over-confidence, over-enthusiasm, though he tried to do so mildly, not to be too damping. He was going to have a lot of practice in that particular art in later years.

But I wasn't really taking him seriously. Dr Coigley had said, 'You probably are', and that was enough for me.

(Some time afterwards, I asked him why he had said that, without the least shred of evidence – just to be kind? 'Not really. Women generally do know.' I think to some extent he was right. Some women claim that they can tell the day after they have conceived, that they experience symptoms of pregnancy well before they miss a period: the only problem is that those very early signs are so vague, and if you are desperately looking and longing for them, it's very easy to deceive yourself.)

I set my little glass specimen phial proudly on top of the bathroom cabinet. It looked terribly definite, and rather official with its Area Health Authority label and hospital laboratory number, and my name in ink. I waited for the next two weeks with impatience, mingled with the very faintest twinge of anxiety which lessened daily as I continued to be overdue. Now I did have some grounds for optimism because this was something that had never happened to me before.

It would have been an impossibly tense time of waiting but it was broken by a short journey we made to Scotland. Stanley was lecturing at the University of Dundee, and I took the chance of going with him for the weekend so that I could stay with old friends and neighbours from my Leamington days, Robert and Irene Boyd, who had moved back to their home country and were living in Perth. They had had one daughter, Kirsty, while they were living near me, and now had another, Morag, who was just over a year. I wanted to see them to catch up on news, and so that they could meet Stanley – but most of all to meet their little girls now that I had a particular and growing interest in children.

I have happy memories of that trip. We went by train, always my most favourite mode of travel, and it was wonderful to ride through the countryside of the north of England again and to see the Scottish hills and moors for the very first time; it was early November, the last of the leaves were still lingering on the trees, the heather was a spread of purple, the colour I remembered from childhood visits to the Yorkshire moors, so softly shading to blue-grey as the sunlight rippled over it.

While Stanley went on to Dundee, I got to know the handsome grey city of Perth, and the two small Boyd girls with their rich Scottish accents and dark, dark eyes. What would having children be like, I wondered. Whatever would it be like? I tried to imagine us with one of these small, dependent people, but I simply could not.

Whether Irene suspected anything or not I don't know and I don't know how I kept my hopes about my pregnancy to myself – perhaps some innate superstition, 'if I tell someone else, it won't be true, it'll make it go wrong', or a touch of caution in case I was wrong and looked a fool. But I did quiz her a bit about her own first pregnancy and the birth of Kirsty in the hospital in Leamington I knew I should be in. Irene had been a radiographer there and knew all the consultants. Also, because of a previous miscarriage, and in view of the mildly risky nature of her job – in terms of child-bearing – she had been under specialist care.

'Och, Mr Begg,' she said emphatically. 'There's no one else I'd have. He's *fantastic*.'

I made a note of the name.

I made a note of something else, too. It was a very cold weekend, with early frosts and brilliant stars in a dark sky. On the Sunday, Stanley finished in Dundee and came to spend the night in Perth. At ten o'clock, we went for a walk.

'Oh, the lovely north!' I said, as I watched our breaths plume up in front of us in the frosty air. We probably wouldn't have such sharp cold in the south until after Christmas. The air smelled of chimney smoke, too – up here, everyone had coal fires, and they were all burning briskly; it was a smell that took me back to my Yorkshire childhood, and to holidays spent in the smoke and grime of Sheffield with my grandmother. I stood still, to sniff it in, enjoy it, remember. And as I did so, I felt a sensation I had never had before, a curious prickling and tingling in both my breasts, near to the nipple. It was a symptom I'd read about but had been quite unable to imagine. Now it was unmistakable. It went on for perhaps half a minute and then stopped.

If I had been in any doubt before, standing there in the starlit moonlit Scottish night, I knew for certain that I was pregnant.

When the test confirmed it, a week later, I suppose my excitement was just a little bit muted because I had been so very sure, but there is, after all, nothing like having something in writing. I don't think I had ever been prouder of anything in my life as I was of the little buff official card Dr Coigley handed to me that morning with a twinkle in his eye.

Form FW8. Certificate of pregnancy. Name of Patient: Susan Wells. I certify that the above-named person is an expectant mother.
Expected date of confinement: 14 July 1977.

The rush of feelings I experienced are common ones. Some woman somewhere is having them every minute of every day of the week, but that doesn't diminish their overwhelming intensity and importance to each individual. I felt extraordinarily *important*, as though I had at last, at last, become a significant, a special, a completely grown-up member of the human race. Until now, it was as though I had somehow been on probation, a sort of trial woman, playing at being adult. When his first son was born, the Prince of Wales told reporters that it felt like 'a very grown-up thing to have done'. I know exactly what he meant.

I felt lots of other things too – excited, apprehensive, like someone embarking upon a voyage into the unknown, a voyage of discovery.

I didn't, as yet, feel anything else – sick, or tired, or faint, or whatever the classic symptoms of pregnancy were supposed to be, but it must have shown. That afternoon I went to visit an old friend of Stanley's, and a new friend of mine, a retired doctor now well into her seventies, and told her I was expecting a baby.

'Oh yes, I knew you were.' She had the most marvellous booming, exuberant voice.

'How could you possibly know?'

'I always do – it's something about the eyes.'

At the time, I smiled in disbelief. Now I do know exactly what she meant. You *can* see something different 'about the eyes' of newly pregnant women.

Stanley took some time to get used to the idea that I was really and truly pregnant. It had happened far more quickly than he, at least, had expected, he had not had time to assess fully its impact on our lives, to know exactly *what* he felt about it. He was cautiously pleased, but it was some months before he began to show a serious interest, rather than a polite and kindly one, in my pregnancy and the coming child. At first I resented that, wanted him to be as high on the news as I was. I didn't understand what I do now – that men simply *cannot*, on the whole, be so completely bound up in a pregnancy because it is not happening to them. It is very difficult to be aware of and fascinated by every minute alteration and symptom in someone else's body, however close you are to them.

He dutifully listened to my detailed account of the smallest physical event, but it was later, when he could feel the baby move, listen to its heart beating, watch small limbs flail out under my swelling stomach, that he became increasingly interested and delighted – and that, too, seems to me entirely usual and understandable.

At my first proper ante-natal appointment with Dr Coigley, he asked me how I wanted to be looked after, and told me in which hospital I would have my baby. I had a degree of choice about the former but I had none at all about the latter. Because I was having a first baby at the advanced age of thirty-five, there was naturally enough no question at all of my being able to have a home delivery. Well, that was fine, there was no question at all of my wanting one. I'd seen too many of my young neighbours in Coventry, ten years before, have problems which were potentially serious because they were having babies at home. Obstetric flying squads were called out, tyres screeching, sirens wailing, blue lights flashing, for post-partum haemorrhages, or a baby born blue from lack of oxygen, with the cord wrapped tightly around its neck.

A first-time mother of my age is an unknown quantity, obstetrically speaking – no one knows how she will perform, and the risks of home delivery are therefore unacceptably high. I happen to believe that they are *always* unacceptably high; emergencies in childbirth can arise within seconds, far too fast for any flying squad to arrive, emergencies which are too serious to be dealt with by a doctor and midwife in ordinary domestic surroundings, emergencies which may put the life of mother and baby at risk or, at the very least, cause pain and great fear and distress; emergencies which are entirely unpredictable, even with all the care and experience in the world; emergencies which can only be safely and swiftly dealt with in a hospital. I have no patience with the romantics who would take any risk, however apparently slight, with the life of a woman or her child in order to give birth in a bed at home, with Dad downstairs boiling lots of water for tea and the rest of the children playing happily in the next room.

Nowadays, women who are low-risk and whose pregnancy and then delivery are progressing normally, are allowed to give birth without the interference of technology, they may not even see a doctor. They are delivered by a midwife, and they can return home very soon, perhaps even on the same day, under the Domino scheme (Do-miciliary midwife – in and out). A woman can go into labour, call her own midwife who will accompany her to hospital, deliver her baby and return home in the ambulance with her six hours later, so that mother and child can be happily tucked up again within the bosom of the family, to enjoy their new life together *almost* from the very beginning with the knowledge that all is well.

Even if the Domino scheme had been available, I would have been considered too high-risk to take advantage of it even if I had wished to do so. I didn't – I wanted my baby to be safely delivered in the best possible hospital surroundings and for us to remain there until I felt fully able to cope at home.

A couple of miles outside Stratford, in a converted and enlarged old house in its own grounds near to the river, was what used to be called a Cottage Maternity hospital; its proper name was the Monroe Devis Maternity Home, and I had heard great reports of its homely atmosphere, comfort and high standard of nursing care. I was told that, alas, I could not be delivered there since it was not as well equipped as a unit in the main hospital; patients with complications, possibly needing forceps deliveries or Caesarian sections, could not be admitted, or, if they were in the middle of labour, had to suffer the miserable experience of being transferred by ambulance ten miles to the Leamington hospital.

The Monroe Devis was not for me, elderly prima gravida that I was (elderly, in obstetric terms, seems to be over the age of about twenty-four!, prima gravida merely means first-time mother). It would have to be the Maternity Department of the Warneford Hospital, Leamington Spa – a gloomy looking Victorian pile, a stone's throw from where I used to live. I was quite certain I wanted to opt for private treatment by a consultant and this, inevitably, would also involve being in a private room rather than the general ward in the hospital; consultants cannot put their private patients in free NHS beds.

I wasn't bothered either way about having a private room – if I felt well, I thought I'd prefer to be in a ward – and I was under no illusions that, in a general hospital, I would get smoked salmon for dinner, private patient or not. Nor did I feel that the NHS offered a second-rate maternity service, and that I was in some way too grand to have anything to do with it.

No, it was when I remembered my mother's horror stories that I lost my nerve and needed to have, from the beginning, the security and reassurance of knowing that I would be looked after and delivered by a consultant obstetrician – just in case. Also, if I was prepared to pay for it, I knew I would be rather more in control, have a greater degree of choice in how things went, and that has always been very important for my peace of mind.

So when I first checked in with Dr Coigley and said that I wanted to be referred privately to a consultant, he agreed readily, accepting my reasons, and asked if I had a particular specialist in mind.

'Mr Begg,' I said at once, remembering Irene's recommendation.

He nodded enthusiastically. 'Excellent choice.'

'He's really good then?'

'Oh, no question – I play golf with him and he's got a very good handicap.'

I wonder how often referrals within the medical profession are made on similar grounds! But, good golfer or not, what I wanted was a good obstetrician with whom I felt safe and at ease. I got one.

I also got, on my journey to keep my first appointment with him, an idea of how suggestible a pregnant woman can be, how near the surface her nerves lie, how ready she is to pick up the slightest suggestion either that all is not well with her and her unborn baby, or that something may have arisen to give her cause for concern.

There is a handy train service between Stratford-upon-Avon and Leamington Spa, the journey quick and pleasant, trundling through the green meadows of Warwickshire – it was a familiar ride and I enjoyed making it again. But I'd forgotten to buy a newspaper or to take a book – most unusual for me, as I am bereft without anything to read on trains, in waiting-rooms, anywhere. Perhaps it was the first sign of the pregnancy amnesia I'd read about! Someone had left one of the more sensational tabloids lying on the opposite seat of the compartment, however, and – any port in a storm – I picked it up, and read the big bold black banner headline.

PILL CAN CAUSE HANDICAPS, DOCTORS AGREE.

There followed a luridly phrased report that women who have taken the contraceptive pill shortly before conceiving have a higher than usual risk of bearing a malformed child, and that the recommendation is for anyone thinking of becoming pregnant to stop the pill at least three or preferably six months before they do so, and use alternative methods of birth control until all the chemical hormones have been completely eliminated from the system.

By the time I had walked from the station to the consulting-rooms, and sat waiting for fifteen minutes or so, not being soothed by their soothing tank of tropical fish, I was in a lather of anxiety, quite convinced that because I had stopped taking the pill one month and conceived the next, I was certainly carrying a handicapped baby.

When I was shown into the consultant's room and a tall, friendly man with receding gingerish hair shook my hand and introduced himself, I didn't give him very much time to take down all my preliminary details.

'There's something I must ask you. I've just read an article in the paper – coming here on the train,' and I poured out all my worries. Mr Begg listened patiently, before heaving a deep sigh.

'I do wish these damn newspapers would *think* before they write. They take a lengthy medical report, which has probably got page after page of ifs and buts, and quote bits of it out of context, blow them up with a sensational headline and have half the pregnant women in the country in a panic, blood pressure soaring – and all quite without good reason.'

'But is it?'

'I think so. Look, let's get it into perspective at least. *Some* research seems to have shown that there *may* be an increased risk of malformation – *may* be – but the link is a very tenuous one, it isn't at all proven and definite. There may be a host of other factors. I'm very doubtful about that report. All right – in an ideal world, perhaps you should stop smoking, stop drinking, and stop eating anything remotely processed, stop taking any medicines, even stop breathing in polluted air, for the whole of your reproductive life. But you can't avoid everything, now can you? You'd become a total neurotic. Besides, the fact is that you have been taking the pill and now you are pregnant, and the chances are you'll have a perfectly normal healthy baby – so stop worrying.'

I did. I never gave the subject another moment's thought. He did ask if I was worried about handicap in general.

'You do know that for an older woman, there is a slightly increased risk of having a child with Down's Syndrome?'

'*How* much more increased?'

'At your age – what are you, you've conceived at the age of thirty-four – not very much. About one in 300 or more, of having a handicapped baby.'

'There are tests to find out whether you *do* have an abnormal baby, aren't there?'

'There *is* a test, but it can't be done until the 16th week and it carries a risk of causing a miscarriage. At thirty-four, I wouldn't recommend that you have it unless you think the risk of handicap is unacceptable, or if there is a history of Down's Syndrome in either of your families.' I thought for a moment. 'No,' I said, 'there isn't. The odds are overwhelmingly good.'

'I think so.'

'Besides, if I had the test and my baby *was* handicapped –

well, then what?' It wasn't a subject I'd considered much until that moment.

'You'd be offered an abortion.'

'I could never do that,' I said, and knew as I said it and with absolute certainty that I never could.

'Then there's no point at all in having the test,' said Mr Begg decisively. 'But if I were you, I simply wouldn't worry about it.'

So I didn't. I did not give it another moment's thought, let alone anxiety. Indeed, mine was probably one of the most tranquil pregnancies on record!

So far as my physical health went at that first appointment, I was clearly very fit and everything was absolutely normal. Because of that, Mr Begg suggested that I go to my own GP and the practice midwife for my routine monthly ante-natal checks, and see him in between – and more frequently towards the end of my pregnancy. He also told me that if all went well with the delivery – and there was no reason to suppose it would not – I could leave the Leamington hospital after forty-eight hours, and be transferred to the Monroe Devis Maternity Home near Stratford for my post-natal care. That pleased me.

Mr Begg sat back in his chair. 'Everything's fine,' he said. 'I'm sure you'll have a good pregnancy. Now is there anything you want to ask me? Anything that worries you?'

'Labour,' I said at once. And told him, briefly, about my mother's experience, and the dread her story had long filled me with.

'Ah, mothers. They've much to answer for!'

'A bit like alarmist newspaper reporters.'

'Yes. There used to be a lot of horror stories about and they frightened quite a few generations of women, but I do think things are better now. What you need is to read as much as you can about what a normal labour will be like, go to some classes, and perhaps talk to people who've had good, straightforward experiences of childbirth – just don't listen to any gruesome accounts!'

I wasn't sure about this advice and I said so.

He shook his head. 'Ignorance breeds fear and fear causes tension and none of that helps us to deal with pain.'

'I'm not very good at pain,' I said.

57

'Well – there's help available, of course.'

'I know,' I said. 'I want to book an epidural *now*.'

I'd read about epidural anaesthesia and had met a woman who'd had it for the birth of her second child, after a most unpleasant labour with her first. She had recommended it warmly. 'I really *enjoyed* Sophie's birth,' she'd said.

'That's what I want,' I said, 'a totally pain-free labour.'

'Fine. There are one or two slight drawbacks I should point out.'

Drawbacks? Ah, I thought it had sounded too good to be true.

'Such as?'

'Epidurals don't always work – we're not sure why, or sometimes they work partially, but that isn't very often. And very rarely they have caused more serious problems, but I'm not going to tell you about those, or you'll fret for the next few months!'

'I still want one.'

'Fine. I'll make a note and book an anaesthetist for you.'

He stood up and we shook hands. 'See you in a couple of months.'

I came out walking on air. I was well, my baby was well, I could have a pain-free labour with an epidural anaesthetic – everything was going to be fine.

In the pale winter sunshine, going down the handsome parade of Regency houses, I did a little hoppitty-skip.

When I next went to see Dr Coigley, and he asked how I was, I said, 'I'm *fine*. I'm really enjoying being pregnant.'

'Yes,' he said, 'yes, most women seem to – the first time, at least.'

What on earth did he mean? If I felt as euphoric and full of fitness as this, I'd enjoy a hundred pregnancies. I had no sickness but I was repelled by the sight of meat. I had to avert my eyes when I passed a butcher's shop, and I was nauseated by coffee, and the smell of alcohol and tobacco; indeed, everything seemed to smell more pungent – I stood in the greengrocer's one day and was overwhelmed by the *leekiness* of leeks! I also got extremely sleepy, but that was all right; I went to bed every afternoon and slept for an hour, and stopped having late nights.

The books said that was what I should do, just as they said everything I was experiencing was as it should be – normal. Goodness, was I normal – every check and blood test – normal, normal, normal. N.A.D. it said regularly on my card – Nothing Abnormal Discovered.

If it had not been so exciting, if I had not been revelling in the experience of being pregnant, it would have been rather boring!

There was only one slight scare. One morning, when I was exactly eight weeks pregnant, I had a very small amount of bleeding. I did not really know how significant it was but it frightened me and I rang Dr Coigley in a panic.

'Is it much?'

'No.'

'Have you any pain?'

'None at all.'

'Hm. Eight weeks. Would you have been due for a period about now?'

I tried to work it out.

'Yes – I suppose so. Yes, I would.'

'It's probably nothing to worry about then. Go to bed for today. If you have any more bleeding, ring me. If it stops, you're probably all right. Don't worry.'

I went to bed. There was no more bleeding. I didn't worry.

I read it all up in the book, though. Miscarriage. No – no, I thought, none of that applied to me. I skipped over the pages and settled down to the section which told me about my baby's development.

'8th week. All the major internal organs are now formed although in a somewhat rudimentary state, and they enlarge and continue to progress towards assuming their permanent shape and position. The heart is beating strongly now that the circulatory system has been established in the fetus . . . The first very tiny movements of the spine begin. The length of the fetus is approximately 2.2 cm.'

I gazed down at my still completely flat, un-pregnant stomach in total wonder.

I'd bought a book on pregnancy the moment I had got back from that weekend in Scotland, although until I had official confirmation, I'd kept it hidden in a drawer and read it secretly when I was by myself. I say 'read' – devoured would be more the word. *Pregnancy* by Dr Gordon Bourne became my bible. I knew most of it by heart, and the pages about the baby's development, with graphic drawings of its growth, became thin with constant turning; whereas before, when thinking about wanting children, I had lurked like a man in a dirty raincoat near the magazine racks, now I went in boldly – hoping I would meet every one of our friends – and bought everything available, *Parents*, *Mother*, *Mother and Baby*, *Parent and Child*, and I filled in coupons to be sent piles of back issues, too. I don't think I read anything but baby books and magazines for nine months.

And I took the train to Birmingham and visited the Mothercare shop, and the maternity wear department at Rackhams too, and came home each time laden with parcels – nappies, clothes, dresses for me, equipment, the cupboards in our not very big house began to overflow. Stanley watched me, patiently, a bit bemused at what was taking over his life. One morning, he opened the airing cupboard for a clean shirt and came out holding a minute white sleepsuit.

'Do they *wear* these? It's like a bodysuit for a frog.' We fell about with laughter.

A lot of people are superstitious about buying anything for a baby before it is born. I was to become so myself, but this time I was totally equipped for the first year of our child's life by the time I was five months pregnant. I bought a beautiful brown carriage pram in the January sales. I went to London to do a radio broadcast and came back with a Moses basket – putting it up on the rack of the train compartment, to the consternation of an elderly businessman sitting underneath who thought it had a baby in it!

Enjoying myself? I've never been so happy. I woke up every morning with that marvellous sense of excitement in the tummy that comes on Christmas Day or a birthday – remembering that I was pregnant, that my baby was growing each day, that in July I would be a mother. My nausea and tiredness faded, to be replaced, just as the books told me they would, with a great sense of vitality and energy. There was no repeat of the slight bleeding, everything continued to be normal.

At my check-up just after Christmas, the midwife asked me if I would like her to book me in for the ante-natal and relaxation classes.

'No thank you,' I said firmly. 'I don't need to learn relaxation, I'm going to have an epidural anaesthetic.'

'Well, fine – but it might be a good idea all the same.'

'Why?'

'Oh, best to be prepared for everything. They sometimes don't work, and you might want to know how to cope with contractions so that if you have some before you get the anaesthetic you'll be happier.'

I looked dubious.

'And the classes are fun, too – you'll meet some other mums, have a chance to chat about things, and they talk to you about feeding and bathing and all that sort of thing.'

'I'll let you know.'

I'm not sure why I hesitated since I was so enthusiastic about doing *everything* pregnant mothers were supposed to do. I think I was steering myself clear of discovering much about labour, and besides, I didn't *need* to know, did I? I wasn't going to feel a thing, my epidural was booked and that was that.

I don't know whether I would have got to the classes on my own or not, but the following week something good happened, and I did go.

I was queuing in the greengrocer's again – because I continued to be off meat, I ate an awful lot of vegetables and had cravings for citrus fruit and green apples. Someone in front of me turned round, and did a double-take.

'Susan! What on earth are *you* doing here?'

It was Pat Gallimore. A couple of years previously, she had acted in a radio play of mine. She'd had a large part and I'd got to know her when we all spent a week in London in the studio. I'd assumed she lived there.

'I'm here because I live here now,' I said. 'I came when I got married eighteen months ago. What about you?'

'I'm married to Charles Gardner, a solicitor. We live in Henley-in-Arden – but I'm often in Stratford to do shopping.'

'And still acting?'

'Yes, I'm in *The Archers* – I play Tony Archer's wife, Pat!'

We went out of the shop together and decided to go and have some coffee.

'Only not coffee,' said Pat. 'I'm rather off coffee just now – I'm having a baby at the end of May.'

'So am I off coffee. Mine's due in the middle of July!'

So we went and drank hot chocolate at the Cobweb Tea Rooms, and caught up on each other's news before we began to discuss our pregnancies. We were both booked in to be delivered at the Leamington Hospital and to have our after-care at the Monroe Devis Maternity Home. It was a delightful coincidence, a pleasure to meet again, and in such happy, shared circumstances, the start of a firm and close friendship between us and between all our children which continues today.

We arranged to meet again for lunch, and then Pat said, 'Have you been to any of these classes? I was told it would be a good idea but I felt a bit shy about going on my own so I haven't booked in yet.'

'Nor have I. Why don't we go together?'

The following week saw us lying on the floor of a large, many-windowed modern room, cushions under our legs, with a lot of other women a good deal fatter and, by the look of it, quite some years younger than either of us. In our enthusiasm, we'd come to the class far sooner than necessary and so most of the others were in the last couple of months of their pregnancies. And looking around the room, we realised, perhaps for the first time, what they meant by elderly primae gravidae: Pat was thirty-three, I was thirty-five, the rest looked about seventeen.

But we enjoyed ourselves all the same, and it was true, there was a lot of chatting, sharing of symptoms and anxieties, a friendly, comradely feeling. We learned about bathing babies and the pros and cons of breast- and bottle-feeding.

I was firmly intent on using the bottle. I had always found the sight of a suckling baby distasteful, and the idea of having one chewing at my own nipples repelled me. Most of my friends in the past had bottle-fed – the breast was very out of fashion in the sixties and I myself was a walking advertisement for the benefits of plain cow's milk. Pat, on the other hand, was a militant breast-feeding supporter, with a little cache, she confessed to me, of special bras designed for the purpose already in her underwear drawer.

I was still adamant that I didn't need or want to know anything about deep-breathing and relaxation for coping with the contractions of labour, because I was going to have an epidural. But it was extremely pleasant, I had to admit, to lie on that floor, supported by those large soft cushions, hearing the rhythmical, gentle breathing of two dozen women, and the soothing voice of the midwife. During the second class, the sun came out and shone on us all through the windows and warmed our faces and our tummies, so that we were as relaxed as a lot of kittens. The following week, this being February and March, those changeable months, the sky grew dark as plums and it began to snow. I watched the swirl of it out of the windows and, after a time, I was so hypnotised by it, and by the quietness, that I drifted off to sleep. When I awoke, the snow outside was quite deep and bright, the room was filled with a beautiful, ethereal whiteness, so that, utterly relaxed and peaceful, I thought I might have died and gone to heaven, so blissfully happy was I!

There are innumerable joys in a successful and wanted pregnancy but one of the greatest for me was the sheer *physical* pleasure of it: the delight in watching my shape change, so that one day when I looked at myself in the mirror, I saw an unmistakable bump, which could not be pulled in; I was full of glee when I was unable to fasten skirt-bands, and proud as I blossomed out into full, flowing dresses.

There is nothing like the exquisite sensation of those first fluttering flicking little movements; no sensation comparable to that in later pregnancy when the little limbs inside kick out and flail, the body turns and twists. I used to lie in the bath every evening watching raptly as my stomach lifted and undulated, and a foot would trace its way across; I could take hold of it, feel a tiny heel, a sharp little elbow under the surface of my own skin. I had never much liked, or been interested in my own body. Now I was attuned to it as to some infinitely subtle, complex piece of machinery – which, of course, is exactly what it is – watching, listening, feeling. I lay in bed with my hands over my tummy, I stroked the baby beneath; I talked to it, sang to it. I noticed, as time went on, that certain things startled it: loud noises, sudden noises – the vacuum cleaner, a power drill in the road – the bath water, if it was too hot, caused it to squirm, as if trying to get away. Other things were soothing – walking, gentle music, my voice.

I was getting to know something about this new small person inside me – he or she who was only a few layers of skin and flesh away, part of me, and yet infinitely separate and unknown, entirely secret and strange. The spring came, the warmer weather – I always seemed to be warm now in any case. I felt as if I were blossoming along with the trees. Difficult to convey how happy I was, how well – how *satisfied* I felt.

Stanley was beginning to enjoy it all, too. On Thursday evenings at seven, there was a BBC TV series about having a baby, introduced by Claire Rayner, and he came rushing home to sit on the sofa and watch it with me. We learned a lot, followed the fortunes of a group of pregnant women, saw their babies being born – wondered, anticipated.

In May, we went for a week to Suffolk, my old stamping ground, renting a neat little cottage in Walberswick; we walked over the flat marshes close to the estuary, saw the most beautiful waders and sea birds dipping their elegant beaks into the gleaming silvery mud, and wheeling about the wide, wide East Anglian skies. We ate fresh fish and chips and great thick steaks – I was permanently hungry at that stage, and paid for indulging a hearty appetite with permanent heart-burn.

We went across to Aldeburgh, and the past I had spent there seemed to belong to another person, another life, yet nothing had changed, it was all still tranquil, still a little town huddled beside the grey North Sea. The previous November, Benjamin Britten had died. I took flowers up to his grave, which was as yet still mounted by a simple, temporary wooden cross, flowers of gratitude for what he and his music and his town had given to me. I stood beside the grave on that bright, but cold May morning, and a blackbird hopped about at my feet in the grass, and I heard the music of *Peter Grimes* in my head, and inside me, the baby lay quiet.

Later, I sat on a children's swing on the village green at Walberswick, and went gently to and fro, to and fro, tranquil, soothed by the rhythm, thinking of the past, but entirely happy to be in this present.

The following week, Pat and I went, with a gaggle of other fat ladies, on a tour of the maternity home, saw girls in beds looking pale and pleased with themselves, girls in dressing-gowns, pushing little wheeled trolleys. And in the nursery, rows and rows of new-born babies, swaddled tight, sleeping stilly, like those sweeties French children have at Easter, boxed rows of marzipan babies covered with fondant. Looking down at them, seeing blue-mauve eyelids, curled fists, pale, pale down on fragile skin, I was transported back to that other nursery; I remembered Aunty Matron and Dybdale, and the smells and sounds and sights of thirty years ago; and suddenly, the reality of it hit me. Strange thing to say – for naturally I had been perfectly well aware for more than six months that I was going to have a baby. Yet, until that day, standing in the maternity home among all those other newly delivered and about-to-be-delivered women, with the midwives and the trolleys, the disinfectant and baby and institutional smells, I don't think it had seemed entirely real – in spite of my swollen stomach, and the piles of nappies and tiny garments in the bathroom cupboard. It had all been a sort of dream or fantasy, a game even. Odd. On the way home, I said as much to Pat.

'I know *exactly* what you mean,' she said – and she was only a couple of weeks or so away from delivery. 'When we were in there, I suddenly thought – I'm going to have a baby!'

I spent a long time that evening trying to imagine what my baby would be like – who exactly it was, what having my own child, for the rest of my life, would really *mean*. I looked around the house, visualising another person there – a baby in a pram, in a cot, a crawling baby, a toddler, a small child. But until you have had your baby, it isn't, somehow, imaginable – babies are what other people have. I did my fair share of looking into passing prams, but those strange little blobs didn't seem to have much to do with me. I found them interesting, in a detached kind of way, but that was all. I panicked then. Perhaps none of this was a good idea after all, perhaps I had no maternal feelings, and what if I found my own baby merely 'interesting' but was detached from it? I stared at my expanding shape in the mirror. Too late now. No going back.

That was a terrifying thought, too. A friend who had had three children told me that the night before the eldest was born, she lay in bed and was suddenly overwhelmed by that thought that there was no going back – only she put it more positively because she's that kind of person: 'There's no other way but forward.'

I rang Pat. 'I've just realised,' I said, '*I've got to have this baby!*'

'Yes,' she agreed, so soon to have hers. 'Quite!'

It was a great comfort having a close friend nearby who was in the same boat.

We went to a reception one evening, and met a lot of old friends who were either interested in my condition, or politely pretended to be. (Pregnant women are awful bores on the subject of their condition; so are newly delivered women and all mothers of young children – it seems to go with the job!) I was introduced to Michael, a colleague of Stanley's who, in turn, introduced us to his friend – and the friend turned out not to be a Shakespeare scholar but, oh joy of joys, an obstetrician – and one, moreover, who was glad to talk shop. We went off into a corner, which spared the rest of the party. Tim was young, and positive and reassuring.

'And,' he said, 'I do recommend that you consider having an epidural – if you're as nervous as you say you are.'

I told him it was already booked and felt even more confident. Indeed, by the time the evening was over, I had actually begun to look forward to the birth, rather than to dread it and turn my mind sharply away from the whole prospect.

Another interesting thing was said that night. We were sitting together with Tim and Michael in a corner of the room.

'And I suppose you don't mind whether it's a boy or a girl?' Michael asked, and I chimed in with the usual reply, 'Not at all – so long as it's all right.'

That wasn't actually true. I *did* care what it was, but I'd never confessed as much, barely even to myself. Deep, deep down, though, I knew that I hoped the baby was a boy. I liked small boys, always had, and I wasn't at all sure about the little girls I'd known – boys seemed so much more open and straightforward. But there was much more to it than that – history was repeating itself already; I was having my first baby at the same age as my mother, but my relationship with her had been difficult and had grown more so. I desperately did not want to have an only daughter, as she had had, for both our sakes – I was afraid that I wouldn't be able to cope with what had always seemed an explosive emotional combination. There were two remedies. To have a son – and to have more than one child. But I'd gone on paying lip service to the accepted phrase – 'I don't mind what we have, so long as it's all right.'

Not Stanley though. He had never actually said it before. I hadn't known what he was really thinking but now he laid all his cards on the table.

'Well, I know what *I* want,' he said firmly. 'I want a little girl.'

I was startled. Not because I felt any conflict between us – but simply because I was so surprised that he dared to admit out loud that he wanted a daughter and so lay himself open to public disappointment. Except, I suppose, that if the baby were a boy, he would not actually mind at all. I hoped I would feel the same, if I had a daughter. I went on, keeping my counsel, wanting a little boy, trying to imagine it.

Meanwhile, on 27 May, Pat did have a boy – Thomas Charles, but from the beginning known as Tom – and a nice easy labour, too, no epidurals, no problems.

I went to see her. She looked extraordinarily well.

'Don't worry,' she said. 'It's really not at all bad – there was

67

just one moment when I thought, "Anything worse than this would be death" – but then, it was all over! It was *fine.*'

I was glad – though I didn't believe I would be so lucky. In spite of the reassuring chat with Tim, in spite of my being so very fit and all the doctors and midwives giving me the thumbs-up, I was apprehensive again, and perhaps fatalistic, too – other people had good, easy labours, but I wouldn't. I'd expected the worst all along, been conditioned to do so by the things my mother had told me. Well – never mind; there would be my epidural. What was there to worry about?

I envied Pat, envied her because for her it was all over (and she was already talking about the next one!) and because she had a son. She transferred to the Monroe Devis Maternity Home, and I went to see her again there, found her sitting on the grass in the gardens overlooking the green fields of Warwickshire and the River Avon beyond, in her nightie in the warm, late spring sunshine. The air was full of birdsong and the smell of fresh new leaves. The trees up the drive were that wonderful bright sappy green. Pat was in the middle of making a long daisy chain, to garland Tom's crib. 'Well,' she said, looking at me, 'you've grown!'

We went into the nursery to look at Tom. He is one of those children who has not changed since he was a few days old, he was Tom then, as recognisably, unmistakably, as he is Tom now. He looked a bit like a frog, peacefully sleeping among the other babies, very small.

In six weeks, here I would be, perhaps making a daisy chain, with the child now inside me, separate at last and asleep like Tom in one of these little cribs that looked, with their perspex see-through sides, exactly like propagators on wheels.

It was no good – I couldn't really believe in it. I felt as if I had been pregnant for ever, I felt cumbersome, I had strange aches and pains. I was like a furnace at night, and I could no longer see my own feet. My body was unrecognisable to me, I did not know it, but I was tremendously well and, in spite of the apprehensions, still incredibly happy. I sat in the sun in our little walled garden under the white lilac tree, and read and read. During those last weeks, I read all three volumes of

Olivia Manning's *The Balkan Trilogy* (better known now, since its television adaptation, as *The Fortunes of War*), and so that book, the atmosphere of wartime Europe that it evokes, is inextricably bound up for me with the state of pregnancy, and the summer sun.

It was the year of the Queen's Jubilee. There were flags everywhere, and Stratford was full of street parties, tables down the road and over-excited children. The weather broke. It rained and rained. The Queen toured Britain under an umbrella.

July came in and, for a few days, we had a heat-wave. I could scarcely move, I was so uncomfortable, so large, so hot. I stayed in the cool of the house during the day, and in the late evening, we took gentle strolls in the shade of the Theatre Garden, watched the rowing boats on the river, saw the swans calmly sailing, waited, waited. Those last days and nights of pregnancy were interminable – I felt suspended, excited, exhausted. I wanted the baby, was impatient – didn't want this dream-like, this *safe* existence to end. Knew that it would.

It did.

At ante-natal classes they talk about it, in magazines and books they present you with the array of possibilities, friends compare notes, but before you have had your first child, you can only wait, in a state of suspense, to discover just how your own labour will begin. Will you wake in the middle of the night with contractions? Will you suffer that indignity you've heard of and have your waters break in the middle of the supermarket? Will your baby be a week early and catch you unawares? Or two or three weeks late, so that you have to be taken into hospital and induced? How? When? And perhaps above all, *will you know?* No one can tell you, it's impossible to predict and each person, each baby, is different. My main concern was that we lived seven miles from the hospital – would there be an emergency dash by car or by ambulance? Would there be enough warning?

My baby was due on 14 July – Bastille Day, as everyone kept on pointing out. I knew that Mr Begg, my consultant, wasn't happy about letting his patients go too far past their due date, especially when they were older. I would be allowed a week, and then induced. That sounded fine to me, I couldn't imagine how I might endure being pregnant another half-hour.

On the evening of 13 July, I lay on the sofa, hot, uncomfortable, mildly cross. I hadn't wanted to eat anything much for a week or so – my stomach felt as if it was full of baby, there wasn't room for food, but Stanley appeared with a great punnet of the most delectable-looking strawberries, huge, moist, dark crimson. Suddenly, strawberries was what I wanted most in all the world. I ate. And ate, and ate, too many, but they tasted wonderful, fresh, sharp-sweet. The juice ran down my chin.

I went to bed, to half-sleep, to try and find the least uncomfortable position in which to lie, to wait until dawn when I might get up and make a drink, and sit in the cool of the garden, the best part of the day. I was even more uncomfortable than ever, with an ache low down in my back, and then, curious griping pains across my stomach. The strawberries! I raced for the bathroom and spent a turbulent half-hour. Returned to bed, forswearing all fruit for the next whenever. Lay, with the ache still niggling in my back. Slept, dreamed the weird, surrealistic, vivid dreams of pregnancy. Was awakened at dawn by a gripping sensation in my lower abdomen that felt quite different from anything I had experienced before. Went to the bathroom where I had what I knew at once was what I'd heard and read about – 'a show' (when the mucus plug at the neck of the womb comes away, marking the beginning of labour).

I remember going back into the bedroom and standing at the window, looking down into the garden, quiet and by myself, for a few moments before waking up my husband. My back still ached a bit, but there was nothing more. The baby was quite still, for the first time, very low down – so that I could rest my hands on the 'ledge' it formed.

It was a grey morning, the sky pearly-looking. The window was open, but the birds had all stopped singing now – during May and June we had been woken between four and five every morning by the chorus of all the birds in the back gardens of Old Town, and a million sparrows in the white lilac tree just beyond our bedroom window. Now, what I heard was the gentle coo-coo of pigeons in a loft at the bottom of the garden that backed onto ours, and the soothing whistle of their owner as he went in to feed them. In a little while, he might release them, to wheel in a great arc about the sky. On the lawn below, dip-dip-dipping into the earth, a male blackbird with a bright, bright eye. Over the brick walls, there were roses everywhere, the last of the first flowering, red, white, pink, climbing up and cascading down. Lots of trees, and greenhouses, and beds of bright flowers and hanging baskets and tubs – Stratford is a gardener's town.

I felt very calm, very still, strangely relaxed and confident now it had come. I stroked my stomach. 'Not much longer, little one.'

But he or she lay low, conserving strength, sleeping? Aware? Ready? Knowing and expectant, like me, or about to be taken by complete surprise, at the start of a journey it had no inkling of? Who could tell?

A little breeze blew, stirring the curtains, bringing the cool smell of outside into the bedroom.

I was ready. I knew. I turned from the window, and went quietly over to awaken Stanley.

Twenty minutes later I had telephoned the hospital, spoken to the duty Sister. 'You'd better come in, dear.'

We went.

Chapter 4

Whenever I think about that day, 14 July 1977, I reflect that ten years or so later, things would probably have been very different – indeed, perhaps in less time than that, for the revolution in hospital practices regarding childbirth was already under way, and was to gather momentum in the course of the next few years. I was at the tail end of methods that had prevailed in hospitals for a very long time. I knew no better, assumed that this was how things were because there was no alternative, that this was the best, the only way. I was docile, I accepted things, I believed doctors and midwives knew what ought to be done for my own good. I've never been a militant person, never joined any protest march. I have many reservations about the extremists in the natural childbirth, or in any other movement, but that they have done women everywhere an enormous service in pressing for so many changes, I have no doubt – even if I believe some have gone too far, particularly in their hostility towards the medical profession and their suspicion of its motives.

But it is thanks to them that women now have so much more choice about labour, that routine induction for convenience and 'social reasons' is now rarer. Women can walk about, sit, stand, kneel, adopt whatever position is comfortable for them in labour, within safe and sensible margins – can even give birth under water, in some circumstances. A happier environment in the labour room, belief that interference by machines and drugs should be the exception and when necessary, not the norm; the practice, in many hospitals, of making sure that the woman in labour is looked after by the same midwife throughout, whenever possible, not by a procession of new and strange ones. So much of this is taken for granted now, even if it may not be absolutely universal.

If I had been giving birth that first time some years later, I would probably not have been admitted to the hospital so soon. I was, after all, in the very earliest stage of labour, I could well have stayed at home pottering about until at least the early afternoon – perhaps later. Or, if they felt happier to have me there, I could have been up and about within the hospital. It would have relaxed me, and might have encouraged the baby to get moving more quickly.

As it was, from the moment we arrived, shortly after nine o'clock in the morning, technology and the efficient routine took over. I was undressed and got into one of those unflattering, billowing shrouds which fall open all the way down the back, exposing your backside to the world, and taken into the delivery room. It looked like an operating theatre – high narrow couch, tiles, gleaming instruments, gas and air machine, huge lights, sink, chrome taps with long arms; it was painted green and cream – of course – and there was a tall window at the far end, frosted over so that it let in a curiously deadened, greyish light. The whole reminded me of the dentist's surgery as much as anything – and I'd had some pretty horrendous times in *those* in the past.

I stepped onto a stool to help me climb onto the delivery bed and as I did so, my waters broke; gallons of warm wetness, it seemed, gushed down my legs and all over the floor, messy, embarrassing – though no one minded, everyone took it for granted.

More indignities to come: internal examination, shaving of pubic hair – routine, then, rarely done for normal deliveries now. For some reason, Stanley was asked to leave the room while this went on, and only allowed back when I was decent again. I lay on my back, feeling vaguely unsafe, as if I might easily roll off the narrow bed, and uncomfortable, too – flat on your back is the most miserable of positions during late pregnancy and, of course, the least efficient position in which to give birth. But that was the way it had to be – nobody's fault particularly, except that of the system.

For that first hour or two, nothing much was happening to me. I had a mild contraction from time to time – but very irregularly, and not especially painfully either. The hospital telephoned Mr Begg to tell him I'd been admitted – he was in the clinic I would have been attending for the last time if I had not gone into labour – and then, because he remembered that I had booked an epidural, they also began telephoning for an anaesthetist. Locating one took some time – it was the holiday season, there had been a couple of emergencies – but I was supremely unworried, sure that sooner or later one would appear, and besides, I wasn't in pain yet.

How long it would have been before my contractions got going of their own accord I've no idea – they weren't going to be given the chance. Because of the risk of infection entering the birth canal once the membranes have ruptured, doctors like the baby to get a move on – and mine wasn't, so they put me on a drip of Syntocinon, which gives the baby a nudge or, rather, a violent shove. One moment I was lying in a slightly dreamy, uncomfortable but pain-free state, the next, my stomach was exploding as a great wave of pain overtook me, and labour began in earnest.

And where, I cried out, was the anaesthetist when I'd begun to need him. I had had no preparation for contractions, hadn't allowed myself to make any, I wasn't expecting pain, wasn't able to deal with it.

Out of nowhere, cheerful and jokey (anaesthetists are generally cheerful and jokey), he appeared.

'Now, roll over on your side – draw up your knees as far as you can – yes, I know you've got a baby in the way but I need your back arched as far as it will go – keep as still as you possibly can and when you feel a contraction coming, tell me – I don't want to slip the needle into the wrong space . . .'

74

I couldn't ask him what would happen if he did – dared not think about it, couldn't talk at all, scarcely breathe, I was so squashed up.

I'd been told that the administration of the epidural was very painful. I braced myself. I felt hardly anything at all – firm hands on my back, a slight pricking, a cold sensation, nothing more, only the pain of my contractions which were not very frequent yet, but felt very fierce. Never mind – hold on.

'How long will it take to work?'

'Not long. You'll gradually begin to go numb – a bit like a local anaesthetic at the dentist.'

I did not. There was just a slightly fuzzy sensation down my right leg.

'Feeling better?'

'No.'

'You should be going pretty numb now.'

'No.'

'Give it another few minutes.'

The anaesthetist disappeared. After another half-hour, I hadn't noticed the slightest numbness and the contractions were every bit as painful.

'You *must* be a bit frozen up, surely?' The Sister seemed to think it was my fault, or else I was just being difficult. 'Now, let's do a little test – can you feel this at all?'

'Ouch!' In so far as it was possible to leap, strapped by drips and monitors to a couch, I leapt. She'd stuck a pin into my thigh.

'Oh dear. Dear me. That hurt, didn't it?'

'It hurt.'

She went off to phone the anaesthetist and sent Stanley back in. (He'd been banished when I was being given the epidural – I'm still not sure why, but perhaps that particular doctor preferred to work without someone peering over him. It is a very skilled and delicate procedure.)

Stanley held my hand through a nasty contraction, and looked anxious. I was to get so used to the sight of him, standing there beside me (no one thought to offer him a seat during the whole of my labour – and he was too uncertain to ask!) looking anxious, holding my hand.

In blew the anaesthetist again.

'As a matter of fact,' he said, 'I wasn't completely sure whether I'd got the needle into the space. You've got rather a difficult back.'

Now he told me.

'Let's have another try. Now, on your side – knees up – right up.'

After another long, slow lot of probing – again, not painful – he said doubtfully, 'Well, let's see how it is now – I think it's in.' He went away rather quickly this time. Too quickly, I thought.

An hour later, it was quite clear the epidural had not worked at all. When telephoned, the anaesthetist said there really was no point in his trying again, I was clearly one of those few people for whom it could not be made to work.

I couldn't believe it, and I was totally panic-stricken, unable to cope with the pain I was now having, not knowing what to do, chastised by the Sister for not even trying to 'breathe through the contractions'.

I had got my come-uppance, then. I heard all those voices cautioning me gently – Mr Begg, Tim, the midwife. 'Of course, sometimes epidurals don't work.'

I hadn't wanted to listen.

The Sister was telephoning to Mr Begg again.

' . . . in a bit of a state – she's a long way to go yet . . .' I don't suppose she knew I could hear her.

She came back smartly.

'Mr Begg says he'll be along in about an hour and I'm going to give you some pethidine. That'll help you – and have you learned how to use the Entonox machine? Gas-and-air?'

I shook my head miserably.

'Well, sit up and I'll show you. Come on – now don't look at me like that, dear, you're only having a baby.'

And so I was. It was just after twelve o'clock.

I went on having a baby for the next thirteen hours.

It wasn't a particularly long labour – not as first labours go, or so they told me afterwards – but it felt like forever, except that pethidine has a very peculiar effect so that time became telescoped, the hands of the clock in the delivery room seemed to whizz round as in some crazy speeded-up film, before going into reverse, or showing the same figure for hours on end. I hated the sensation that drug gave me, of being out of control, drunk, but unhappy. I couldn't make my thoughts work properly, or the right words that I had prepared so carefully come in order out of my mouth. I felt odd, floated about, didn't quite know what was going on, yet the pain didn't seem to be any the less, I was just even less able to cope with it.

I remember all manner of things from those hours, a jumble of incidents. Stanley looking anxious – then telling me he was going out for some lunch. Lunch? How *could* he go off and eat lunch? I was outraged, and even more so when he came back, telling me he'd eaten ham and eggs and drunk brandy. Mr Begg appeared from time to time but later when I wanted to ask him something, they said he'd gone home for supper. I was even more outraged – what could he be thinking of calmly driving off to eat *supper*? Anything might happen to me. It didn't, of course. A perfectly normal labour progressed, that was all.

It was, for most of its course, no better and no worse than a thousand others. It was my response to it that was so bad because I was so frightened, tense, and ignorant. I breathed in a great deal of gas-and-air through the nasty rubber mask, helped by one of a procession of midwives who came and went, on and off duty, but I never really got the hang of it. I just felt sick, and a bit more fuddled.

It was not the dreadful, terrible labour of all my mother's lurid stories, but it hurt. And it dragged on.

'Never again!' I remember shouting out to Stanley at one point. 'Just remind me about this – I'm never ever, ever doing it again.'

But he, on his feet for sixteen hours or so, didn't much fancy doing it again either.

14 July went. In the last hour or so, nothing seemed to be happening. I had a frantic desire to push, everyone got ready – the urge faded again. Nothing went on happening. The baby had got itself into an awkward position and the

fetal heart monitor showed that it was beginning to grow very tired. So was I, and my contractions were making no progress at all. It was not a particularly unusual situation, not dangerous, but it would be best for both of us now, the doctor said, if he helped a bit. They do not like to intervene with forceps too soon, but there comes a moment when the intervention is judged to be the best means of helping an exhausted mother and baby to a safely concluded delivery. That moment had now come.

Stanley was sent outside the room again, which was the worst of all, but Mr Begg was firm. And very kind, very reassuring.

There was a blur of pain that was perfectly appalling but did not, thank God, last for very long, and then he was saying, 'Tell Mr Wells to come back in – quickly.'

I looked towards the door as it swung open. There was Stanley. I saw his face change – he shot me a glance of amazement, disbelief, excitement. 'It's here,' he said, 'I can see it.'

Afterwards, he told me that when he came into the room, he saw part of a baby, looking as if it were quite dead, the colour of dark grey slate or stone, and that as he looked, its colour changed, flushed pink as it breathed.

'It was as if it just came to life – all in a few seconds.'

I couldn't see, but I could feel. No more pain or discomfort, then a slip and a warm slither between my legs – and that first unforgettable, heart-stopping cry – of what? Rage? Fear? Anguish? Protest? Or just life?

I could see a baby in Mr Begg's hands, slimy limbs flailing everywhere, kicking as he struggled with all the slipperiness to cut the cord.

'And what have we got? What have we got?' A second's pause, as he tried to see. 'We've got a little girl.'

But of course, of course, it was a girl. I'd never really expected anything else. I saw Stanley's face again, intent upon the little body, open with astonishment and joy.

'Ten past one,' somebody said.

'What's the date?'

'July 15th,' said Stanley.

'St Swithin's Day!'

And then the end of the bed was raised, and someone was putting a pillow behind my head and a cotton blanket over me.

'Here you are,' said the midwife, 'one daughter,' and handed her to me.

I looked down. 'But I know you!' I thought. 'I know you already. I've always known you.'

It lasted only a moment, but it was vivid, this extraordinary feeling that here was someone as familiar to me as my own self: I *knew* her – she wasn't a stranger, an unknown child, she was herself and we had met long ago.

'Hello, Jessica,' for that was who she was, at once.

She was very red, her mouth was an O of rage and misery, her tiny head misshapen, like a tomato that had been squeezed at the sides – her face marked by the pressure of the forceps, used to pull her gently those last few desperate inches to the shore.

But in the middle of her crying, she looked back at me – warily, her eyes clear and apparently all-seeing. We squared up to one another. 'And I know you, too,' the look said.

Then the midwife took her, and gave her to her father, and I saw for the first time the expression on his face I was to see a thousand, thousand times – tenderness, overwhelming surprise that this small person should be, happiness in her, delight – or, more simply, just love, instant, complete, self-abandoned love.

I expected to fall in love with her at that moment, too – it's what mothers are supposed to do, I knew that. But love wasn't what I felt then – or, at least, not of that particular kind, though I felt protective at once, and sorry for and tender towards this little bruised, angry, reddened person who'd had such a long, hard journey into this strange, new, bright world. Other than that, though, I felt strangely detached from her – interested, curious, a little nervous; I expected to love her at some point but, for the time being, I found myself reserving judgment.

I didn't dare tell anyone that, I felt too guilty and unnatural. I wish I'd known then what I found out later, that it's very common not to fall instantly in love with your own baby and some mothers take weeks or even months before they do and there's nothing unnatural about it.

She didn't stay with us very long. If delivery had been quicker and forceps had not been used, they would probably have encouraged me to put her to the breast then and there, while I was still on the couch. I would not have had any milk yet but the colostrum – the first fluid which contains so many vital protective antibodies for the baby – would have been ready. Although I had decided I would not breast-feed, the instinct to suckle the baby is very strong in those first few moments. But no one suggested it, and Jessica was whisked away.

They took her off for a bath, and a night in observation because of the trauma of the forceps. I sat up and had a cup of tea, feeling completely wide awake and not remotely tired – quite clear-headed. The moment I'd seen my daughter squirming in Mr Begg's hands, it was as though I'd had a jugful of cold water doused over my head; all the wooziness, tiredness and confusion that the mixture of pethidine and gas-and-air had caused were rinsed quite away, I was totally alert and focused on the baby.

After I'd been stitched and washed and had had my tea, after we'd talked and talked about her, gone over it all, the way one does after a great drama, Stanley had gone home, exhausted but euphoric, to telephone his mother. She lived with his sister in Canada, but it wasn't the middle of the night for them, it was quite a civilised time to receive a call. Then, I hoped, he'd sleep long and late.

In the lift on the way back to my own room, an Irish midwife with red hair bent over me. 'Mrs Wells – sure and I've just given your baby a bath and a drink of water and what was she doing but being wide awake and taking it all in, looking at me when she should have been sound asleep.'

I liked that. It was the first indication of what kind of person she was – wide awake, taking it all in when she should have been asleep – oh yes, that was how it was to be.

I stayed alert for the rest of the night – only dozing occasionally, and starting awake again, from weird dreams, to wonder where I was, and then where she was. It was the first night we had been parted for nine months – and I missed her dreadfully, missed the little body moving about inside me, the drumming of the tiny feet in my ribs. I felt peculiarly flat, light and empty, like a deflated balloon.

I was woken at five o'clock from my short fitful half-sleep by a noise like the squawking of a thousand seagulls – the dawn chorus from the nursery. (At that time, all the babies in that hospital were taken away from their mothers at night – an excellent thing since it meant the new mother got at least a few nights of uninterrupted sleep. But now most babies sleep beside their mothers in the ward; only sick or especially fractious ones are removed.)

Gradually the noise subsided as the babies were wheeled down the corridor to Mother, and food. I had been told that Jessica would need to stay under observation for six hours or so after her birth. I supposed she would be given water, perhaps a bottle feed. Out of the window, a grey sky, rain pattering against the pane. I couldn't go back to sleep, felt stiff and sore – but most of all, lonely.

I heard footsteps and trolley wheels squeak on the polished floor of the corridor outside, but for ages no one disturbed me. I wished they would. I wanted to know how Jessica was, to see her again – I'd forgotten what she looked like and I thought she must be feeling as strange and lonely as I was. How different, bundled up in sheets and blankets in a cot, from being curled naked in water tight inside the womb. I wanted to hold her, to tell her that I was still here, it was all right, to reassure her with a familiar voice, familiar smell.

They came to wash me, bring a bedpan, tea, breakfast – cheerful, brisk, busy.

'Do you know how my baby is?'

'Oh – no. I'm sure she's fine, I'll go and find out for you. Back in a minute.'

Only they never were. Nine o'clock came, ten.

I rang the bell.

'Please do you think you could possibly find out how my baby is, and when could I see her?'

'Of course – I'm sure she's fine. I'll be right back,' but she wasn't.

A doctor put his head round the door. 'Mrs Wells. I'm the paediatrician. I've just checked your baby over – she's super.'

'Can I see her? Do you think they could bring her in to me now?'

'I don't see why not. I'll go and ask Sister.'

Half past ten. Suddenly, I was hysterical – why wouldn't they bring her? There must be something wrong after all and they didn't want to tell me. Perhaps they'd lost her. Perhaps . . .

I put my finger on the bell and kept it there. When the nurse came running, I burst into tears. 'What's wrong with my baby? *Please* will you find out when I can see her?'

She disappeared swiftly, making a clucking noise. Two minutes later, the doors of my room opened and a cot appeared, pushed by Sister.

'Now then, Mrs Wells. Whatever's the matter? Here's your baby – she's fine. What on earth were you getting so het up about?'

It wasn't anybody's fault in particular, yet it was everybody's, an accumulation of thoughtlessness.

But it was all right now, it was over, she was here. The Sister wheeled the crib up to the bed, and I looked down. She was pale now, not red, pink-and-white baby coloured, neat and clean and tight under the white cotton blanket. A fringe of fine golden hair, tinged slightly ginger in the light; and the clear, faint mark of 'a widow's peak'. Her face was still marked and moulded slightly. Her eyes were wide open. She looked *exactly* like my mother. I stared; then, suddenly, she looked quite different, not like anyone.

'Hello,' I said, rather tentatively. 'Hello,' and my voice sounded strange to myself in the room. She stirred slightly, her eyes still wide open, a light, bright blue.

'You'll be all right,' I thought.

But I still didn't know what I felt about her, not really, was still holding back, loving, you might say, but not in love. Happy, though I didn't feel wild, hysterical joy, just complete satisfaction, contentment, relief, a deep, secure kind of feeling.

Closer to the surface, though, I felt excited, gleeful at the thought of all the people who were being told, the days of cards and flowers and presents and visitors to come, the novelty of it all. And it is the most marvellous time, like one long party and birthday and Christmas all rolled into one, and everyone smiles all the time and you are Queen of the May. Having a baby successfully, especially the first time around, is *fun*.

It went on being so all that first weekend, and into the next week. I stayed in the Warneford Hospital at Leamington three nights, and then we moved over to Stratford, and the little maternity home by the river: here the flycatchers darted out and back from the post at the end of the tennis court in the warm July evenings, and the smell of lemons being grated for the lunch-time lemon meringue pie caught your nostrils as you pushed the crib back to the nursery after the early morning feed – for they had proper cooks there, and real home cooking; and at night, we got Ovaltine or Horlicks, and giggled together after lights-out like schoolgirls in the dorm, until Sister came in smartly and ticked us all off. There were about a dozen of us in the long ward overlooking the garden, and it was friendly, sisterly, happy, a bit silly, and all the girls looked seventeen and the husbands who came visiting, even younger. Stanley and I felt like grandparents.

Oh, happy, happy week, when there were enough midwives to go round, with plenty of time for us all; there was a strict regime so that we were obliged to lie on our beds and sleep for an hour in the middle of the morning, after Sister had taken us through our post-natal exercises. The babies were brought in at four-hourly intervals to be fed, and taken away again afterwards, except when visitors came, and the visitors were strictly rationed, too, so that we didn't over-tire; it was husbands only in the evening. I don't suppose there is anywhere like it left in the country, nor anywhere which sends its mothers home so well rested, so 'set up'. I daresay it gave us a false sense of security –

four-hourly feeding and an uninterrupted night's sleep (they gave them all bottles in the night then, even the breast-feeders, unless the mother insisted on being woken), but at the time it was an innocent, peaceful paradise, and I was in no hurry to go home.

And on the day after we arrived at the nursing home, something else happened. In the big hospital, Jessica had been with me, all day, in the crib beside my bed and only taken away after the last feed at night. I'd been able to talk to her, pick her up and hold her, feed her when she needed it. Yes – I was breast-feeding, too. On that first day, the Sister had marched in, picked her up, unbuttoned my nightdress and attached her to me. My faint protests that I was intending to bottle-feed blew away on the wind as Jessica clamped her tiny jaw onto the breast, and sucked contentedly. 'There,' the Sister said, 'nothing to it, is there?' Apparently there wasn't. So I breast-fed, and found it, to my astonishment, the easiest and most pleasing of activities.

In the maternity home on that second morning, Jessica was upset for some reason, but they swept her away nevertheless, said she would 'soon settle'. I suppose I thought they knew best, but a little later, going past the nursery on my way to the telephone room, I heard her crying and crying. I went in. All the other babies were sound asleep, only Jessica cried, loudly, heart-breakingly, inconsolably. I picked her up and held her trembling little body close to me, and her sobs lessened. She went still. The top of her head in the crook of my neck felt damp, smelled that amazing, indescribable new-baby smell; I cupped my hand around it, a perfect round and fragile as an egg.

Beyond the tall windows, white clouds sailed in a lavender-coloured sky, and the leaves of the chestnut trees were darkly, heavily green. When I looked down again at my daughter in my arms, she had fallen quite asleep. And I felt a surge of love for her that was like a great wave breaking, passionate, protective, tender, total – the first time I had felt it. I couldn't understand why it had not come sooner, how I could have been holding back, uncertain of myself in relation to her, shy, detached, nor how I could have worried about having a daughter or ever wanted a boy.

84

I stood there quietly holding her in my arms for a long time in that now-silent room, overcome by this new feeling, this extraordinary love until, in the end, the martinet of a Sister bustled in and peeled her off me, and shooed me away to have my rest, and I wandered miserably down the long corridor, bereft of my baby, seething with rebellion, in thrall to love.

Chapter 5

Nature is a capricious, treacherous, wholly unpredictable force. 'Labour isn't a bed of roses,' a friend had written to me while I was pregnant, 'but you forget all about it in no time at all.'

I had found that hard to believe and after all, my mother had not done so. But my friend was right. Within twenty-four hours of the end of my labour with Jessica (during which I had made Stanley promise faithfully to remind me that I would never ever do it again), I was cheerfully talking about doing it again. I didn't want a very small gap between children, wasn't sure I'd be able to cope but, by the time Jessica was three I thought I would want another. We'd decided to call a boy, if we'd had one, Nathaniel, and I still favoured that, but oddly enough, it was our next daughter I talked about – Daisy Maria (Maria, as in 'fire' not Maria, as in 'fear').

Stanley duly kept his promise, and often reminded me what I'd said, but I waved him away.

'It wasn't *that* bad,' I said, genuinely having almost forgotten, 'and it doesn't go on forever. Besides, first births are always the hardest – the next time, it will be much quicker and easier. You'll see.'

He looked unconvinced.

But it didn't take very many weeks of living with the infant Jessica to silence me on the subject of having another baby, even though I thought I knew for certain that I did not want her to remain, as I had been, an only child of older parents.

I wonder, looking back, just how awful a baby she really was. Perhaps, compared to some I have read about, she was no worse than a wakeful but average first child. I'm not sure what I'd expected. Certainly I'd stayed with friends who had young babies, and sometimes they had cried, but apparently, for decipherable reasons. I suppose the problem with Jessica was not simply that she cried, and we did not know why – it was that she wanted to be awake for so much of the time when I needed her to be asleep, and I had not realised how much of my life would be eaten up by attending to her. I had not yet come to terms with the fact that when you have that sort of young baby, you can look after them and not have time to do very much of anything else at all.

I was tired, of course – bone-tired. You are, after pregnancy and birth and when the body is thrown into reverse and you are making pints of milk every day.

'Look at cows,' Dr Coigley said, 'they just chew grass all day when they're in milk, they don't try to do everything else as well.'

Jessica liked feeding, and after a couple of days at home I realised that the four-hourly routine in the maternity home had been an artificial one, and I am sure she had cried a lot and been topped up with bottles of milk and water behind my back. The only thing to do was feed her on demand, and hope she would ease herself into a sensibly spaced routine quite soon. She did not. 'On demand' meant little and often – every hour was the norm. I had plenty of milk, except at the end of the day when I needed to rest and recoup, and she wanted to go on feeding, and sucked and sucked in frustration at the empty breast before exploding in hunger and rage.

She woke three or four times every night, to be changed, fed, changed again – but not then to go back to sleep, not for at least another hour. Stanley would get up at dawn and take her downstairs, to allow me a chance to go back to sleep for a couple of hours. Most early mornings when she was wide awake, he simply put her in the big brown pram, and pushed her around the sleeping streets of the town, seeing butchers swilling out the pavements in front of their shops at five o'clock, and lone fishermen pedalling off to their vigils under green umbrellas on the river bank, and milkmen and paper boys. Once a police car drew alongside him.

'Morning, sir. Mind if I ask you what you've got in that pram?'

He shot the two officers a bitter look. 'A baby,' he said between clenched teeth. They grinned sympathetically, and left him to it. What had they expected him to say – 'Lead from the church roof'?

In the evenings, when we had eaten and Jessica still cried if I tried to settle her down, Stanley took her into his room and played Mozart and Elgar to her, and showed her his beautiful collection of pictures on the walls. Otherwise I sat on the sofa, endlessly feeding her, reading my way steadily through Dickens and Hardy again, and the short stories of Katherine Mansfield which didn't seem to mind being interrupted, or watching all sorts of television programmes I would not normally bother with, or falling asleep as she sucked and sucked. I loved her dearly, she was endlessly interesting and entertaining but many a day I could have chucked her in the river. I was so tired, tired of feeding, tired of tramping around the town with her, trying to get her off to sleep, tired of being tired.

She must, in the end, have settled down, but she never came to terms with sleep, not until she was four and at school all day. She woke in the night to be fed until she was at least nine months old. She stayed awake all evening, and was ready to begin her day at dawn. She needed company, stimulation, conversation, diversion, attention. Later, she woke when she was teething, had her first colds, her first nightmares – anything, everything. There was nothing *wrong* with her, she was healthy and normal and everyone – doctors, nurses, health-visitors, friends, the books – assured me that her alertness and lack of interest in sleep, were signs of intelligence. And so she apparently was, reaching every milestone early, stretching herself forward to do the next thing and the next, fascinated by everything around her.

Whenever I looked at her and thought that she really must not be an only child, that the tensions between us were already too great, I put the thought to the back of my mind.

Sometimes I mentioned Daisy Maria – and got a desperate look from Stanley, but mostly I lived for the day when Jessica would sleep more, entertain herself sometimes, demand a bit less of us.

Just before her first birthday, Stanley took up a new post as Shakespeare Editor of the Oxford University Press, with a commission to prepare a completely new Oxford edition of the playwright's works; and so we left Stratford-upon-Avon for Oxford. For a year, I was miserable and lonely, spending too much time cooped up with Jessica, knowing no one, missing Pat and little Tom, and all the rest of my Stratford friends; missing the town itself. Oxford seemed impersonal, big, I couldn't get used to it.

That first winter was a bad one. It snowed after Christmas, and the snow lay and the cold winds blew for weeks. When I trudged up to the local shops, I had to shove the push-chair over the rutted ice on all the dull suburban side-roads of North Oxford. I felt low, in need of a break, sunshine, friends – and most of all, in need to get back into touch with myself again. I had not really done any work since Jessica was born, apart from scrambling to finish a column about books every month in the *Daily Telegraph*, and I felt the need of it badly, missed using my mind and my imagination, missed writing, panicked that I'd never be able to again.

One bleak, grey February day, when Jessica had a cold and was getting back teeth and had woken several times a night for the previous week, I sat down in a chair and began to sob and, having started, couldn't stop. In the end, I was so miserable and lonely, I rang up Stanley and he came home at once, comforting, concerned, and we all went off in the car to have tea and cakes at Brown's in the Woodstock Road.

As soon as I felt better, I said that there were three things I needed to do. Book us a holiday in the sun. Find someone to come and look after Jessica so that I could work for a few hours each morning. And make some new friends. Stanley agreed readily.

The following day, I telephoned the agency that I have relied upon to find me sterling helps ever since. Yes, they said, they were sure they had just the right person – would I like her to come and see me tomorrow? Euphoric, I put Jessica into all the paraphernalia of a toddler's winter clothing, and pushed her up to the travel agent's, to pick up a sheaf of sunshine brochures. On the way back, she wanted to walk – and very slowly and carefully walked right up somebody's front path. Before I could grab her back, the door opened and there appeared a small snow-suited child of exactly the same size. They stood and stared solemnly at one another while I tried to encourage Jessica to come back; then an extremely pretty woman emerged behind her daughter.

'Hello. Do you live down here? I don't think I've seen you.'

'No,' I said, 'two streets away. We're new – well, fairly – we don't really know anyone.'

'Oh, then won't you come in? Come to tea,' she said, and introduced herself as Polly Mitchell, 'and this is Milly.'

It was my first Oxford friend. From that day, things began to look up. We booked a two-week holiday in a remote bit of Corfu for the end of May, Polly and I got on well, and the little girls seemed to enjoy one another's company. And our helper started from nine until twelve, daily, the following week.

There was a summer-house at the bottom of our North Oxford garden which was reasonably comfortable and wired up for electricity, so that I had a study away from the house, that essential in every writer's life – indeed, as Virginia Woolf has it, every *woman*'s life, 'a room of my own'. I began to work again, on an edition of the short stories of Thomas Hardy, for Penguin English Classics, on a new radio play of my own and, as a challenge, six weeks of scripts for *The Archers*. It was the sort of thing I had never done before, didn't even know if I could do, but the producer, Bill Smethurst, had spurred me on to try by suggesting to me that the job wasn't as easy as it looked. I had sneered a bit. 'Right,' he said, 'why not see what you're made of?'

I picked up the gauntlet. It was great fun, it paid well, and it gave me a discipline and a deadline, to get me back into the habit of being a professional writer again.

I went down to my little hut at the bottom of the garden as soon as Jen arrived to look after Jessica every morning and, as the work began to go well and I got used to it, I felt the most marvellous sense of exhilaration, to be writing again, to have time and space and quiet to myself, and to have a long break from Jessica so that I enjoyed her much more when we were together. I felt as if I had crawled out of a long dark tunnel. I could even cope with the continued lack of sleep, and the fact that Jessica was now having five-star, mega-tantrums, the legendary sort, kicking and screaming like a child possessed by demons, in shops, in the street, on buses.

It was at the end of an arduous day – scarred from steering her through a particularly bad one of these battles, clinging on to my new-found freedom and partial independence, that I burst out to Stanley: 'Only child or not, she'll just have to cope with that as best she can, and so will we, because the last thing I could face, now that I can see light at the end of the tunnel, is going through all that again. I categorically do not ever want to have another baby!'

Part III

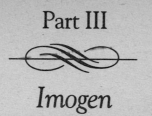

Imogen

Chapter 6

In the summer of 1980, we moved out of suburban Oxford into the country. When I wrote about it all later, in *The Magic Apple Tree*, I called our house Moon Cottage. That is not its name but during those first few weeks of June and July, I so often stood at the top of the stone steps that lead down into the garden and saw the moon rising, new as the paring from a silver coin, or full as a golden pumpkin, behind the branches of that apple tree, that the fictional name was inevitable.

The cottage lies at the end of a lane leading from the church. Go on a few yards down the slope and the lane runs out into a bumpy, stony track between hawthorn and blackberry hedges leading down to the open fields and woods and that mysterious stretch of wild, ancient country called Otmoor, below.

The village is small and old, the central, original core of it built of stone, like our own cottage, in the 1740s, though the church dates back another six hundred years.

We discovered the village when we were invited to lunch by an old friend of Stanley's who lives a hundred yards up the lane, and though it was dank chill November, I knew at once that this was where I wanted to be. And that night, I dreamed about the village, and saw Moon Cottage in that dream, though I did not then know it, only felt happy at seeing it, and remembered it clearly when I awoke. A few weeks later I drove out to see a cottage that had been advertised for sale, walked down the lane, and stood at the top of the seven stone steps – and there it was, but real this time, no longer in a dream. The same house though.

When I was a small child living by the sea, we had often taken the slow country bus ten miles inland to see friends of my mother's who had a farm, and a daughter of my own age. She and I ran riot among the corn and climbed the haystacks, and lay down in buttercup meadows and gorged ourselves among the raspberry canes, and the air smelled of cow dung and chickens and warm grassland, and I was in paradise. At the back of my mind, it had always remained there, the countryside, the quietness of it, the space of open fields and sky, I had always known that one day, somehow, I would live there.

Now we would, most of all because I wanted to bring up my young daughter in the country so that she would have a store of rich memories by which to sustain herself later. Because of Stanley's job, the need for Jessica to have the best schooling, and for us to have access to trains and libraries and shops, I knew we would not be able to isolate ourselves too far in the depths of the countryside. Finding our village was a stroke of the best fortune because it is very quiet and self-contained, and overlooks miles of farmland, ancient grassland and woods, is set up on a hill, and best of all has no through traffic; the main road is a couple of miles away but it takes only twenty minutes to drive into the centre of Oxford, ten to reach the motorway to London.

From the moment we arrived, I felt as if my roots were being sunk deep down, and I might have been there for half my life.

That September, Jessica went off to the nursery class of the Oxford school we had chosen. I collected her at lunch-time every day. I had the cottage, the garden, the quiet lanes and, sometimes, it seemed, the whole of Oxfordshire to myself. I planted and dug the garden, and sowed seeds. I walked, I made friends, and over the next months, we acquired a black kitten called Polly, a terrier called Tinker left by the old lady in the tumbledown cottage next door, and a run full of nice brown hens. And I began to keep a daily diary, and to write *The Magic Apple Tree*, my book about our life at Moon

Cottage. I was very contented indeed. As the seasons slipped by, I had everything, as they say, that I could ever want.

Jessica was at nursery school each morning and I did begin to feel that I had a great deal of time to myself, and that perhaps I could afford to give a bit of it away to other people. I didn't quite see myself as a member of the Voluntary Brigade in a hat with a badge, but I wondered if Oxford's John Radcliffe Hospital, which was only a few miles away, ever needed helpers.

I went to find out. The general hospital was rather overstocked with volunteers at that time, so they sent me across to the tall white slab of a building known as the JRI – the maternity hospital. They were in need of someone, temporarily at least, to push the shop-trolley around the wards one morning a week. Why not?

I felt that eventually I could be even more usefully employed as a volunteer in some more demanding job but, for now, it was fun, I was needed, and above all, I very much liked the atmosphere of the hospital. It is a light, airy, spacious building, full of windows, full of activity.

Full of babies. As I went slowly from floor to floor, ward to ward, along the polished corridors, my nostrils full of the nostalgic smell of hospital – I heard babies, saw babies, smelled babies. Babies in cribs or in the familiar perspex-sided propagators, babies in arms, babies being changed, bathed, fed, babies awake and crying, asleep and dreaming. I stood while mothers in nightdresses chose stationery and drinks and sweets and toiletries from the trolley, and saw the sunshine filtering through the wide windows onto beds, cots, cards, flowers – babies, babies, babies.

I'd forgotten it all, but now, now I remembered – the atmosphere, the excitement, the joy, the sleeplessness, the congratulations, the pain, the pleasure.

The rational part of me, the top of my mind, was dismissive. It remembered everything only too clearly, and my vow never ever to have another baby, and it was absolutely right. But something else had already begun to take me over – and that force is quite irrational, has nothing whatsoever to do with the mind, it is the force of nature, a purely biological urge, it is feeling, not thinking, desire not reason.

For a while, though, I did not admit to it, genuinely did not know that it was there. I only knew that my visits to the JR awakened vivid memories, nostalgia for a particular time of my life, sadness that it was gone forever – powerful feelings.

Around this time, my friend Pat in Warwickshire had an early miscarriage. She had had two previously, before Tom was born – and she had wondered then if she would ever be able to have children. I was sad for her now but I did not identify closely with her experience – a miscarriage was something that happened to other people, like infertility, car crashes and death.

Meanwhile, my stint of trolley-duty came to an end, and I looked elsewhere for a voluntary job, contacted Sobell House, the Oxford hospice in the grounds of the Churchill Hospital. Tiny babies were out of my life again, and I never thought about them. But the desire for a baby has nothing to do with thinking.

I had been having some trouble with the intra-uterine device I had had fitted after Jessica was born, and began to think about a more permanent and problem-free form of contraception. Sterilisation? Fine, but for which one of us? I mentioned vasectomy to Stanley who was, if not *happy* at the idea – I suppose all men have natural reservations – willing to consider it; our GP, Dr Sacks, thought it the sensible choice as we were sure we wanted no more children, and referred us to a specialist. The appointment was made for some weeks ahead, in the early autumn.

My *Magic Apple Tree* book was finished. As always we returned for a couple of weeks to Stratford during the summer, where Stanley ran the Royal Shakespeare Theatre Summer School and attended the International Shakespeare Conference, and then, in September 1981, Jessica began full-time school. She was four, lively, bright, funny, articulate. She slept more or less normally now, and so, blissfully, did we. By day, she was delightful company, she and I had our squabbles, we both burned on short fuses, storms blew up, died down. I loved her dearly, and she was happy where we lived, happy at her school. Happy.

When she was two or so, she had had an imaginary dog for some time. She called him 'Tree Trunk'. Now when we were out for a walk one day, I suddenly asked her if she remembered him. 'Oh yes,' she said, 'but Tree Trunk has gone now. I've got a little sister instead.'

And so she had, her little sister became a member of the family, eating with us, going out in her pram, sharing Jessica's room, occasionally taking the rap for misdemeanours. I didn't ask whether she minded that her sister was imaginary, or if she would like a real one. Dangerous ground.

Meanwhile, the specialist's appointment card for Stanley was pinned on the notice board in the kitchen.

Then two things happened. For a while, I'd been trying to lose a bit of weight and not succeeding, and in despair one evening, I said, 'The only way I'm going to get rid of half a stone is to go to a health farm for a week.'

'All right,' said Stanley, 'I'll give it to you as your fortieth birthday present.'

Forty!

No, it was no good, I simply couldn't take forty seriously, it was a joke, that was all. I rang Pat.

'No, no,' she said. 'You can't be forty, that's what our mothers were, and their friends. Forty isn't for us!'

No. But when I looked ahead to February, I saw that actually it was for me. My thirties were running out. I didn't really mind at all, not a jot – except that people over forty didn't have babies – or rather, they did, but not easily. I looked it up in a book.

'After forty, fertility begins to decline sharply.'

That went home. I brought up the subject with Stanley.

'Well, yes,' he said calmly, 'but surely you don't want another baby, do you? Just remember!'

I remembered. Yes, of course, he was right.

That night, I wandered down long white corridors in my dreams, looking and looking in room after room in which there was baby after baby, all smiling, all beautiful – but none of them mine. Where was mine?

I spent the next day in the garden. It was still very warm, although it was early October, a golden day. I picked the last of the peas and cleared the sticks and dead stalks and burned them, and watched the thin smoke coil up blue into the air, smelled the pungent, unmistakable smell of autumn. In the field over the wall was a fox, keeping close to the hedge, perhaps the same one who patrolled the garden each and every night, sniffing round in case I had forgotten to lock away the ten brown hens.

And the ten brown hens clucked in their run, a contented, country sound. I went to collect the eggs, still warm. A perfect day, peaceful, satisfying.

I went inside to change, feeling good. In half an hour, I had to set off to collect Jessica from school. I washed, got out of my garden clothes, and crossed the room to take a clean shirt from the wardrobe. And as I did so, I had – what? – a sight, a 'vision' I suppose, so vivid, so strong, it was almost truly real –

I saw a small child, a toddler of one and a half or two, running across the room to me with open arms. It was not Jessica, but it was my child, my other child, our next child, a small daughter.

I felt it, saw it, imagined it so intensely that I all but reached out my own arms and bent down to her to catch her up as she reached me.

I sat down on the bed. The room was quiet. Empty.

But I knew at that moment and acknowledged it openly, that I wanted, and would have, another child. I went from a strange state of suspension, of not letting myself think about it, to one of complete certainty. It overtook me and settled upon me. Changed me irrevocably.

I was considerably shaken, but happy, too. Something was released within me, so that I felt light-hearted, excited, free, I looked forward.

I rang Stanley and told him how worried I had become. He was too, he confessed, and suggested I try to talk to the surgeon. As soon as he was off the line, I picked up the telephone again and, surprisingly enough, got through to the consultant without much trouble. I explained who I was, and that my husband had an appointment with him for the following week. Then I faltered, uncertain, quite, how to talk to him, anxious lest he should curse me for a stupid woman who didn't know her own mind from one minute to the next, and had wasted his valuable time.

'The thing is,' I said nervously, 'that now it's come to it . . . you see, we don't feel happy about the prospect of permanent sterilisation . . . it suddenly seems . . . a bit too irrevocable, and . . . well, I've just seen my fortieth birthday looming ahead – and it's made me wonder if we might not want another child . . . before it's too late . . . and altogether . . .'

Gently, kindly, he interrupted me. 'Mrs Wells, I'm very glad indeed that you rang. Let me assure you that if you – either of you – are in the *slightest* doubt – even if in the end it proves to be only temporary – there is no way I would *consider* performing a vasectomy. None. You've done absolutely right to ring me.'

It seemed unimaginable, within only a few days, that we had been about to put paid to our chances of having another baby for good. What could we have been thinking of?

Or that was how I felt. Stanley, as always, was less certain, more cautious. But it was very clear to him how passionately I felt, how I had been completely overtaken by this new, urgent desire for another baby, it was not simply a question of his letting me have my own way – he respected the force of such deep feelings. And he adored Jessica, loved being a father, and was so very good at it. He is the most patient of men with his children, self-sacrificing, attentive, gentle, generous. If he spoils, it is in ways which are not so very important; if he is indulgent, it is not with material things or because he wants to curry favour, but because he loves to give which is not – or not always – the same as 'give in'.

Perhaps I rushed him into the idea of another child, swept him along, as I had done before. But I knew for sure that at heart he did not mind, would love a second baby as much as his first. Above all, I knew it would be right for Jessica, she should not be an only child: her 'little sister' should not remain imaginary.

At the beginning of November, I had my contraceptive coil removed.

That Christmas morning, I woke before the others and lay in the dark for a while, seeing the dim outline of the full pillow-cases of presents, heaped on the sofa beneath the bedroom window, feeling that stir of excitement that, since childhood, has never failed me on Christmas morning. But before Jessica woke and came bounding in, before the day was all open and spilled out at my feet like a package, I was quiet, and thinking to myself, 'Next Christmas, there will be two children – two stockings to fill, this time next year, we shall have another baby.'

Early in January 1982, I knew that I was pregnant. I had conceived as quickly and easily as before, no problems. Well, but that was right – I didn't have them, did I?

Chapter 7

It was lovely to be pregnant again and I felt, as before, extremely well – no sickness yet, no tiredness, but I noticed the changes in my body, those strange pricklings in the breasts, the way the veins showed through the skin more, seemed bluer, more enlarged.

In February 1982, my fortieth birthday came and I laughed at it, gleefully. When I reached thirty, I'd been shocked, age had seemed to be overtaking me, at too great a rate. But forty? Forty was absolutely fine and even if I couldn't go to a health farm, what better way to celebrate than by having a baby? Stanley was cautiously pleased too – though I think he needed longer than me to get fully used to the idea.

I was busy, in some demand for broadcasting again. I went off happily to London to record the radio programme *Quote Unquote*, and then to do *Call my Bluff* for the first time. I'd always liked the occasional public side of being a writer, it raises the spirits to make a foray into the entertainment world, makes a change from solitary, serious work.

The only slightly disconcerting thing during the afternoon and evening at Television Centre was that I kept getting very mild stomach cramps – a little like the period pains I'd had as a girl, only they weren't strong enough to be called pains, and nothing else untoward happened, and they subsided by the time I was on my way home.

It was about this time that I renewed my acquaintance, and my friendship, with another pregnant 'older woman' – the novelist Angela Huth. We had first met some years before when she was introducing an edition of the Radio 4 arts programme *Kaleidoscope* to which I was contributing. We had then lost touch until she rang me to say she was living not far from me in Oxford. We met spasmodically, but then there was another break because we were both busy with our own lives and because Angela had been preoccupied with trying to have another baby. Having had a son who lived for just two days in 1962, she now had one almost grown-up daughter, Candida, and had only succeeded in keeping her by spending virtually her entire pregnancy in bed.

Recently married again, to James Howard-Johnson, and wanting to have a child with him, she had been through another tragedy. After a hazardous pregnancy, she had finally given birth, at the age of forty-one, to a son – Jed. But Jed had been born with Down's Syndrome, with many physical complications arising from his condition. He had been gravely handicapped and lived for just nine months. (Because of her 'incompetent cervix' Angela had been advised not to have any tests to see if she was carrying a Down's Syndrome child although, at her age, the risk was increasing. Whoever could blame her? She was desperate to give her baby every chance – and fate had played one of its cruel tricks.)

Now after two three-month miscarriages since Jed's birth, she was pregnant again, fit and well – though taking care. She had had all the tests – including, after much deliberation, the one to see if she was carrying another Down's Syndrome child – and they were fine, her baby was normal and she did not miscarry. I admired her very much, but although I had felt tremendously saddened by everything that had happened to her, I still did not identify with them. She was another of those women who were unlucky in their pregnancies. I was not. We were different. We wished one another well: Angela's baby was due in April, mine in September.

There was another surprise, too. We had been going to spend a weekend in Stratford and hoped to spend a day with Pat and her family. But when she rang to say she'd better warn me that Tom had chickenpox – just in case I didn't want to take the chance of Jessica getting it – I said, 'It isn't Jessica so much – it's me. I think I've had it but I'd better steer clear of those sort of viruses just now – it's better if pregnant ladies don't get chickenpox.'

There was a small silence. Then Pat said, 'Susan, that's quite extraordinary because, you see, so am I!'

Her baby was due at the end of July, we were six weeks apart exactly, just as before. Shrieks of surprise, congratulations, delight.

A week later, Jane Coles, a producer from the BBC, drove up to see me. The television programme *Omnibus* wanted to make a twenty-minute film about *The Magic Apple Tree* to coincide with its publication in May.

She wanted to bring a crew and to film life going on around 'Moon Cottage', with all of us taking part, and then to take in the village itself, and perhaps a church service. In those days, I still went to church sometimes and took Jessica. Stanley, a pious and respectful unbeliever, sometimes came too. We didn't go to the village church, but to St Nicholas, Old Marston, five miles away on the fringe of Oxford itself, yet still with a true village community. I had greatly taken to the warm, ebullient, welcoming vicar, Paul Rimmer, and to the vigorous life of his congregation – if not to what Stanley called the 'Andrew Lloyd-Webber-style music' of his choral services!

In *The Magic Apple Tree* I had described a Mothering Sunday service in which the children went up to the altar for posies of spring flowers which they took back to their mothers, and the whole congregation later went outside and joined hands in a great ring, the whole of the way around the church, to 'girdle it'.

Jane planned to film that at St Nicholas, and over lunch in the village pub we talked about her outline scheme – and then about Mothering Sunday, which led us on to the subject of mothers and my pregnancy. It shouldn't interfere with the filming, I said, since I was perfectly fit and well and likely to remain so.

She said I was lucky, she envied me. She herself was forty too, and had been wanting a family for years, but couldn't conceive.

'I did just once think I was pregnant,' she said. 'Perhaps I was – but anyway, nothing came of it. I've accepted it now.'

My confident, complacent state must have hurt her but she gave no sign, she was genuinely pleased for me. In her place, I thought I would have been bitter. I wondered what it was like to long and long and try and try for a baby, to go through all the indignity and physical and emotional strain of tests, and get nowhere. How did such women survive, how did they bear it? Not to conceive easily, not to have a baby when you chose – I couldn't think how anyone coped with it. Thank heavens I didn't have to.

In March, on the day before the film crew were due, I had a small amount of bleeding. It alarmed me for a moment – but I quickly remembered that I had had the same thing with Jessica and all had been well. I didn't worry. Only I did notice that I suddenly felt less pregnant. I no longer minded the smell of coffee or alcohol. And my breasts seemed to have shrunk back, the veins were no longer prominent.

Nonsense.

Early the next morning, a little more bleeding. I telephoned the doctor, and was told to take it easy.

'Stay in bed?' I asked.

'Not necessarily, there's no evidence that it does any good. If you're going to be all right, you'll be all right; if you're going to miscarry, nothing will prevent it.'

He sounded friendly but quite casual.

I went to bed. When the film crew arrived, I told Jane they would have to manage without me. She agreed at once, urged me to stay where I was and not move, said the baby was by far the most important thing, they could perfectly well make the film without me.

They did and it worked, I think, far better for my *not* being in it. They filmed the view from our garden across the fields at dawn on a misty morning as the sun broke through, Jessica trundling about the garden with her small wheelbarrow, and planting bulbs under the magic apple tree, and our hens pecking about, the cat, the dog, and later, the Mothering Sunday service in Old Marston church. It was quite beautiful.

I looked at it again the other day, and knew the book, and I, could not have been served better.

Meanwhile, I lay in bed, anxious, alarmed, frustrated, while the filming went on downstairs and outside, feeling out of it, but sure I was doing the right thing. So long as I lay down there was no bleeding. When I got up and moved about, there was, occasionally, a little.

I rang the doctor again. What was going to happen? He didn't know. Time alone would tell. Wasn't there anything he could *do*?

'No,' he said firmly, 'it's in the lap of the gods.'

The next morning, I'd had enough, I wasn't prepared to wait for the gods any longer. I was miserable and tense, desperate to know what was going to happen to my body – my baby.

I had been booked in under a private obstetrician again, one recommended by Dr Sacks.

'He's young,' he said, 'and the best. His name is Mark Charnock.'

My first appointment with him was in a couple of weeks' time. Now I telephoned his secretary direct and told her what was happening, how anxious I was.

'I'll get in touch with him,' she said at once, reassuringly. 'I know exactly where he is – in the infertility clinic. I'll call you back.'

I felt better at once. She sounded so nice, so warm, capable and confident. I had done the right thing.

It was only twenty minutes or so later when she rang back, to ask if I could go up to the John Radcliffe Hospital in an hour's time, where Mr Charnock had made an appointment for me to have an ultrasound scan. He himself would see me after that, as soon as his clinic was over.

I rang Stanley who came at once to fetch me, much relieved that this vague state of uncertainty and suspense was over, and that something was happening.

When I had been pregnant with Jessica, ultrasound scans had been available only in the Queen Elizabeth Hospital in Birmingham, and since nothing had gone wrong, I had not been sent for one. They were not, at that time, routine. I didn't know what to expect but I wasn't worried at all about the procedure – only about what they would find. And the moment we stepped through the glass self-opening doors on to the blue carpet of the reception area, and into that familiar, nostalgic maternity-hospital smell, I felt safe, glad that someone would be looking after me, doing the best for the baby. It was a feeling that never ceased to support me through all the visits of the next few years. Going into the JR seemed like going home.

So, for the first of what would be many, many times, I undressed in the cubicle in the radiography department, put on the cotton gown, then went through the scanning room where Stanley was waiting. I climbed onto the high couch, and felt cool oil being spurted onto my bare tummy, and then the flat surface of the small scanner held by the radiographer being swept to and fro. He had red hair and a friendly face, and looked at me comfortingly over half-spectacles.

'Watch the screen.'

I did so. A sort of black-and-white television set was to one side of us, with a strange, furry picture – a lot of close-together lines, blurred white circles. It looked like part of the weather forecaster's chart, or else the surface of the moon.

'There,' he said, and pointed. 'That's your abdomen. Now, here's the uterus – and – ah, that's it. There's a fetal sac.'

Another blob, pear-shaped.

He held the scanner steady.

'I can't see any sign of life – there doesn't seem to be a heart-beat – perhaps a bit early to see – let's measure it.'

Two little blips moved across the screen.

'How many weeks pregnant do you say you are?'

'Nine – nearly ten.'

He shook his head. 'No,' he said, 'that's not nine weeks. It's either six –'

'No – not possible.' I was quite sure it wasn't.

'Then I'm afraid things don't look too hopeful.'

What did he mean? What was he saying?

'There's a fetal sac all right,' he explained gently, 'but no baby inside. Not any longer.'

I felt cold, I couldn't believe it, took Stanley's hand.

108

'Probably there was one but it simply failed to develop.'

'Now what will happen?' I was suddenly afraid, as well as unhappy.

'I'll write a note to Mr Charnock – you're going to see him, I gather? He'll decide what he wants to do – I think I know what that'll be, but it's up to him. Do you know where to find him?'

'On Level 7. We're to wait for him there.'

'Fine. The lift's just opposite the doors into this department. Someone will be at the desk up there.'

He put his hand on my arm, to steady me as I clambered down from the couch, and kept it there for a moment.

'Don't fret,' he said. 'We had several miscarriages after our first two children – and then suddenly, another daughter, just when we'd more or less given up and my wife was well over forty. You'll get there, I'm sure.'

It was the first of many such comforting reassurances from so many people in that building. I felt he was on our side, that he understood, and I was grateful to him for having told me something about himself. Doctors so rarely do. It helped me a great deal.

I dressed, and we went up in the lift, to wait for the consultant. The Sister who met us knew we were coming, and took us into a small waiting-room.

'He might be quite some time,' she said. 'There are some magazines – and there is a tea-bar down on Level 1, you could get a drink and a sandwich.'

I wasn't hungry, but it was one o'clock and Stanley was. He disappeared in search of food and drink, and I got up and stood, looking out of the window.

Very far below, I could see tiny figures walking along the paths, between the maternity and the general hospital which stood behind it – nurses in capes, doctors in white coats, men with trolleys; on the road, ambulances drawing up at the main entrance. I found it interesting and reassuring. Opposite, rows of windows – wards, labs, offices. Above, a dull grey sky. It was a view, a scene, I was to become very familiar with.

Stanley came back with coffee and rolls and we waited, not quite knowing what to say to one another. I skimmed the magazines and didn't take much in. Then, after half an hour or so, the door opened and the man who was to become so bound up with our lives, the focus of so many of our hopes and fears, came into the room.

Afterwards, on the way out, Stanley said, with an amused look at me, 'Well, you'll be quite happy in his hands, won't you?'

I knew what he meant. Mark Charnock was, as my GP had said, very young indeed to be a consultant, only in his late thirties, tall and extremely handsome. Well, it's always a bonus to have a good-looking doctor! But I felt in good hands for much more obvious reasons. I had liked the way he talked to us, explaining everything fully and clearly, putting the options to us so that, within limits, we could decide with him what was the best course of action, rather than, as so often, being *told* what to do. I was to get very used to this over the following months and years, it was Mark's usual approach.

He had looked at the radiographer's notes and felt that although there didn't seem to be much hope that the pregnancy was viable, it wasn't a good idea to rush into taking me into hospital at once, and giving me a D & C (dilation and curettage, to scrape out the contents of the womb), it was better to be on the safe side and wait – just in case.

'How long?'

'I suggest a couple of weeks. Then give you another scan to see what's happening.'

Stanley looked worried because he was due to fly to America to a conference in ten days. At once, Mark said, 'Fine, then let's just give it a week. That should be long enough.'

'And what in the meanwhile?'

'Just carry on as normal, take it easy but no need to stay in bed. And if you begin to have any pain or bleeding, or anything that worries you, ring straight away.'

He took out his card and wrote something down.

'This is the hospital number. You can contact me here through my bleeper, or my secretary will know where to find me. And that's my home number: if you need to ring in the evening or at night – at any time – don't hesitate.'

That impressed me most of all – a doctor who handed out his private number!

We left the hospital. I didn't feel very confident about the pregnancy but I *did* feel absolutely confident in my doctor.

A week later, we went back. The scan showed virtually nothing – the fetal sac had shrivelled, and there was definitely no life inside it. I was booked in to have my D & C two days later.

'Oh pooh, miscarriages,' an acquaintance said to me recently, 'miscarriages are nothing – everybody's had a miscarriage.'

And yes, so they have – what are the statistics? One in five of all pregnancies? I scarcely know a married woman who has not had one at some point in her child-bearing years. However, there are miscarriages and miscarriages. To be rushed into hospital as an emergency with sudden dramatically heavy bleeding and extreme pain, and lose a fourteen-week pregnancy without warning, is a very different matter from losing one six weeks earlier in the undramatic way that I did. To have your tenth successive miscarriage at the age of forty after fifteen years of marriage and never to have had a child is infinitely worse than losing a third pregnancy when you are twenty-eight and when you already have two healthy children and every prospect of going on to have two more.

Nevertheless, I take issue with that woman's dismissive attitude, for the misery and grief one suffers at a miscarriage, and the depression afterwards, are out of all proportion to the seriousness of the event and bear no relation to it. Nearly everyone I have ever talked to about it and who has suffered one says the same.

It can be – as it was my first time – a trivial physical event, not painful or even uncomfortable, not especially frightening, but the shock and unhappiness it brings in its wake are enormous. My head took in what I was told – that there was nothing basically wrong with me, and that the miscarriage would in no way affect any future pregnancies or their successful outcome. This was a common occurrence, and although no one knew the reason for it, in the vast majority of cases the body was being efficient in rejecting a fetus that was not viable, or a baby which was in some way seriously handicapped. In other words, the miscarriage was almost certainly a *good thing*.

That was what I heard and understood and knew was reasonable – but reason was irrelevant, it was not the head that was reacting with such violence but the heart. When you lose a baby, however early, you suffer a bereavement, and you have to mourn and grieve, and give yourself time to get over it. And the emotions always affect the body, which in any case has suffered a hormonal upheaval. In my case, because the pregnancy had died in-utero but not been rejected naturally – what is called an incomplete abortion – I felt, during that week of waiting, like a walking coffin, knowing that a minute scrap of life had died and was being carried about inside me. And for weeks afterwards, I felt ill – tired, sick, occasionally giddy, drained. I also felt profoundly depressed and, as always with me when in an emotional turmoil, tense and anxious, I got agoraphobic, couldn't drive my car, had panic attacks and sudden machine-gun bursts of palpitations, I broke out into cold sweats, I felt faint.

It all alarmed me, because I was sure there was something seriously wrong. Well, so there was. I'd miscarried, I'd lost the baby I had expected and wanted to have. Suddenly, I felt mortal – and very vulnerable. It was a great shock to discover that those things I had believed only happened to other women had happened to me. I was never again to feel safe and confident and serene in my child-bearing, never again to face a pregnancy in that blissfully self-assured way I had done with Jessica. I was to look back on those days and envy my old self.

But I was still sure that I would conceive again easily, whenever I chose to. When I went to see Mark Charnock after having the D & C, he said although the traditionally cautionary advice had always been to wait five to six months after a miscarriage, to give the body a chance to rest, he saw no reason why I should do so this time. I was physically well, nature would see to it that my bodily cycle got back to normal quite quickly, and the best cure for the mild depression I was bound to experience would be to start another baby whenever I felt like it.

Also, he pointed out tactfully, I was now forty, and time was precious. I came out of his consulting room feeling confident again. My pride, as much as anything, had taken a blow but although I did not feel myself for some weeks, I was climbing back fast.

Mark had said, 'If there's any problem, anything you're worried about, do please ring. Otherwise – well, see you when you're pregnant!'

Stanley returned from his American trip in April, *The Magic Apple Tree* was published at the beginning of May. Watching the *Omnibus* film, made that sad weekend two months before, I remembered how I had felt, lying upstairs in bed, not knowing what would happen to me, while the filming went on all around. It was nice to see what they had done, and I admired it tremendously. The miscarriage seemed far away now. We went for an idyllic week to Salcombe in Devon, where we enjoyed empty beaches, warm spring sunshine, and all the lanes and meadows full of flowers. The only thing wrong was the news of the Falklands war, which raged on the other side of the world, depressing and violating us, in a hotel full of retired Rear-Admirals, rooting for victory.

But the bays of Salcombe are so beautiful, the views of the sea and the freshly green countryside were so satisfying, we all felt rested and re-charged. I came home and cast my eye over the diary for the coming months, feeling I had better not plan anything definite for very far ahead because, any day now, I would be pregnant.

I was not. The summer came, and ripened. At the end of July, Pat had a daughter, Harriet, born as easily and speedily as her brother. They were in the same hospital and we went to see them. The maternity home had not changed, the Sisters were all still there, the sun shone, my new goddaughter lay, small and blonde-haired and seraphic in her crib. I felt the deepest envy. I would have hated my friend, I think, except for the fact that she did not gloat – and that I was sure I was pregnant. Only a few days but –

But no. I was not. I began to panic, bought a few books, secretly, about infertility – which I now understood could mean not only difficulty in having a baby at all, but delay in conceiving a subsequent child, for a variety of reasons, known and unknown.

I had identified, in the spring, with all those women who had suffered miscarriages, knew at last what they felt like. Now I was beginning to understand some of the strain and misery of the infertile. It seems a little ridiculous, looking back, that that is what I ever considered myself to be. Time puts everything into a proper perspective and it is easy to forget how keen the edge of my fear was. All that was happening was some delay – perfectly well within normal limits, in view of my age, but I had conceived twice before at once, and now I could not. Why? What was wrong?

I began to take my temperature, to try and pinpoint ovulation (now it would have been a whole lot easier, you can buy testing kits at the chemist, so that you know *exactly* the right days you are fertile), and insist that Stanley be at home and 'on duty' during the time I was most likely to conceive. And for the second half of my cycle, I fretted, examined myself minutely for early signs of pregnancy, became so sure, so sure, that my breasts were a little fuller, that I felt slightly nauseated, that coffee did not appeal to me – that I was one, two days late so surely, surely I must be –

No. Month after month, I burst into tears of anguish, frustration, misery. I counted ahead – nine months from July – August – September – October, and saw my baby recede into the far future – I was going to be forty-one after all, not forty, when I had my next child.

I thought of very little else at that time. I did manage to write another book, a ghost novel called *The Woman in Black* and while I did so, and Jessica was on summer holiday, Julie Tranter, the daughter of her headmistress and a medical student at the John Radcliffe, became my 'mother's help'. She and Jessica were tremendously happy together. I wrote my book in seven weeks – and at every available opportunity, quizzed Julie about obstetrics and gynaecology, fertility and infertility. I was obsessed by my need to become pregnant and, in a strange way, that is what the desire becomes – not for a baby so much as simply to succeed in getting pregnant, being in that state. The baby is almost incidental.

It was a miserable time, but it gave me a precious insight into the lives of a great many other women I simply had not considered very much before. I even joined an organisation called Child which has a monthly newsletter for infertile couples, with the latest medical information, reports about research – and case histories from poor, sad couples desperately trying any treatment and paying anything for it, in their quest to become pregnant.

It put my own situation into proportion a bit too. Yet I often wonder how much it really does help to realise that so many others are far worse off than oneself, whatever the problem. Because it is your own state, your unhappiness that obsesses you, your misery and despair and frustration and anger are all you can feel, and they do not necessarily bear much relation to the facts of the case. I was experiencing emotions I had not known before, my reserves of confidence and pride were being fast eroded. I could hardly bear to look at pregnant women in the street. When I heard a friend tell me she was pregnant, I *hated* her, wanted to stop my ears, I was bitter with jealousy and hurt pride. Babies were being born everywhere and I could not bear to think about them.

I must have been weary company for Stanley during this time, but he endured my anger, put up with my obsessive need to have a baby, willingly gave himself up to it, with the patience and quiet understanding I had come to expect of him – expect, and rely upon – though never take for granted. And he had been sad at the miscarriage, too. Although I think he now wanted another child, he was not obsessed by it, consumed by it, as I was. How could he be? How could any man?

It was a miserable summer and autumn, and I dreaded Christmas. When I climbed up on the steps to reach down the box of decorations, I wondered what point there was in pretending it was going to be a good season of the year. Celebrating the birth of a baby? Oh, yes, we'd hoped to be doing that this Christmas, only there was no baby.

I don't think I have ever felt so bitter, or so sorry for myself. There seemed to be not much point in anything. Even Jessica seemed far away from me, happily involved in her school, her friends, her new-found delight in being able to read.

But just the very last day or two before Christmas, I realised that this time it was not a false alarm – I really was pregnant. I put a star in September in my new calendar, and spent the holiday in a haze of triumph and euphoria. When Pat and her family came to us for Boxing Day, I looked at Harriet, rolling over on the floor in her vigorous efforts to get at the sparkles on the Christmas tree, and thought, 'This time next year – by next Christmas.' And told Pat, gleefully.

In the middle of January 1983, I had another miscarriage – it happened in the same way as before. Another 'missed abortion' followed by the inevitable D & C.

I didn't have time to become too depressed, or to work myself up into a state about not being able to conceive because I did so again the very next month – but by now, I had lost my confidence. I felt no joy when the pregnancy test was positive and the ultrasound scan showed a tiny heartbeat. I felt only apprehension. I no longer believed that I would sail through everything. Instead, I began to wonder what dreadful thing would go wrong next.

Several things did. I contracted a particularly virulent strain of flu with high temperatures, and a serious chest infection which gave me, for the first time in my life, bouts of asthma. It was terrifying. The infection would not respond to antibiotics and I went on feeling extremely ill, and very depressed, too.

It was nearly three weeks from the start of the illness before I came downstairs one Sunday afternoon to sit by the fire with a rug round my knees and watch television with Jessica. I still felt awful, but perhaps it would cheer me up to be away from my bed for an hour or so.

In the middle of the film, the telephone rang. Stanley answered. It was the warden of the block of sheltered flats into which my father had moved just before Christmas. After years of trying, the Council had agreed to take him into Oxfordshire because we lived there, his only relatives, and he was now seventy-six. He had been so happy to move, felt safer, only four miles away from us in Old Marston, instead of fifty-four miles away in Coventry.

Now, just three months later, he had gone for a long walk

116

in the cold, and on his way back, dropped dead in the street a few yards from his flat.

It was an appalling shock. And the next morning, with my temperature still high and the chest infection worsening, I began to bleed a little. When Stanley, in the midst of all the dreary but urgent business that has to be done in the wake of a death, also had to telephone urgently to Mark Charnock, it was to discover that he had just left for a three-week holiday in his native South Africa.

It felt as if the end of the world had come. I remember sitting weeping helplessly on the end of the bed, feeling more ill than I had ever felt in my life, and quite unable to face the thought of anything, or to cope with my father's death and possibly another miscarriage. I just wanted to be dead myself.

Two hours later, I was being admitted for rest and observation to Level 7 of the John Radcliffe. I was stuffed full of new antibiotics, and treatment was started for asthma, with a Ventolin inhaler, as well as physiotherapy. Otherwise, I was simply to rest.

When I crawled into that high narrow hospital bed and put my head on the pillow, I have never been so relieved to be anywhere. I felt safe, I knew that somehow or other, I would be made better. Whether or not they would save my baby I did not know. I had lost all faith in my own ability to have a successful pregnancy. Why, why, *why* couldn't I? What kept happening? What was wrong with me? No answer – except that in this case the influenza, plus the high temperatures, had probably damaged the developing fetus, and the shock of my father's death had not helped.

I lay, day after day, unhappy and lonely, looking out at the lights from the general hospital opposite, seeing the ambulances like toy cars so far below, and the tiny people walking about, not reading, not thinking and, all the time, dreadfully conscious that the body of my father was in the mortuary somewhere in that building across the way.

Polly Mitchell, my first friend from North Oxford, came, on the day of the funeral, to take me from the hospital, to be with me, and bring me back from the church at the bottom of the hospital drive; my father was buried in the cemetery I could see from the other side of the hospital. I didn't go to the committal, I was ordered back to bed. The day was bitterly cold with a cutting north-east wind, but I felt too numb with misery, too ill, too anxious, to take very much in. That night, Stanley came to see me, looking white and strained. He had had to carry the burden of the arrangements, look after Jessica, worry about me – he was exhausted.

But gradually, I began to feel better. And to feel at home in the John Radcliffe. In the next room was Margaret who was trying to keep a baby after six or seven miscarriages. She was forty-two, she had not yet had a child, and now they had admitted her for the full term of her pregnancy – her baby was due in July. I used to go in and talk to her, and be helped by her calm and cheerfulness. Her room had been turned into a mini sitting-room – she had a television, a sewing machine, books, a magazine rack, a radio, but she had to rest in bed for much of the time. After work, her husband came fifteen miles or so to spend the evening with her before driving home again. I marvelled at their patience and determination.

By the end of the next week I was feeling much better, though my chest infection had a firm grip and simply would not clear up (in the end, it was May before it finally went).

On the Saturday morning, Stanley and Jessica came to fetch me home. I had been well looked after by Mark Charnock's Senior Registrar, a huge, cheerful, bearded New Zealander who looked like – and probably was – a rugby prop forward. I was told to take it very easy, that things were looking good, the bleeding had settled down. All my forms had been filled in, I was booked for delivery in September – but I couldn't believe in it. When I answered all the questions about what kind of delivery plan I had, if any, whether I wanted to breast- or bottle-feed, it was as though I were acting in a play. I refused to look at the babies in their cribs as I walked out of the building. Because of my miscarriages, having a baby had become an unreal idea, a successful outcome could have nothing to do with me.

I was as depressed, as low, as pessimistic, as fatalistic as it was possible to be.

Perhaps it was as well that I had no hopes for then they

118

could not be dashed. That night, I had a miscarriage, at home in the bathroom. Stanley telephoned for a friend in the village to come and be with me while he contacted the hospital. Pam Edmonds-Seal, tall, quiet, calm Pam, drove down within minutes and sat, holding my hand. Her daughter was at school with Jessica which was how we had met. Pam is a nurse, her husband, John, a consultant anaesthetist. I was in good hands – and above all, safe, sure, sympathetic hands. And Pam, who is a devout evangelical Christian, said they would be praying for me, too – she had, in any case, prayed for a long time that I should have another baby, and she was sure, absolutely sure, that I would.

Only not this time.

The next morning, I was re-admitted to hospital.

Chapter 8

On New Year's Eve, 1983, we gave a party – it was a happy evening, a gathering of a couple of dozen close friends, to eat and drink around our fireside. Until even a few weeks earlier, I would not have thought I could possibly face and organise such an occasion, but as much as anything, I think I wanted to see the back, publicly, of what had been a particularly awful year.

I had felt ill – if not seriously ill, then several degrees below par physically – for much of it, and I had had no hesitation at all in agreeing when Mark Charnock advised me very firmly not to try to become pregnant again during it but to give myself at least six months to rest and recover. I had used up all my reserves, and knew that I had. There was nothing at all to fall back on – I was down, as it were, to the bone and below. I was exhausted, I had no energy, no stamina, no resilience or resistance, I went from cold to cold, infection to infection, picking up every bug that was passing. However, I am, I think, physically a pretty tough person, and I knew my body would soon regain strength, my immune system would learn to fight again. No, it was not the physical reactions to everything that had happened so much as the mental and emotional ones that were so frightening.

For about a year, I was depressed – not just a bit miserable, a bit low, but properly, clinically depressed. When I woke each morning, a sense of doom and misery that there was another day to face seemed to lie like a stone in the pit of my stomach.

I had no interest in anything very much — family, work, the world around me, holidays, friends — everything was an effort, a drag. I was irritable, and short tempered. I nagged at Stanley, turned on Jessica, could not bear anyone's company for long, but was afraid to be by myself for fear of —? Of nothing, really. Just fear. I was gripped several times a day by uncontrollable fear, panic, when I wanted to run away somewhere, pull a blanket over my head and hide. I was agoraphobic and claustrophobic. I hated crowded streets and shops, dared not drive, and when I walked in the fields around the cottage, I felt terrified that the sky would fall in on my head or the ground would swallow me, that all the birds were swooping down to attack me. I had night sweats, waking with nightdress and bedclothes wringing wet, I had palpitations, felt sick, felt faint or giddy, the world seemed to shift suddenly before my eyes, but worst of all was the leaden grey misery, the sensation of feeling that I was constantly on the edge of an abyss — and yet knowing that I was a fool to have these feelings. I felt embarrassed, ashamed of them all, I could scarcely bring myself to talk about any of it, but kept most of what was happening to me bottled up inside. I cried a lot, I rang Stanley a lot at work, suddenly in the middle of the day, to beg him to come home and stay with me. He always did.

It was scarcely surprising that I should have such a violent reaction given the things that had happened to me, all at one time, but I fought against it, could not understand or accept, or stop feeling tense, anxious, restless, angry with myself and longing to be well, be normal.

It was a long, slow haul back to relative well-being. What helped?

Time to a large extent, I think, simply the soothing passage of time. Gradually, imperceptibly, I began to feel better physically, and to improve slightly in mood and emotions — but my nerves seemed to be electric, and to lie very close to the surface.

In my search for health and wholeness, I consulted a great many people, and read a large number of books. I also talked to a few close friends. Dr Sacks, my GP, was sympathetic and extremely helpful, and sent me to see a psychiatrist who put me at once onto a course of mild anti-depressants. They helped, though the side effects were rather annoying – I have always reacted badly to medication. But talking, recounting the list of symptoms and receiving reassurance about them was perhaps most important of all. If your heart suddenly races, you feel a terrible sense of dread, you are faint, your eyes play tricks, your hands tremble, you have a lump in your throat that means you find difficulty in swallowing – you believe, not surprisingly, that you have something seriously wrong with you. I certainly did. I lay awake each night, certain that I had cancer, heart disease, motor neurone disease, a brain tumour – yes, it's funny now, perhaps, but at the time it was not. Most of all, I think I was afraid that I was going mad – and that is the most terrible fear of all, that you might actually lose your reason.

A year previously I had consulted a homeopathic doctor in Oxford, Lee Holland, about Jessica's asthma. Now I went to see him about myself. I would never visit an alternative practitioner who was not a qualified doctor but knowing that Lee was, I felt confident and I reached out desperately for help from any source. I began to read a lot about homeopathy and other branches of alternative medicine, and at the time, I believed much of it; if I had been a cancer victim, for example, I would have put all my faith in alternative therapies. Now, I am ambivalent about them, to say the least, but although I doubt if any of the little white pills and powders that Lee gave me did anything at all for me – I think any effect homeopathy has is almost certainly as a placebo, albeit very powerful – I certainly found talking to him and listening to his helpful, practical and very calming and reassuring advice, a most positive thing.

My aim in reading books was to understand what was wrong with me and try to cure it, so that I would be fit and well to start trying once again to be pregnant. I ransacked the shelves of bookshops and libraries and I devoured anything and everything to do with pregnancy, problems, miscarriages, infertility, and in each one found something, some snippet of information or advice, which was useful. I read books about positive thinking, relaxation, healing, meditation, hypnosis, manuals of self-help for depression and anxiety.

I took what I wanted, and what was relevant to me, from

each and discarded the rest. I watched any television programme – often in the middle of the day – which looked as if it might help me to understand what was happening to me, and there were a great many; every one gave me something – and, perhaps, best of all, often showed me another woman telling her story, sharing her own problem, assuring me and thousands of others that we were not alone and that recovery was possible.

Gradually, bit by bit, I improved. I spent hours talking to friends, to Pam Edmonds-Seal, to Judy Bogdanor, a GP whose son was at school with Jessica, to Pat Gardner on the telephone.

To God. I did a lot of talking to God in those days, a great deal of anguished, desperate praying for help. I bargained with him a lot – I would do almost anything if only I could have a baby. And in the depths of despair and at the height of panic, I just cried out for help. At the time, I always got it immediately. There was always an absolutely instantaneous response – a friend would ring or turn up on the doorstep so that I could talk to her, or else I would simply stop crying, stop feeling afraid. I also always knew, somewhere, somewhere very deep down, that in the end it would be all right, that in time I would get what I wanted. *But* – I also knew, somehow, that it was not yet, that a lot had to happen, things weren't going to be straightforward.

I'm always suspicious of those who claim to have an answer to prayer, to know what God is saying to them – and my whole attitude to God, my religious beliefs, have undergone a profound sea-change since those days, I am not the person I was. Yet I would not be telling the whole truth if I did not set down what surely happened at that time – that I never prayed without help appearing in some form, and that my inner certainty about what would happen in the long run, and after a great many things had come to pass, was correct. It wasn't as clear and easy to understand as I make it sound, but I cannot in all honesty deny it.

It had been a year of deep unhappiness, shock, depression, fear, a year that seemed to go on for ever, but things make a pattern. Looking back on it, I see how much I learned that year, how much I came to know myself, how, at the end of it, I understood a bit more, had grown up a bit more – because I have never doubted that life is a journey of self-discovery, and a process of learning and growing.

Only perhaps I could have done with a bit less of it all at once.

Still – I was the one who'd started it. And I was going to finish.

I had plenty of examples of determination and persistence. Margaret, who had been lying so cheerfully and patiently in the room next to me in the hospital, waiting, waiting, had a little daughter quite happily and safely in July. I'd been in to the hospital once or twice to see her during her wait, talked to her about myself, watched her getting larger. Now I went in with flowers and gifts, and rejoiced over Katie, lying peacefully in her little crib, the outcome of all the months of waiting. Well – if Margaret could do it . . .

And there was Angela Huth whose daughter Eugenie had arrived after all the years of unhappiness.

Two more special babies were born during that year, two more happy endings to two sad, frightening stories.

A couple of years earlier a friend, the actress Emily Richard, had been a week from her due delivery date when, one afternoon, she realised that she had not felt her baby move for some hours – perhaps for most of that day. She had gone to the hospital where, at first, a junior doctor had reassured her that all was probably well. But Emily, with that sixth sense of all pregnant women, had still been unhappy. In the hospital car park, she had met her consultant and told him of her anxiety. Instead of telling her to stop worrying, he had taken her back inside to check things for himself. Emily had been right, after all. A scan revealed that her baby had died in the womb.

The following day, she had gone through a full labour – with the physical help of an epidural anaesthetic but nothing, of course, to dull the emotional pain – and gave birth to a little boy. The fact that the dead baby was discovered to have had a rare and severe condition was an explanation, but no real comfort. Almost nine months and all for – nothing.

I remember how thrilled we had all been at the news of Emily's pregnancy, how much she had enjoyed it, how she had longed for her baby and we had all said what a marvellous mother she would make –

I wept and wept for her.

Now, in what seemed a very short time (although, in fact, it was three whole years of frustrating waiting, and trying for a baby, of tests and disappointments during which I had been so preoccupied with my own attempts to become pregnant) Emily gave birth to a daughter, Dora, and all was well again.

She, like Margaret in Oxford, had been delivered by Caesarian section, as seems often to be the case with 'special babies' – I suppose doctors feel more in control, unwilling to trust to nature if something has gone badly wrong before.

I talked to Emily a few weeks later, trying to keep the bitter note of envy out of my voice – for the feelings of jealous rage when I saw any pregnant woman, or heard of a successful birth, were often hard for me to control. But how could I feel anything but joy for Emily and her husband, Edward? And admiration, too?

I heard with some alarm about Emily's Caesarian, during which she had remained awake (that famous epidural again) to see Dora born. That was one thing I did not fancy, the surgeon's knife, but the chances were I would never have to suffer it – I felt entirely pessimistic then about my ever having another baby. That was what other people did. (I knew, of course, that I would never be able to have a Caesarian under epidural, because of its complete failure with me when I had Jessica.) Still – Angela, Margaret, Emily – they were all tremendous sources of inspiration. If *they* could do it . . .

And then there was Gillian Morriss Kay, a colleague of Stanley's at Balliol College, where he was then a Senior Research Fellow. Gillian was a lecturer in anatomy and she and I had met at the College Christmas dinner.

Earlier that year, she had given birth to a little boy, Toby. Her husband, Roy, had a grown-up son and daughter by his previous marriage, and they had been delighted to be starting a new family. Gillian was about forty, but her pregnancy had gone very smoothly, until a face presentation was diagnosed a few days from the birth. Sadly it transpired that the cord had prolapsed beneath the face, Toby was asphyxiated during labour, and a massive post-partum haemorrhage put his mother's life at risk, too.

That had been in July. By the new year following, Gillian was pregnant again, and I had kept in touch with her all the time I had been ill, though we had rarely met because I had scarcely left the house all spring and summer. As I recovered, Gillian blossomed, and in September, a year and two months after Toby, Matthew was born, another Caesarian delivery of another 'precious baby', another mother and child fit and well – another inspiration. I remember longing, aching with longing, as I went up in the lift to the old familiar seventh floor of the John Radcliffe, and pushed open Gillian's door. Room 19, the nicest room, overlooking the big cricket field and the trees, and all the roof tops of Headington. I looked at Gillian, bursting with health, looked at the tiny Matthew.

'If *she* can do it . . .'

But I wondered how many more times I would come into this hospital, bearing flowers and tiny garments, how many other people I would come to see with their babies, whether it would ever, ever be me.

'But I *am* going to do it, you know,' I said to Mark, on that New Year's Eve. He and his wife Margie had both become friends, and Margie sat at the other side of the room talking to someone, happily pregnant with her second baby, due in early June.

I must, at last, have been feeling better. The fact that we had arranged this party proved it. I no longer woke in the morning unable to face the day, I was a bit less afraid and tense, though I still burned on a short fuse. Life had begun to interest me again. And with that and my renewed physical health had come a great surge of fresh longing for another child, fresh determination.

We listened to the chimes of Big Ben. I looked a new year in the face.

'*I'm going to do it,*' I said to Mark, who stood beside me.

He raised his glass to me. 'To 1984,' he said.

Chapter 9

In fact, though I did not yet know it, I was already pregnant again. From the moment I had begun to feel even slightly better, the old obsession with having another baby had been tightening its grip upon me, and as everyone began to get into gear for Christmas, it had dominated my thoughts and been the focus of all my energies. It's curious that I remember so little else about those years, only those things that had to do with pregnancy and babies; not surprising really since we were trying so desperately to increase our family. I went on working, we had holidays, Jessica grew and her horizons expanded, season followed season around our cottage in all its rich detail. I was not unaware of it all, or uncaring, only dominated by that overwhelming other thing.

I felt guilty sometimes, though I knew I was not alone in my obsession. I read enough about other women in books, talked to enough friends, to understand that the desire to have a child had a force, a power, that could take over any of us, but I still thought at odd moments of detachment that I ought to relax all this, that it was getting out of hand, out of proportion. I had one child, after all – more than a lot of women had managed to achieve. Was I not neglecting her, missing out on those precious years of her young life – because of my obsession? Did she notice? No, at this time I think I can honestly say that she did not. Partly because her father and I took great care not to let her be affected, and because she has always had such a strong, close relationship with him that she could afford to have a mother whose whole attention and energy was not fully concentrated upon her – in any case, I'm not sure that it is ever a good thing for a child, especially an only child, to be too overwhelmed by parental attention and concern. They need room and time to breathe and grow in their own way, privately. Also, Jessica had a school in which she was completely happy and fulfilled, her life was full of friends, learning and all the activities of bright little girls.

When I had miscarried for the first time we had explained to her briefly that we had been going to have another baby, but that it had died very, very early on, when it was only just beginning to grow, that we had not known why, and that although we were sad we would one day be able to have another.

She talked about it rather a lot for a time, obviously thought about it – yet I do not think there was much real distress in it for her, nor any very clear understanding of what had actually happened. She was, after all, not then even five years old. We had not told her about the subsequent pregnancies, she simply knew that I was ill.

So it would have been very surprising if, when I realised that I had once again managed to conceive, I had told her – yet I did. Why I did was bound up with something that even now, even though I have thought and thought and thought about it for years since, in an effort to make sense of it, I cannot fully understand. It has to do with my own particular psychology, I suppose, and with what I was thinking and believing at the time – and – what? No, I don't know, I only recall that it was so, and the absolute and total strength of it.

What I had was an unshakable inner confidence, a single-minded certainty that I would conceive again and that this time all would be well. There was no reason behind that conviction, all the evidence was piling up against it. I was almost forty-two, with a recent history of three miscarriages and almost a year of physical and emotional illness. I *might* succeed, but there was nothing inevitable about it, everyone who had anything to do with me expressed encouragement but always caution, too; hope – but with reservations. Yet I knew, I was quite, quite sure, that this time all would be well.

I had the example of so many friends who had succeeded against all the odds. I wrote a letter to the medical adviser of a women's magazine and had a reply which for months I kept close to me as a sort of talisman. I have it still. It reads:

'So that in spite of your recent unhappy obstetric history, and even while taking your age into account, I would encourage you most warmly to go ahead when you feel fit and ready, and conceive again, and would advise you that the odds are still strongly in favour of your succeeding and achieving a successful outcome to your pregnancy.'

It looked so good, so reassuring. I was so grateful to that unknown 'medical adviser' – I still am. It was a lesson to me, too, that writing to people like that, for advice and information, would produce more than a bland general or impersonal reply. There is a place for such people, the doctors on magazines and in the media, in much the same way as there is a place for Samaritans – to whom sometimes I also turned for support and encouragement, though I was never suicidal even at my lowest.

But there was something more than all this general encouragement and cheer, something else made me more sure than all the books I read about positive thinking: it is important because it goes to the very heart of everything I was feeling then and because of what was to happen.

Another Christmas had come, another year I had climbed up to the high shelf and wearily got down the lights and the box of decorations, and thought bitterly how I had been so certain last Christmas, that by the next one we would have another baby. One year seemed to merge into the other with only disappointment in between.

This time, on the day after Boxing Day, I had gone for a walk by myself. It was a grey, dull kind of day, and I was glad to see the back of 'the festive season', though it had been lovely, as always, and fun. We had enjoyed it in spite of the emptiness inside.

But now, I was suddenly absolutely frantic, *desperate*, in my longing to have a child; it had somehow overtaken me that day in a great wave of yearning, and the six-month respite from pregnancies that Mark had ordered had been up since the autumn. I walked up the lane and climbed the path between the gravestones to the church which is set on a high mound above the village. Inside, it was cold and smelled of the damp and must of all the ages, and quite empty. The flowers for the Christmas services, great heads of chrysanthemums, the swags of ivy and holly, and the garlands of greenery, were still alive and fresh-smelling. And there in the corner was the crib, the sort you find in country churches the length and breadth of Britain; it comes out each year from its old newspapers-and-tablecloth wrapping in the vestry as it has done since the turn of the century. It has vaguely Italianate plaster figures, chipped here and there and with peeling paint, odd-looking beasts, and the donkey's tail newly restored with some rather bright brown wool. But the straw in which they stand is real enough and fetched from the yard of the farm next door.

In strictly Christian, religious terms, I am never sure what I think about the Christmas story, except that it is a good one, it is meaningful, it speaks to the hearts of men, has all the right symbols, it is moving. I don't believe it literally and I don't believe that matters.

Now, though, it meant to me the birth of a baby – and certainly one born in strange circumstances and against all the odds! I knelt down beside the crib in that cold, cold church, and I prayed – no, begged would be a better word – to have another child. I believed that there was a God who could hear me, and one with the power to answer my prayer. I didn't believe in the similar existence or power of the Virgin Mary – but in a way, I suppose, because of the situation, I was praying to her, too.

And what I received, there in the cold, was the feeling of absolute certainty that I *should* have my baby, and that all would be well. I went into the church feeling uncertain, vaguely depressed and overwhelmed with wanting. I came out quietly sure, calm and certain. It was going to be all right.

The power of prayer? An answer? The force of my desire? The need to be convinced? I do not know, but whatever it was, it had worked. I was not to lose my rock-solid, sure and certain confidence – not for some time.

And so, because I was so entirely sure that *this* time all would be well, when I knew I was pregnant again, I told Jessica – though remembering even as I did so how cautious Pat had been with Tom when she was expecting Harriet. She too had had miscarriages enough to feel she could never take her child-bearing for granted, and she had been almost six months pregnant and growing really rather large before she had told Tom about the baby. Perhaps I should have been similarly cautious, but I was so full of joy, so glad to be feeling well again – and above all, so *sure*.

The other day, when clearing out some old filing boxes, I came across a sheet of paper in Jessica's handwriting. It was a chart, accompanied by funny little drawings of what looked like bits of frogspawn, and then tadpoles.

'Our baby has grown to 2.2. cms. Its heart is beating. It has arms and legs, and its head is a lot bigger than its body.'

'The eyes have grown but not the eyelids. The inner part of the ear is complete, the outer part is beginning to grow. The head is still large. It has ankles and wrists, fingers and toes.'

We had been looking at Gordon Bourne's *Pregnancy* together to find out about the baby's development. She was fascinated and excited, and getting to know this new little person.

Miraculously, it seemed, so was I. As soon as my pregnancy was confirmed at the beginning of February, Mark decided on a campaign of positive action – we did not know why I had miscarried before, but we would do everything, absolutely everything that might be vaguely helpful to give this one a chance. I would lie low for the early months, though I did not have to be in bed, I was to take life very gently indeed, potter about at home, have a sleep every afternoon. I had been reading about the needs of the baby in early pregnancy in an American book which promoted good nutrition – something I still do firmly believe in, and never mind the weight-gain problems – and at once I put myself onto a high-protein diet with plenty of whole milk, cheese, eggs, whole-grain, fruit and vegetables, lean meat, fish, pulses. Every morning, I made a whip of milk with added skimmed milk powder and brewer's yeast, two eggs, honey, and a banana. Packed with goodness –

desperately fattening! I did not smoke anyway, and I stopped drinking alcohol – I only ever have wine, and have always been nauseated by it in pregnancy, so that was easy. I became really rather bovine, I sat and did needlepoint every afternoon, I read, I went for gentle walks, I slept. No excitement, no late nights.

I also had the district nurse twice a week to give me HCG injections. HCG stands for Human Chorionic Gonadotrophin. It is a hormone produced in large quantities by the embryo, and is detectable in the urine of a pregnant woman very soon after she has conceived. It has been suggested that perhaps women who miscarry are low in HCG at a vital stage in the pregnancy, and that boosting the levels by injection will give the hormone support needed, so that miscarriage does not occur. This may or may not be so but certainly HCG can do no harm; if the pregnancy is not viable, no amount of the stuff will prevent a miscarriage and if there is an excess, it will simply be excreted. By the 16th week of pregnancy, the need for any boost to the pregnant woman's own hormones has passed.

Perhaps the effect of the injections did have something to do with this new pregnancy continuing. That may have been the old power of placebo – or the sort of voodoo which really does work, when a specialist prescribes something and a nurse arrives twice a week and plunges a great syringe of the stuff into one's backside. As one doctor said to me, 'If you believe it will do you good, then it really will do you good.'

At least I felt *something* was being done which might work, at least we were all making every possible positive effort to help this baby on its way. And I knew someone for whom HCG had succeeded. Anne Robinson, who has typed this book, as she has typed many another for me so impeccably and swiftly, sent me a note after she had typed up an article I wrote about miscarriage. She said that she had had numerous miscarriages and despaired of ever having a child, before eventually reading about HCG and finding a doctor in Cambridge prepared to try it out on her. She kept that pregnancy, and has had three more children since. Another success story, more inspiration for me, as well as another link in the great chain of women friends, united because of the problems and tragedies in our histories of child-bearing.

So, while Stanley went off to work and Jessica to school each day, and the nurses buzzed in with their syringes of HCG, the weeks went by and then the first signs of spring arrived. It always comes a little late just here; we are on the cold, exposed side of the village – my daffodils are always two weeks later than those of my opposite neighbour – but in the end, there are those warm days when the earth smells unmistakably of spring, of new leaves and freshly growing things, and the mornings begin to draw out and all the birds of Oxfordshire start to sing and sing.

And still, all was well. I had had no problems, no bleeding. I felt the baby move – those funny, butterfly flutterings. I could no longer do up my skirts. We held our breath. Since Jessica, I had not got beyond 9 weeks. Now it was 10 – 12 – and then 14. And it was at 14 weeks that I went to see Mark for another routine ante-natal check – not that we any of us dared regard a single thing as 'routine' now – but my confidence was growing with every day that went by, and the end of the nasty HCG injections was even in sight – then I really *could* relax.

I sat in the consulting-room. 'Well, everything's looking fine.' It was – we had just heard the baby's heartbeat on the portable Sonicaid, my blood pressure was, as usual, nice and low, and my weight-gain nice and high.

'Perhaps we'll have another scan next week – see how big the baby is and check that all looks well,' Mark said.

'Could Jessica come and see it? It would be very exciting – and make the baby much more real to her.'

'Why not? Just check with the radiographer, but they're usually quite happy.'

I made movements to get up.

'But – there is one question we haven't really discussed – and now you're 14 weeks, we have to.' I sat down again.

'Amniocentesis.'

'Ah.'

'Have you thought about it? We've never done more than touch upon it generally until now because the previous pregnancies have ended before it became relevant.'

Had I thought about it? Oh, yes. I had spent a very long, careful time thinking about it, and talking to Stanley about it, too, as well as reading up on the subject and listening to what others who had been in my situation had told me. Margaret, Gillian, Emily, Angela – they had all been in my age bracket and all had had the test. What about me?

Over the age of about thirty-eight, a woman's chances of bearing a handicapped child – and, more specifically, a child with Down's Syndrome – increase dramatically. When I had been pregnant with Jessica, the odds against had been acceptably long. Now I was forty-two. Statistically, I had a 1 in 60 chance of having a Down's baby. There are other handicaps too, of course – Spina Bifida is one – but these are not so clearly related to maternal age, and I had never really worried about them.

In the past, a great many older women bore Down's Syndrome babies because there was no way of detecting their presence in advance. Nowadays, most of them are born to young mothers – because there is a slight chance of having a child with such a handicap at *any* age – because any woman over the age of thirty-five is automatically offered testing.

Within the last year or two, a method of testing for Down's Syndrome called CVS (Chorionic Villi Sampling) has begun to be used. In early pregnancy, the fetal sac is surrounded by tissue called the chorion (some of it later becomes the placenta) and a sample is taken from this via a needle which is inserted gently through the cervix. This sample is tested for any chromosomal abnormalities, including Down's Syndrome, and the results are obtained in only two to three days, as against those from the amniocentesis procedure which take three weeks.

CVS can be done as early as eight weeks into the pregnancy. It carries a rather higher risk of miscarriage than amniocentesis and is not universally available – but the advantage is that if a woman *is* found to be carrying a handicapped child, termination of the pregnancy can be done safely at this very early stage, and is a far less distressing procedure for the mother, and for everyone else concerned (including, we can only presume, for the fetus).

134

But CVS was only at the early experimental stages at the time I was pregnant and even if it had been available, with my history of miscarriage, it would not have been recommended.

No, the only test I could be given was amniocentesis. It is done at around the 16th week. Ultrasound is used to locate the exact position of the baby in the uterus, and a large hollow needle is then inserted through the mother's abdomen into the fluid that surrounds the baby, some of which is then drawn off. The mother has to rest for the next twenty-four hours and to wait for up to three weeks – until she is 19 or 20 weeks pregnant, while the cells are grown in a culture in the laboratory. If a child with Down's Syndrome or one of a number of other detectable handicaps is present, a termination of the pregnancy is offered. But at this late stage, this means inducing a labour and, to all intents and purposes, giving birth. The whole process is a distressing one, and carries a risk of miscarriage – because the fetal environment is disturbed – though this is low when the test is done by a highly skilled doctor using ultrasound in a specialist hospital.

All of this I knew. I had thought, read about, discussed it ad infinitum. And from the very beginning, I had known absolutely and unquestionably that I could not possibly have the test. Not out of cowardice – though I did not much like the sound of any of the procedures – but because I felt totally, passionately that I could not do anything to put this child at the slightest risk – and that even if it was discovered that I was bearing a Down's Syndrome baby, there was no way at all I could have an abortion. I do not think I had realised before just how strong were my convictions about this. I was not condemning any other woman who felt she must have the tests and if necessary terminate her pregnancy – felt, indeed, that she was right, had a moral duty to do so, and not to bring a handicapped child into the world. I would not presume to speak for or judge anyone else. I simply knew that I could not do it, that for me it would be wrong, and out of the question. The strength of my feelings was overwhelming and they went very deep. Stanley, too, had them. That being so, there was, of course, no point whatsoever in having a test, even if it carried no risk at all.

135

Ultrasound can detect quite a number of handicaps and malformations, and if that had revealed such a problem with me, I felt I would simply have been given time to prepare myself, but the only certain test for Down's Syndrome was amniocentesis.

'No,' I said firmly to Mark, 'absolutely out of the question.'

'You've obviously thought about it.'

'Yes.'

'Fine, then I respect your decision. No test.'

I did not for one moment regret it, and Stanley was as one with me on the whole subject.

But of course the issue of the test itself, whether it would cause a miscarriage and so on, was not the central point. I now had to face the possibility that we might have a child with Down's Syndrome. How did we honestly feel about that? How do I feel now? Easy when you have not had to experience it to give glib, sentimental replies.

I believe very strongly in the sacredness of life, and in the right to life. I also believe passionately that a person with a handicap of whatever kind has as much right to life as any other. And it has been proved to me times without number that within a handicapped body, alongside, as it were, even a grave disability, lives a unique and sometimes very special human being.

I also felt that I had taken the responsibility of conceiving another baby – I wanted it, so I had to carry that responsibility through to its conclusion, and love and care for the child once it was born, and no matter in what state. I had given it life – but I had no right to take that life away.

But that is still not the whole story. A Down's Syndrome child is a burden, on parents, on siblings, on the state, for the whole of its life. Who knows whether it is not also a burden upon itself?

Today, the opportunities for them are greater than they have ever been. The quality of their lives can be better than anyone could ever have imagined, their horizons have expanded, the very best that can be done for them and made of them, is.

But it does not do to be starry-eyed. As the grandfather of

one greatly-loved Down's Syndrome child said to me recently, 'When you've said all that – they're not good news, they're *still* not good news.'

I have seen enough sad and stressed families, their lives restricted and wearisome as well as full of anxiety, because of the burden of bringing up a handicapped child. Marriages can be wrecked by it (though some are strengthened) and the strain on normal brothers and sisters is grave. And now, because modern medicine is able to conquer their physical problems so efficiently, Down's Syndrome children live to adulthood and beyond, to middle and old age, and think of the problems *that* gives rise to.

No, even though I have seen happy, loved and loving, light-hearted handicapped children, even though I can understand the belief that they are in some curious way specially chosen by and favoured of God, I am clear-eyed about them.

Nevertheless, we had to face the possibility of having one to bring up because there was no way we could have done anything to harm the unborn child, or terminate its life.

And that, really, was that. Once the decision had been made, I can honestly say that I never worried about it for a single moment, never had any doubts that it was the right, the only possible decision for us. I scarcely gave the whole subject any thought, I simply settled down to look forward.

At last, at last, here was a pregnancy I could begin to *enjoy*, as I had so enjoyed the first. I read Dr Bourne's book until you would have thought the print would have come off the page.

'The head is now rounded . . . the face is formed, with the mouth, nose and eyes properly developed. The sex of the infant is now obvious . . .'

'The approximate length of the baby is 16 cm.'

Every day, unless it was wet or the wind blew too coldly off Otmoor, I went for a walk. Snowdrops were followed by crocuses, the catkins and the pussy willow filled the lanes, then daffodils, then the willows beside the stream at the bottom of the sloping field below our garden began to show the first flush of pale, pale green.

At 16 weeks, I said a fond farewell to the district nurses, and began to go about just a little more. I was still going to be extremely careful, but I also still had my total inner conviction, my calm assurance, that all would be well, and now there was positive evidence – I had got past those dangerous early weeks. From now on, it would be plain sailing, through the rest of the beautiful spring and then the summer, to August, and the baby's birth.

At Easter, Stanley went off to his usual International Shakespeare jamboree in the USA and Jessica and I went down to spend the holiday in London with our friends, the Ewbanks. Jessica had grown up knowing them and their family almost as well as she knew us, it was a home from home. She could go off with the children while I read and rested, knitted and vegetated in utter contentment. And over that week, I also had an experience which brought home to me sharply just how close the baby was, how affected it could be by what happened to me, and made me feel, as I had not quite allowed myself to feel yet in this pregnancy, that here was a person I already loved desperately, even though I did not 'know' it, and towards which I felt all the urgent, passionate protectiveness I had already for Jessica.

It was Easter Sunday afternoon, sunny and bright though not especially warm. We had eaten a delicious celebratory lunch and then I had slept; later I was sitting talking to the big Ewbanks over a cup of tea in the kitchen. Jessica was playing in the garden with the children. Occasionally we could hear their shouts and laughter, and the grinding and clattering of roller skates as the older ones skated with varying degrees of competence up and down the driveway at the side of the house.

Suddenly there was a crashing sound, and the sort of screaming and crying that had us on our feet and through the back door in a split second. Jessica was being helped up gently by the eldest daughter but, having fallen over the kerb stone and hit her face smack onto concrete, all she wanted was 'Mummy, Mummy, Mummy'.

As I rushed to pick her up, seeing blood all over her and imagining the worst possible injuries, the baby inside me began not so much to move and kick as to leap, to flail its limbs in urgent panic, like a fish trying desperately to leap out of its tank. We went indoors and cleaned up Jessica, but it took a while for her to calm and quieten down, and all the time that I held her and we were both so distressed, the baby, sensing my emotions, went on thrashing about inside me; I had never felt anything like it. Only after an hour or more, when everything was fine, the anxiety over, and I was calm again, did it gradually settle and go still, as though sleeping in exhaustion.

I sat in an armchair, with my hands on my stomach, instinctively trying to clasp the baby tight, needing to comfort it as much as I had Jessica, realising for the first time just how close was the link between us, the effect of my emotions, what I did, what happened to me, on that tiny person.

That afternoon, the baby ceased to be unknown. I suppose I had been keeping myself a little detached from it, too, holding back for fear of something going wrong yet again. Now the danger time was passed, I was able to commit myself totally — and after this afternoon, could not have done anything else. I had been as careful as it was possible to be, but now I was trebly so, suddenly acutely conscious of the vulnerability, as well as the preciousness, of this new life.

Chapter 10

My sense of well-being, and the inner certainty I felt, continued and increased. Stanley returned from America safely; Jessica came up to the hospital with us and, after the radiographer had checked privately first that all was well, came in and saw me lying on the couch, with the black-and-white television picture beside me.

'Oh – it doesn't look like a baby at all,' Jessica said. I saw what she meant – I was well used to the scan-monitor by now, and knew what to look out for, although it was getting actually *less* clear as the baby grew. At the beginning I had been able to distinguish a complete little form quite clearly, limbs, head, trunk. Now, things were more blurred. But the radiographer carefully pointed out to Jessica the baby's head – body –

'There, can you see that little regular movement – like a pulse? That's your baby's heart.'

I saw her face light up. 'My baby!'

'And there's a foot – look, a leg – can you see it kicking?'

She could. She turned to me in delight.

'It really *is* a baby!' she said. I joked about it not being a kangaroo, but I knew what she meant. It really *was* a baby.

Every time I went to see Mark Charnock, all the signs were good, everything was as normal as could be.

We had made no plans to go away on a holiday during this pregnancy. I would not have wanted to be far from home, and my own doctor and hospital. It seemed astonishing how casually we had taken off for the depths of Suffolk when I was expecting Jessica – and friends who flew half-way round the world when pregnant filled me with unease, they still do.

But we thought we would like to have at least a weekend away, and some friends who had moved to live in the Worcestershire countryside had invited us to call in to see them, so we decided on a weekend in a hotel nearby. I mentioned it to Mark, who thought there was absolutely no reason why I shouldn't go.

'You're well past that dangerous early stage – well, dangerous for you – and everything is looking absolutely fine. Of course you should go, it isn't the depths of the jungle, after all!'

No, but all the same, I began to feel uneasy. I put it down to traces of that old phobia I had had the previous year, when I had been ill and felt unsafe anywhere far away from home. It was odd though, because recently I had relaxed, and had been feeling so much more sure of everything – and I still had, deep down, my conviction, which I carried like a torch, that all would be well. I *knew* it.

All the same, I looked on the map to see how far away we would be from a large hospital. There was Worcester, which I knew had a good maternity unit, fifteen miles or so away.

But I still felt a great reluctance to go, and as we were setting off, an anxiety settled like a stone in the pit of my stomach. All the way, I noted the roads – how easy would it be to get to a hospital? How quick? Why was I like this, why? No reason. I was 22 weeks pregnant and all was well, *very* well.

That first night, I lay awake in the hotel room, feeling the baby's movements, and going over and over in my mind what we would do if something went wrong, whether we would ring the hotel porter or an ambulance or . . . but *why*?

On the Sunday, the weather was beautiful, a perfect May day in the English countryside. We went to lunch with our friends, and when all the others went for a walk I was sent off to the spare room to sleep. I lay, under a quilt, with the sun shining through the cottage window and making patterns on the sloping ceiling, hearing the afternoon quiet of the depths of the country – but I could not sleep. I simply lay, feeling anxious and uneasy, not wanting to be alone in case something went wrong, longing for the others to come back, wondering how long it would take to reach the hospital, through these remote, winding lanes.

But still why – why? I had had no sign whatsoever that anything was wrong. It was *not* wrong, I was fine, but I was tense. I could not lose the sense of dread, it was like a grey cloud just over my head.

After tea, I agitated for us to be away, desperate to get home I didn't explain why, could not have communicated my feeling of anxiety, my fear that something awful was about to happen, it seemed too silly.

Why? Why?

I have never been so glad to see home, and once back I felt better, could relax again, but not completely – the vague sense of unease was still there, though underneath it, very deep, my confidence remained untouched. It's hard to explain the mixture of feelings except to say that they were in layers, and the sense of unease was on top of and more conscious than my sense of certainty.

Twenty three weeks. And then 24. The weather changed, it grew colder. The winds blew from the north, some of the flowers that had come through early were looking pinched and miserable, the countryside seemed to retreat a bit, back into its shell after such a wonderfully warm and beautiful spring. I even put tights on again though that was getting a bit uncomfortable, I was really quite large, looked more pregnant than 24 weeks. I didn't mind at all . . .

May 21 was Stanley's birthday and we went out to dinner at the smart Quat' Saisons restaurant, then still in North Oxford. The food was delicious, but there was a particularly noisy party showing off at the next table, and smoking a great deal, and tobacco was the only thing that still made me feel nauseous. Was that the only reason I didn't really enjoy myself, felt uneasy, and was so glad to get home?

On Wednesday, 23 May, I had an ante-natal appointment with Mark. No problems anticipated. But the previous afternoon, I could not relax when I went for my rest, and for some reason I picked up one of my many books about pregnancy and childbirth. It was specifically about miscarriage. I read it, perhaps, because I wanted reassurance though I have no idea why I needed that. Or have I?

Yes. Sometimes in my life – and perhaps I have not actually realised it until afterwards – I have had a vague but a definite advance warning of something, a sort of foreknowledge as if someone has been desperately trying to tell me that something is going to happen, though I have not always taken in fully what they have been saying. I think it is probably quite a common experience, and I have no explanation of it. I only know that it has happened.

I read avidly through the book, passing quickly over all the sections about early miscarriages which could not apply to me now. It was almost as though I was looking for something. The book was punctuated by accounts, in their own words, of various women's experiences of miscarriage. One particular such account I read as if my life depended on it. A woman told how the membranes had ruptured unexpectedly, causing her to have a late – 22-week – miscarriage. And there was another, rather similar story, in which it happened a bit later.

Suddenly, I caught myself at what I was doing, and shut the book firmly. It was as though I were *looking* for something new to worry about, now that the early dangers were over, being hypochondriacal about my pregnancies. It was stupid and unhealthy, worrying and feeding my worry was not an especially helpful way of passing the time. I was perfectly fit and well, all the omens were fine. Why torment myself with details of other women's problems? Nothing was going to happen to me.

But if I was really worried about anything, well then, I was to see Mark the next day, and he would check me over very thoroughly, and put my mind at rest.

He did. I drove myself down to his consulting-rooms on the Wednesday morning, feeling well and cheerful, but glad to be there. He did all the usual checks. No problems.

'Is there anything you want to ask me?' he said as usual, just before I got up from the couch.

I hesitated. 'I've been a bit anxious.'

'Well, I think anyone who has had a problem in pregnancy is going to feel a bit anxious from time to time, with another one. It's quite normal. But there really is no need – things are looking very good. You're fine – your baby is fine.'

Because I felt, somehow, that I ought to have a problem, I mentioned a slight discharge I had been having occasionally – was that anything to worry about?

'I shouldn't think so, but let's take a swab quickly and send it away. Just on the offchance.'

He did so.

'Really, everything looks all right,' he said, as he washed his hands. 'I'm sure that's nothing.'

I said goodbye, and went home feeling much relieved and reassured. If there was anything even vaguely troubling me still, I dismissed it. 'Free-floating anxiety' – I had had it in my life before. I would simply ignore it from now on.

On Wednesday evenings during the University term, Stanley always went to the Fellows' dinner at Balliol. On this particular Wednesday, though, it was a special occasion, a biennial event known as the Snell dinner, and for this, he was required to dress up. Jessica and I made all the appropriate admiring noises as he came downstairs in his black velvet dinner jacket and crisply pleated, embroidered white shirt, with impeccably tied bow-tie. I put the finishing touches to him with a clothes brush.

'Meanwhile,' I said as he departed, 'Cinderella and Buttons will stay at home by the fireside!'

Six-year-old Jessica giggled. 'Girls' night,' she said. That's what we had taken to calling it when he went off to College and she and I were alone. We had supper on trays and we watched *Coronation Street* together. I rarely see television, but I have followed that cheerful northern soap since I was an undergraduate and Jessica has taken after me.

So on this particular evening, we settled down cosily with our supper trays as the familiar wailing signature tune came up and the ginger cat settled itself for the ten thousandth time on that Salford terrace roof.

Outside it was grey and chilly for late May. We were glad to be indoors. I was feeling fine.

Half-time came with the advertisements and, leaving Jessica to enjoy them, I got up to take away my empty supper tray. As I crossed the sitting-room, quite abruptly, and painlessly, and completely without any warning, I felt a gush of something warm and wet run down my legs. I put the tray on the table and went quickly into the cloakroom just off the hall. But I think as I did so, I knew – it was almost as if I had been expecting this. I had no fear that it could be blood, was sure, even before I looked, that what I felt gush down was the warm amniotic fluid from the uterus. I had, after all, experienced this before, on the day I went into labour with Jessica.

But having read, only the previous day, those graphic accounts, I knew even more accurately what had happened.

Although my heart was beating very fast, I felt curiously calm and in control. I called to Jessica that I would be with her in a few moments – she was engrossed in the programme again – and went to the telephone. The hospital number was pinned on the wall beside it. I dialled Delivery Suite direct and asked to speak to the Sister on duty.

'My name is Mrs Susan Wells. I'm a patient of Mr Charnock and I'm twenty-four weeks pregnant. My membranes have just ruptured – I've lost quite a lot of water.'

'You're quite sure?'

'Pretty sure, yes.'

'Are you having any contractions?'

'No, there's no pain at all.'

'Bleeding?'

'No.'

'Right. Can you come in straight away? Do you need an ambulance?'

I thought fast. Pam?

'I think I can get someone to bring me.'

'If you can't, get an ambulance and tell them I said so.'

I dialled Pam Edmonds-Seal's number, praying that she would not be out.

She answered and I told her quickly what had happened.

'I'll be down at once. You pack a bag – and we'll take Jessica for the night, don't worry.'

The last person I got hold of was Stanley. I was put through at once to the Senior Common Room at College – they were just about to process in to dinner, but the steward managed to grab him and bring him to the telephone.

'Now, you're not to worry –' those famous, fatuous words when giving anyone awful news. 'My waters have broken – I've got to go into hospital at once. Pam is coming down to take me and she'll have Jessica for the night. Will you meet us at the John Radcliffe – now, *don't worry!*'

Then I went in to Jessica, as calmly as I could.

'Jessica, I must turn off the television, I've got to tell you something.' She looked alarmed, guessing from the quiet, urgent tone of my voice that all was not well. She had known crises of this sort the previous year, and I saw, now, the wariness in her blue eyes.

'The bag of water that the baby is living in has burst – and some of the water has started to leak out. I've got to go to the hospital at once – Pam is coming to take us. Will you come up with me now and help me to pack a bag?'

Without a word, she took hold of my hand and came, but as we passed the front door, I saw Pam's figure behind the glass. She came inside and gave me a quick hug.

'Now you're not to worry!'

We both laughed rather weakly.

'I'll take Jessica up and she can show me where things are for the bags – you sit there.'

I sat.

'Is it all right?' I asked her. 'What about your family? Is it –'

'They're fine. I put supper on the table, they can cope perfectly well. John said if in doubt, call the ambulance but I think you look OK to come with me. Are you having any pain?'

'No. None.'

That was quite true. So far as I could tell, the water had stopped leaking, too – there was nothing. The baby was quite still.

Five minutes later, we were in the car and on the road to the John Radcliffe. Jessica was in the back, very quiet, a bit white.

'Has the baby died?' she asked suddenly.

146

'Oh, no. The baby's fine.'

'What will happen?'

I looked at Pam, realising that I had absolutely no idea.

'Your Mummy will have to go to bed and rest, that's what,' Pam said in her soft, wonderfully calming voice. 'They'll do a lot of tests to make quite sure the baby is all right and then she'll have to lie very still.'

'Will they fill the water up again – like a hot water bottle?'

We managed to laugh a bit at that, too.

And then we were outside the main entrance to the John Radcliffe – going in through the doors. That reassuring hospital smell. I breathed again, felt safer at once, in the right place.

And, turning round, I saw Stanley coming in at a half-run, behind us, his car parked anyhow behind on the kerb, looking completely incongruous in his velvet dinner jacket and black tie. But his face was creased into such an expression of anguished anxiety that suddenly, the awfulness of what was happening hit me, and I crumpled. He took hold of me.

'I went over two sets of red lights,' he said.

But I couldn't muster any energy to admonish him or to worry in retrospect. He was here, we all were, that was all that mattered.

And then the Sister came out and I was saying goodbye quickly to Jessica and she was going off with Pam. I knew she would be cared for and loved and reassured as much as possible. I wasn't going to worry about her, though I wished it weren't happening and that she was not having to go but was tucked up safely in her own bed at home.

– Oh, and me, and me, I thought, as I climbed onto yet another of those high, narrow hospital couches.

One of the things I remember most vividly was how very quiet it was on the ground floor of the hospital that evening. By day, and during the week, the main entrance area is a constant bustle of people coming in and out, visitors, doctors and nurses, porters, outpatients, ancillary staff of every kind. Telephones ring at the reception desk, lifts open and close, doors swing, trolleys bang in and out. I like it, and it's a busy, purposeful, cheerful world.

But at night everything is very still once visiting time is over. The outpatient areas are empty, offices locked, upstairs on the levels, the wards full of mothers and babies are livelier; down here, there is a carpeted hush. To one side, through the swing doors, is the Delivery Suite; further along, intensive care called Observation Area, and the Special Care Nursery. Behind their doors, there is activity, but, although sometimes frantic, it is confined within its own area, and quieter. When I came in, there had been just the porter on reception who rang at once for Sister. It was strange, felt empty, oddly hushed – I was to get to know that atmosphere well over the following few weeks.

But now, I lay on the couch in a bare but not uncomfortable admissions room, looking up at the inevitable clock. Stanley stood beside me, drawn and worried.

Then the Sister came back in, serious but trying to be reassuring. She was a Yorkshire woman. I felt happy with her. She asked all the routine questions and took a swab for testing, to make sure I was right and that what had leaked was amniotic fluid.

'I've telephoned Mr Charnock. He'll be in before long – he'd just started his supper.'

Poor Mark – a long day, and now this. I wondered what he must have thought.

Later, he told me. He had been about to eat when the telephone rang, hoped fleetingly that it might not be for him. When they told him my name and what had happened, he said he had been so startled, shocked, that he hadn't quite taken it in.

'Mrs *Wells* – Susan Wells? Are you sure? I saw her in clinic only this morning, everything was fine.'

Perhaps it still was, perhaps I'd got it wrong. The bladders of pregnant women are notoriously weak, maybe . . .?

The Sister came back and took hold of my hand.

'You were right,' she said. 'Your membrane has ruptured – that was amniotic fluid.' Her voice was quiet. 'You do realise how serious this is, don't you? What it could mean?'

'I know it's serious, but what will happen?'

'Generally things don't happen. It'll probably be a question of wait and see. To begin with, of course, you'll be staying here until your baby is born – whenever that may be. Once the membrane has gone, there is always the danger of an infection entering the uterus so we want you under observation.'

'Will they induce the baby? Straight away?'

'Oh no – you haven't had any contractions at all, have you? No, you're not in labour at the moment. But of course you might start at any time. Once the waters have gone, nature often completes the birth process.'

'But not always?'

'No.'

'If I don't go into labour?'

'Well – let's wait and see what Mr Charnock says.'

We didn't have to wait long. Poor Mark, yet another bolted meal – I wonder obstetricians don't suffer from terminal indigestion and gastric ulcers, but perhaps their bodies get used to it and adapt themselves.

He is a calm, steady sort of man, never apparently agitated or upset – 'laid back' would perhaps be a good way of describing him, if that did not imply that he was a bit too relaxed. But he is generally optimistic, generally cheerful and positive. Even when he had had to give me bad news before, though sympathetic and serious, he had always presented it 'bright side up'. Now he came in through the swing doors in his dark 'consultant's suit', and he looked as grave as I have ever seen a man look, no bounce, no optimism, his voice very low-key, measuring his words carefully.

'Susan, I am sorry about this – I could hardly believe my ears. And just when we saw you this morning and everything looked as if it was going so well.'

'There wasn't any sign of this, was there?'

'Absolutely none – nothing at all. It's a bolt from the blue.'

'But why has it happened – *why*?'

He shook his head. 'I'm afraid we have to say we don't know quite often in obstetrics. But there is one thing – we don't have to blame an amniocentesis because you didn't have one. And we would have probably done so.'

'Even as many weeks after it as this?'

He nodded. 'It would have been a possible cause.'

It was the one great consolation of the evening – that I did not have to blame myself for having made the wrong decision, for having allowed the test, and caused this. It was nothing to do with anything I had done.

'Now – for tonight, I'll put you into Observation and I'm afraid we'll be disturbing you quite often – I want to keep a close eye on you.'

'If I go into labour?'

'Let's hope you don't.'

'But if I *do* – does this baby have any chance of survival at all?'

The Sister spoke. 'Not much,' she said. 'They can work miracles in the Special Care Nursery – they do wonderful things. We've kept babies at 26 weeks, even 25 –'

'But not 24 –'

She shook her head. 'It's just that bit too early – they really are too immature to survive.'

'The aim, if you *don't* go into labour, will be to get you as far down the road as possible to a date when your baby *does* have a good chance. That will mean full bed rest in here. But let's get the next twelve hours over before we look ahead. They are absolutely crucial.'

Once you are in hospital, and particularly in an emergency situation, you lose all sense of time – I'd noticed that before. When they wheeled me into my room beside the observation desk in intensive care, it was past eleven o'clock.

'Poor Dad,' said the Sister, patting Stanley sympathetically on the arm. 'All dressed up and nowhere to go – he didn't even get his dinner!'

We said goodnight. It was very quiet in there – just one or two figures humped in beds, and some empty areas as I came through.

'We're quite quiet tonight,' said the Night Sister, 'long may it last.'

But in Maternity, they can never be sure – who knew when a totally unexpected emergency like me might not be rushed in?

When everyone had gone, I lay feeling exhausted, slightly weepy and disorientated. But throughout the whole evening, from the moment the waters had broken until now, the rock-like calm and sure confidence that had upheld me since the previous Christmas had been there, and was much closer to the surface now. Everyone around me had looked grave and anxious, and I was alarmed by the speed of events, and yet I had a certainty that everything was going to be all right, somehow this baby would survive – and so would I. I never doubted it.

Faith – trust – blind optimism – stupidity – what was it? I don't know, but it was there and it sustained me.

Surprisingly, I did manage to sleep that night, though they came first to take a urine sample and then every fifteen minutes at first, and later, every thirty, to take my blood pressure and to check that I had no pains. But the nurses used a torch and spoke in whispers, and I think the reaction to what had happened knocked me out so that they even managed to take my temperature two or three times without waking me.

The next morning, I woke to find Mark at the foot of my bed, all dressed, shaved and spruce – time seemed to telescope together. I could hardly take it in that he had been home, gone to bed, got up again and begun a new day. He was also looking considerably more cheerful.

'I'm very pleased so far –' he said, 'cautiously optimistic. There are no signs of infection, you haven't gone into labour. We'll get a scan this morning and see how things are looking and then decide what next. Is there anything you want to ask me?'

'Yes,' I said urgently, '*please* can I have something to eat and drink?'

It was a very long time indeed since last night's supper and my mug of coffee had never got made.

When I went along to the ultrasound scan, the radiographer was rather silent.

'Is the baby all right?'

'Yes – bit still, but that's not surprising. It can't move about easily without the usual amount of fluid.'

'But surely I didn't lose it all – there must be some left?'

She moved the scanner about again. Then switched it off abruptly. 'Not a lot,' she said.

By the time Stanley came in later that morning, I had been

moved out of the ground floor, out of Observation, and up to the old familiar Level 7 and one of the rooms on my favourite side, overlooking the cricket ground. I'd also had a good breakfast and a very great quantity of tea. The world was looking better.

We had to make arrangements about Jessica. She had spent a good night at Pam's but they were going away the following day – the Whitsun Bank Holiday and half-term were upon us. We decided to contact my other close friend in the village, Louisa Lane Fox, who had been most supportive and concerned during all my years of trying to become pregnant. Jessica had stayed with the family several times, and Louisa loved her – it was a relief to know that in a crisis there were so many people we could turn to for help.

While we were talking, Mark came in. He was feeling happier, he told Stanley – the immediate crisis of the previous night had passed.

'The thing now is for as many days – and hopefully weeks – to tick quietly by as possible. Every single day counts. Now the longer the baby can stay in the womb, the greater its chances of survival when it is born. We want it not just to grow but to mature more. I would hope to get Susan's pregnancy to 32 weeks – by then a baby really has every chance of doing fine, down in the Special Care Nursery.'

'So I'd be induced then?'

'Yes. There's still a risk of infection and by then, if the baby is all right, we prefer to deliver, not wait and take any further chance.'

He explained that sometimes, with bed rest, the membrane could grow over again but meanwhile, the amniotic fluid would be replaced from my body continuously though, unfortunately, it would be like filling a bath with the plug out – the fluid was going to leak away again all the time if the membrane remained ruptured.

'So I have to stay here in bed – for as long as eight weeks?'

'That's right. You'll need plenty of books, you can work, get Stanley to bring in a television for you, and radio, anything to keep you happy. But you can't get out of bed – not for any reason at all.'

I groaned. If there's one thing I hate more than any other, it's bedpans!

Still, everyone was looking so much happier today. I had been right, I *knew* things would be fine, didn't I? And the prospect of spending the next eight weeks in here was not a bad one. I had a nice view from the window, the food was reasonable to good, and think of the reading I could do. I had a telephone. I could have visitors. Oh, yes, there were worse prospects. Besides, if it meant saving the baby, I would do absolutely anything at all they suggested.

The only worry was leaving Stanley and Jessica at home. But the moment word got round, offers of help came pouring in – friends at school would have Jessica, neighbours would help with the school run, they invited Stanley for meals – my phone never stopped ringing. We were overwhelmed by friendship, support, love, caring, practical help.

We would make the best of it all. I settled down that night feeling content, relieved, almost happy. Everything would be all right. I ticked off the first day on my mental calendar – only another sixty-three to go – just until the end of July. Say it quickly and it was hardly any time at all!

Chapter 11

The rest of Thursday and all Friday passed pleasantly enough, and I began to dig myself in for the long haul, recalling that two months was only a quarter of what some women spent flat on their backs, trying to maintain a pregnancy.

Messages began to arrive, and flowers and books; Stanley brought in my post, and some paper and pens so that I could keep up with at least a small amount of work – I was reviewing books for *Good Housekeeping* magazine, then as now, and I reckoned I would be well ahead with my copy by the time the baby was born. Friends telephoned, several visited – indeed, the day passed rather quickly. Perhaps two months would seem like no time. And all the time, the baby inside me continued to move although, in a womb without much liquor, not with the vigour it had been able to show previously. I imagine it felt a bit like wearing a wet-suit that was rather too tight.

I don't remember anything about the morning of Saturday 26 May except that I didn't want to eat any lunch – I wasn't nauseated, just completely un-hungry.

In the afternoon, I had two visitors. Judy Bogdanor, my doctor friend, full of cheerful stories about her two sons, and optimistic noises about my situation. Outside the windows, it was wet and grey and I began to feel shivery while she was talking – I supposed it was the sight of such a bleak outlook for the May Bank Holiday.

A little later Ann Campbell, the mother of a schoolfriend

of Jessica, arrived bearing a campanula cascading with flowers of pellucid mauve-blue. 'You're to nip off the dead heads every day,' she said. 'That'll give you something to do, and by the time the baby is born, it will have tumbled over the edge of the pot and grown down to the floor!'

I looked forward to that. But while she was talking, I was feeling uncomfortable – I shifted about in the bed. Stiff, probably – well, not much point in getting fed up after just two days – not when I'd got another two months in here. Then, as I was trying to find the position that did not give me a low backache, I felt a swift but to me unmistakable tightening, like a belt drawn in around my lower abdomen. A contraction, surely? I waited. Nothing else. When supper came, I still didn't feel like eating, and I asked to have an extra blanket.

'It *isn't* very warm tonight,' the nurse said when she brought it, 'you'd never think it was the end of May.'

Stanley came, but he couldn't stay long – he'd left Jessica with our neighbour, and she also had all her grandchildren staying for the holiday. I didn't feel like talking much. I was feeling tired, and suddenly rather out of sorts.

For the hour or so after he had gone, I felt increasingly unwell – hot then cold and shivery, and I had a niggling low backache, interspersed with that occasional, painless tightening.

The nursing auxiliary who came around at the beginning of the night shift to do the observations frowned over my thermometer. 'You've got a bit of a temperature. Do you feel all right?'

'Not too good. A bit hot and shivery.'

'Perhaps you're in for a cold?'

'And I've got backache.'

She rang for Sister.

They spent the next hour trying to decide whether or not I was in labour. Whenever I felt the tightening, one or other of them felt my tummy, but it was always soft.

'Hold on and see what happens.'

To take my mind off things, I tuned in to the hospital radio – and even called up Radio Cherwell to answer one of the questions in their musical quiz, something I had never done in my life before. And got the answer right.

It was to be the last bit of light-heartedness for rather a long time.

By half past ten, I was feeling more unwell, and my backache was considerably worse. They sent for the Sister on duty in Delivery Suite. She put her hand on my tummy. 'Definitely,' she said. And then turned to the midwife. 'I know you couldn't feel Mrs Wells's contractions – it's not surprising with someone who is only 25 weeks pregnant – but always remember, the mother is usually right.'

Five minutes later, my bed was wheeled along towards the lift.

'Where are we going?'

'Observation Area – I want to keep a close eye on you. We'll ring Mr Charnock and see what he wants to do.'

What he wanted to do, he explained carefully when he arrived – it was a television sports programme I'd interrupted this time – was to try to stop the labour before it got past the point of no return. The aim was still to keep my baby inside for as long as possible.

'I've put you on a drip of something called ritodrine – that will stop your contractions. We'll keep it up for the rest of the night, and hopefully by tomorrow morning things will have quietened down. But meanwhile, I'm going to ring Stanley and ask him to come in.'

Fortunately, Stanley had not gone to sleep. Jessica, of course, had. What should he do?

'Tell him to ring Louisa.'

Jessica vividly remembers that fateful night when she was awakened gently, told that Daddy had to go to the hospital, was wrapped in a duvet, and driven to Louisa Lane Fox's house at the other end of the village. I was grateful, then, and I am still grateful, that she was able to fall out of her own bed into theirs with so little anxiety, that she had love and care surrounding her on so many sides.

When Stanley arrived and was sitting beside my bed, Mark explained again what the aim was, and the way the drug would work.

156

'Is it harmful?' I asked, my anxiety-level rising steeply with every contraction.

He shook his head emphatically. 'But it does have some side effects and you may feel a bit unpleasant. We can adjust the dose a little but I do want to make sure we give you enough to stop the labour.'

'A bit unpleasant.' Yes. I can be amused now at the obstetric understatement, but at the time, it wasn't in the least bit funny. A good many unpleasant things were to happen to me over the course of the next few days and weeks, physical miseries, quite apart from the emotional distress. Nothing was ever as awful as that night on the ritodrine drip. I would submit to a great many nasty medical procedures before ever agreeing to suffer it again.

Ritodrine is a drug similar to those used by asthmatics to dilate the breathing tubes during an attack. It relaxes the uterine muscle and has the effect, temporarily at least, of stopping the contractions of labour. Side effects include a very rapid increase in the heart-rate, tremor, headache and acute anxiety.

Whether its use is effective in the longer term or even, sometimes, desirable in the shorter, is debatable.

Time became blurred, hour after hour went by and all I was conscious of was the insane, desperate need to get the drip off my arm and out of my system. At one point, I knelt up in the bed and tried to tear the whole thing down from its stand.

And the next worst thing to being on the drip must surely be having to sit by and watch someone in the throes of having it administered.

There was no one else in the Observation Area that night, the rooms were empty and quiet. Stanley had been given a camp bed in my room upstairs and had gone there to try to sleep. The Sister sat at her desk, in the still, yellow pool of light. Sometimes she came over to me, held my hand, wiped my forehead, tried to reason with me. Twice she telephoned to Mark to explain my extreme distress – but each time, the message came back:

'He's very sorry, but for the sake of the baby, you really *must* stay on the drip until the morning.'

Part of my misery was that I had a temperature and the temperature was climbing. At dawn, she came to sponge my face, to try and make my bed as comfortable as she could, and to check the vaginal pad I was wearing – a routine procedure but, as she removed it, I saw the alarm on her face.

'I think,' she said, 'that you've got an infection. There's a very nasty discharge – and your temperature is up a bit more.'

By now I felt so awful I didn't care, didn't really take in the seriousness of what she was telling me. All I wanted was to be anywhere, to run away, to *get off that drip.*

I heard her picking up the telephone once more.

'Mr Charnock – I'm sorry to wake you again . . .'

When she came back to my bedside, she didn't say anything at first, only untaped the tube and pulled it gently out of the vein in my arm, then dismantled the drip stand and took it all down.

'You've taken it off!' I couldn't believe it. I wanted to weep with relief. Almost at once, the banging of my heart slowed down, the blood stopped pounding in my ears like storm-waves.

'Yes.' She came and stood beside me, held my hand. 'You've got a bad uterine infection. The Registrar is coming in a minute or two to put you on an antibiotic drip – and if your labour doesn't restart naturally soon, we'll have to give you something to get it going. . . . With that infection, your baby will be safer out than inside you now and we need to get it delivered.'

I turned my head away and looked out of the window. A grey dawn was seeping in around the drawn blinds and I could hear the birds starting to sing.

'After all that,' I said weakly.

'Yes.'

'Never mind.'

And for a little while, I did not. I was only limp with relief at being free from the terrible drip which had been like some instrument of torture to which I had been tied down.

Then, as the Registrar came in and began, with Sister, to get things ready, I suddenly realised what was going to happen. My baby would be born and I was just 25 weeks pregnant — it was far, far too soon. Did it have the remotest chance of life? I couldn't see how. And I had a uterine infection, the one thing everyone in midwifery and obstetrics learns to dread. I knew enough about it, and the possible complications, to feel very frightened, antibiotics or no.

Things had gone badly wrong. The confidence I had felt for so long had taken a dreadful knock, but it *was* still there, far, far below, like a flickering lamp in a dark and violent storm. It *would* be all right — wouldn't it?

Within ten minutes, my arm was strung up to a drip again and antibiotics were going into me fast: they had rung upstairs for Stanley, and I was feeling regular and uncomfortable contractions. No need for them to start my labour — it had never really stopped. My baby was on its way.

By comparison with the labour I had the first time — indeed, in comparison with most labours, I suppose — this second one was relatively quick, and not particularly difficult. It began in earnest around seven in the morning, and was over at 10.45. But the secret, if there is such a thing, of coping with contractions is relaxation and co-operation, not resistance, and inevitably my body resisted every one, tensed against it instinctively because I knew it should not be happening, it was too soon for this baby to be born. I was ill, I was afraid, I was sure the child would not be alive.

Sue Clayton, the Sister who had admitted me on the previous Wednesday evening, hearing that I was in labour, came in specially to be in charge. Since Mark was seeing patients at another hospital during the early part of the labour, it was one of those small things that counted for so much, to see a familiar face, to be looked after by someone I felt confident with.

She was positive, encouraging, caring. She was also very concerned — an infection in the Delivery Suite is always taken seriously and, by this time, it was clear that mine had got a firm hold.

Stanley stayed beside me. How different it all was from that last time. Now he had a comfortable chair and, having been through all of it before, knew what to expect. But his face was grey with anxiety because, he, too, knew how wrong things were, and was afraid of the outcome.

After an hour of fighting against the contractions, the midwife suggested I have an epidural.

'That'd be no good,' I wailed. 'They don't work on me.' Stanley filled her in about the previous experience.

'Hm,' she said, and rang the bell. 'It's still worth a try.'

Anaesthetists are always somewhere else, doing something else, I thought, as the clock hand went round. Then, a cheerful, bearded face appeared, hair topped by one of those silly disposable dishcloth caps.

'I'm Mike Ward, your friendly neighbourhood anaesthetist.'

I liked him. Sue was explaining rapidly to him about the previous problem with epidurals, as well as my toxic state.

'That's all right,' he said, 'never beaten yet.'

Well – he wasn't. Not exactly. He got the needle in, but the contractions were coming strongly and quite fast by now and I simply had not been able to keep as still as he wanted. The line between success and a mistake in administering epidural anaesthetics is a very fine one.

'Damn,' I heard him whisper. The Sister glanced up. 'I've done a dural tap.'

I didn't know what that meant and, in any case, a contraction came crashing over me like a wave. When it receded, he said, 'It's fine now – the needle is in, you'll start to go numb very soon.'

Ha! I'd heard that one before. Then, after another contraction, Sue was by my head, her hand on my arm.

'There's a slight problem. The first time, you moved – and the needle went into the wrong space. It's perfectly all right now, the second one was fine, but it means you'll have to lie flat on your back for the rest of your labour and for twenty-four hours afterwards. And that means *flat*. Not even a pillow. Otherwise spinal fluid can leak out.'

'What would happen then?'

'You could get a very nasty headache – not just an ordinary headache, but a really serious one, with intolerance to light – the sort that doesn't respond well to painkillers. To avoid that, we keep you flat until the tiny puncture wound has healed over and no fluid can leak out.'

It was a question of 'one more thing', but for the moment I didn't worry much because, indeed, Dr Ward had been absolutely right.

'Have you noticed anything?' he asked.

'Yes, I haven't had a contraction for quite a few minutes.'

'Yes, you have – you're just not feeling them. The epidural has taken effect.'

Sure enough, my legs felt numb and heavy – and I had absolutely no sensation from the hips down. The relief was dramatic, wonderful. Even though I had needles taped to my back, and the antibiotic drip going into my hand, even though I could not sit, or even be propped up slightly, I felt better.

I could see the midwife's bent head.

'You're fully dilated,' she said. 'This isn't going to be long.' She crossed the room quickly, rang another bell. 'Find Mr Charnock,' she said. 'I want him here – *now*.'

At which, the door opened, and Mark came in, looking his usual calm, cool, collected self. I breathed an even deeper sigh of relief. A few minutes later, from the opposite door, two gowned and masked figures appeared, pushing some sort of huge trolley – I couldn't see it properly.

But Mark caught Stanley's look of alarm. 'It's a resuscitation trolley,' he said. 'Those are our paediatricians.'

One of the reasons for my having an epidural had been to relax me and relieve my pains. The other, even more important, had been so that the baby could be delivered in as slow, careful and controlled a way as possible, guided by the midwife. The epidural cancelled the natural urge to push out the baby that is overwhelming in the second stage of labour – with such a tiny, fragile, premature infant, my forceful pushing could have caused serious damage to the head.

I felt nothing, only saw Mark's bent head, heard a murmur as he spoke to the midwife. He let her deliver the baby. It seemed to take a long time. But there was no triumphant moment, no sudden cry, only a tense silence, a group of intent, anxious faces.

Then a flurry of activity.

'Your baby's out – ' Mark said. I saw the Sister turn, the paediatricians close in, and then bend under a grill-like heater, heads almost touching, I did not see a baby. Low voices.

Stanley gripped my hand on one side, the anaesthetist held the other. Squeezed it.

'It'll be OK.'

What will? Who will? Oh, what was happening? I saw a flash of silver, heard a crackle – it reminded me of something, something ridiculous, out of context. Cooking, that was it. Stanley at the oven.

'What's that?' I asked the doctor. 'What are you doing?'

'Wrapping your baby in special tin foil, to stop it getting cold.'

That was it! Stanley cooking a chicken, wrapping it in foil, ready for roasting, but I couldn't laugh.

'They're putting a tube down into your baby's lungs, it couldn't breathe for long without it at this stage.'

My baby. I had a baby. What? Who?

'What *is* it?'

They had been so busy, they hadn't yet checked. Besides, it is not easy with very premature babies to distinguish the sex immediately. Eventually, I heard a voice, muffled by the gauze mask.

'Girl.'

I turned to Stanley. 'Oh, it's a girl. I wanted a girl.'

Though until that moment, I hadn't realised that I had. I wanted to see her, touch her, let her know that it was all right, that I was there.

But the doors swung open. I heard a warning bleeper, and then she was gone, away fast to the Intensive Care Nursery, wrapped in her tin foil, tied to tubes and wires, like me, surrounded by plastic and metal and strangers. But alive. That was something. Amazing. Alive. I hadn't dared hope . . .

After that, there was the usual clearing up and cleaning up. The Sister explained that, because of my infection the room would be sealed off with tape across the doors, and later would be completely sterilised; until then, no one would come into it and it would not be used.

I was put into a clean gown, lifted and turned. I got a fleeting idea of what it must feel like to be paralysed – what with the anaesthetic, the tubes and wires, and having to lie completely flat.

I still felt numb – in every sense. I held onto Stanley's hand tightly. He looked desperately tired.

'She'll be all right,' I said. 'They'll look after her.'

He nodded slightly.

'We haven't given her a name.'

He looked at me. 'She's Imogen,' he said.

Yes, Imogen, of course she was. We'd mentioned it, when we had dared to begin discussing names at all, it had been the next Shakespearean name we favoured. But I had given more attention to boys' names since that is what I had been sure I would have: Nathaniel had been our choice for a boy's name.

'What is the date?'

'May the twenty-seventh.'

'Tom's birthday.'

Pat Gardner's son was seven. I thought of the year he and Jessica had been born, all the excitement and rejoicing. How different.

'You'd better go and ring – tell Jessica.' But how? And tell her what?

'Not on the telephone,' Stanley said.

'No.'

Mark came over. 'Now, you're going off to get better in Observation Area. The antibiotics are beginning to take hold, your temperature is down. But you'll have to be on them intravenously for a day or so yet – we want that infection well and truly knocked on the head. And I know it's a bore having to lie flat but you really must, the headache after a dural tap can be pretty incapacitating, so don't be tempted to sit up even for a few seconds.'

'Mark – what about the baby? What will happen?'

His face clouded. 'I'll go round there in a moment – I'll be able to learn more about her condition.'

'Will she live? Has she got any chance at all?'

163

He was silent for a moment. 'Susan – I don't know. I just don't know.'

It was very quiet again back in Observation Area – on the Sunday morning of a Bank Holiday weekend, no one is about in the hospital unless they absolutely have to be.

Stanley went home to get a couple of hours' sleep, and then to go and talk to Jessica. I lay, flat on my back, tied up to a paraphernalia of drips. Outside, rain lashed the windows and the wind howled – people said it was cold, too, all the spring flowers were being battered down.

Inside, they left me alone to sleep. But I couldn't. I could hear the nurses talking at the desk outside, and the clatter of the Scholl sandal-clogs they wore on the polished floor. It's the most comfortable, cool footwear for them, but I suppose it hasn't occurred to anyone how much noise they make. And then there is the squawk of the intercom.

But it wasn't only that a hospital ward is not the easiest place in which to get sleep. The problem was that so much had happened in the last twelve hours, my brain was spinning round and round. I went over and over the confusion of events, trying to take them all in, to make sense of things. I kept on going back to the delivery room in my mind, and to that tiny body I did not even see – to the flash of tin foil, and the sight of the incubator disappearing fast out of the swing doors.

Somewhere in the depths of the hospital, in a room I had not been into and could not imagine, I had a baby daughter – alive, so far as I knew. But what did she look like? What were they doing to her? It felt very strange to be empty again, not to have the little feet kicking about inside me, yet to have no baby in my arms, or in a crib beside me either. I felt anxious about her, I wanted to go to her, to let her know that the person whose voice and smell she was familiar with still existed. Yet she was a stranger, too, because I had not seen her, couldn't visualise her at all so that my emotions for her were confused. I cared about her, but I could not yet feel love.

I still felt quite ill, too, though each time the nurse came to take my temperature it had gone down very slightly. The

164

epidural numbness had almost worn off; I was not sore, only uncomfortable and stiff, and longing to sit up. But I felt disorientated and light-headed, restless, weak – I suppose I was in a state of shock, as well as being a battleground between a virulent infection and some powerful antibiotics.

My response to desperate situations has always been to talk out my anxieties and fears, to go over and over what has happened, how I feel, pour it all out to someone – not my husband, or anyone too close to me, but a friend or a doctor, someone with experience and understanding, someone positive.

As the day wore on and my head still buzzed and I felt the pressure of the events become almost unbearable, I wanted more and more to unload everything. But Mark had gone and the nurses seemed to be busy.

In the middle of the afternoon, I had an idea. I asked if they would wheel in the portable phone, and I rang Judy Bogdanor hoping she would be at home.

She was. When I began to explain what had happened, she interrupted. 'I'll come now.'

And she did, arriving in half an hour full of professional concern, but giving me reassurance at once, too, telling me I looked fine, reading the chart and saying the observations showed the antibiotics were beginning to work. Just seeing her made me relax. And then I talked. I went through everything, from the moment my waters broke until now, voiced all my worries, asked a thousand questions. At the end of it, I felt weak and exhausted – but better.

I also realised that I felt ravenously hungry. Have you ever tried getting anything to eat in a hospital, outside set hours for meals, and especially on a Bank Holiday? Judy's quest for food for me – *any* food – was, she said, an adventure for the determined. The canteens and all the outpatient tea-bars and the hospital shop were closed. She herself had left her husband and sons eating a large tea: she described it – sandwiches, toast and honey, biscuits, scones, cake, until I begged her to stop.

'If I'd known,' she said, 'I'd have brought you some.'

We laughed – it was the first slightly funny thing that had

happened for a long time. In the end, she found a nurse who ransacked cupboards and fridges until she came up with a rather elderly white-bread cheese sandwich. It was cold and dry, and curled at the edges, but they made me a cup of sweet tea to wash it down, and the edge was taken off my hunger.

'Is there anything else I can do for you?' Judy asked.

'Yes. Will you go and see the baby? I want to know where she is, what she looks like, what's happening to her.' I hesitated. 'But I suppose there'll be restrictions – they won't let you.'

Judy stood up. 'Don't go away,' she said.

And went out. I heard voices at the nursing station in the corridor, then on the intercom. More discussion. Footsteps going away. Silence.

A burst of rain pattered against the window. I felt very tired indeed, my body seemed to be floating, the wind seemed to blow through my head into a strange, jumbled dream. I wondered what time it was, how Jessica had taken the news, what she was thinking. She and Stanley wandered into the dream, carrying armfuls of daffodils.

I didn't sleep for very long, but it was wonderfully refreshing, the first unconsciousness for thirty-six hours. When I awoke, Judy was back, sitting again on the chair beside my bed.

'I've been to see your daughter,' she said.

I tried to sit up – remembered – fell back flat again.

'Tell me, what is she like? What did they say?'

Judy knew exactly what I wanted to hear – not a general, vague picture, but every possible detail.

'Well – she is very, very small – a *tiny* baby. If I had to describe how tiny . . .' She gestured a possible length with her hands but she couldn't have remembered accurately – no baby could be *that* small.

'She hasn't any clothes on, but she's covered in a sort of bubble-plastic, and she's lying on a lamb's fleece. She's wearing a little knitted pink bonnet to keep her head warm. Her eyes are closed. She has a ventilator tube down her throat, and she's attached to all sorts of wires for monitors,

166

and tubes and drips.' Poor little love – I knew exactly how she felt.

'She's a lovely healthy pink, and quite wriggly. Her incubator is right next to the observation window so I could see her close to, very clearly.'

I tried hard to picture it all. Couldn't really.

'The main thing is,' Judy said again, 'the one thing you notice – is that she is just so tiny.'

She left shortly after that. It had been so good to see her, so good to talk, and to have her description of Imogen. I was more grateful to her than she could ever know.

Not long afterwards, the midwife came in. 'Three things –' she said, 'will you feel like supper?'

'Yes!'

'Fine, but you ought to have something light tonight – soup and ice-cream maybe.'

I thought of the cheese sandwich. It hadn't been light and it hadn't gone very far, either.

'Next – your husband telephoned, he's coming in soon. And last but by no means least –'

She held something out to me. 'A photograph of your daughter.'

A photograph?

'They always take Polaroid pictures of the babies as soon as possible after they've been admitted to the Nursery – you can see what she looks like now.'

She went out. I looked down at the small square of celluloid. And there she was, exactly as Judy had described her, a tiny little red naked thing, with a pink bonnet, one curled hand. I couldn't see what her face was really like because of all the tubes and wires – and the picture wasn't completely in focus. But this was my new daughter, alive, perhaps with a chance?

The confidence that had taken such a knock welled up inside me. Suddenly, I knew that we would be all right, both of us – that she would live. I don't think I had ever fallen completely into despair – I had my obstinate certainty deep down. Now it resurfaced and took a strong hold of me.

When the staff nurse brought my supper – soup and ice-cream – I asked her if she had seen Imogen.

'I certainly have. She's a little fighter, I'll tell you that. You realise she'd no right to get as far as she did – ?'

'I did wonder . . .'

'She was full of your infection, as well as being so premature, but they've got antibiotics into her now. If she has a chance anywhere, it's here – we've got one of the best Intensive Care Nurseries in the country,' she said proudly.

After that, we giggled a bit, trying to work out the best way I could drink soup while lying flat.

I had assumed that I would not be able to see Imogen until I was on my feet again – and that wasn't going to be for several days. I resigned myself to the wait, confident that she was in the best hands in the world, only anxious about how strange she must be feeling, bewildered, perhaps ill or uncomfortable, feeling that everything was suddenly different, out of the familiar dark, watery environment. What I had to do was get better and recover my own strength so that I could give myself to her as soon as possible.

But that evening, I had a surprise. While Stanley was sitting with me, telling me about Jessica, the door opened and two midwives came in, together with the Sister I recognised from Delivery Suite, the one who had been summoned to see if I really was having contractions the previous night – though it felt like a lifetime ago.

'Come on, Dad,' she said, 'take your jacket off and roll up your sleeves. You're going to be pushing from behind.'

'Where are we going?' I asked as they began to move my bed.

'To visit your daughter, of course.'

'Like this?'

'Like this, on your bed, drip trolley and all – if we can manoeuvre you round the corners.'

Whether they've done it again since, I don't know – but I bet nobody who took part in it has forgotten that expedition – my bed was wheeled out of Observation Area, and along to the entrance corridor of the Intensive Care Nursery. Stanley pushed, Sister pulled, and the midwife wheeled the drip trolley. It was a bumpy ride, it felt extremely perilous – and rather odd, as the ceiling went whizzing by.

In the corridor we stopped beside a wall covered with photographs – babies, babies, babies, and toddlers and little children, all peering brightly out at me. On each one was a label – the child's name, and date of birth, and the number of weeks' gestation it was at birth.

'These are our pin-ups – our success stories,' the Sister said.

I read. 'Christopher – 28 weeks. Sarah and James – 32 weeks. Nicholas – 30 weeks. Mary – 27 weeks.'

'Here's the star.'

There was a series of pictures. Jacky – 25 weeks, in an incubator, a tiny little pink girl on a ventilator, just like Imogen; then, over the weeks, getting larger, looking like a real baby, without tubes, being held, being fed – and so on, right up to a walking, bright-eyed two-year-old.

I felt a stir of excitement. She had been a bit larger than Imogen – but the same gestation. If *she* had made it . . .

Slowly we passed along the line of happy photographs. Then through a doorway – a lot of manoeuvring – would we make it? Maybe not – a push and a pull – and the bed was in. Bright lights in my eyes, and an atmosphere like a greenhouse.

'This is the hot room. The tiniest babies and the very sick ones come in here – they have no temperature control at this early stage, so we have to do everything we can to keep them warm.'

There were three or four nurses in the room and they, in turn, bent over me to say hello before diving back to the incubators they were in charge of. As well as being hot, the other thing I noticed about the room was the peculiar noise – a series of intermittent bleeps and pips and blips and hums that emanated from the battery of machines and monitors all around the room.

We waited for a moment beside a sink, and Stanley was shown how to scrub his hands with a special cherry-red pungent-smelling antiseptic in a tipped-up plastic bottle.

'Always come to the sink and scrub your hands as soon as you enter the room and before you go to your baby – and certainly before you touch her.'

Because I still had the drip in one hand, they washed my right one as best they could for me, and dried it on a paper towel.

'Now then, come and be introduced.'

There was yet more manoeuvring as they pushed my bed as close as they possibly could alongside the incubator. I was beginning to feel slightly sea-sick.

'There she is – look, right beside you.'

I turned my head. On my eye level, as near as could be, separated only by the transparent plastic ledge of the open incubator, was my daughter.

I had heard what Judy and the nurses had said, and seen the photograph, I thought I had taken it in and that I could even visualise her. But I had had no idea really, was not prepared at all.

She was unimaginably tiny, it is impossible to convey the smallness of her, and absolutely perfect. Her head, her arm, her hand, her finger, her nails, her ear, her leg, her toes – they were absolutely right, completely formed and normal – but all in miniature. Her *whole hand* was only as large as the top joint of my thumb.

She was indeed pink, she looked like a boiled lobster – which was normal for a baby of that maturity. The ventilator tube pulsed up and down regularly, lifting her little chest as it fed the oxygen into her lungs. And she was moving all the time, fluttering her fingers, kicking her legs gently, wriggling her arms – and as I watched, I remembered those movements inside me, my body felt them again.

I looked at Stanley for a moment.

'She's so *small*,' I said. 'Oh, how can she *be* so small?' He nodded, but then we both looked back, unable to take our eyes off that perfect, minute creature, our daughter, battling for life.

'You can touch her . . .' the nurse who was looking after her said. 'Here – put your hand out.' And she lowered the side of the incubator, lifted a corner of the plastic covering.

Very gingerly, holding my breath, I rested my hand on the side, and stretched out two of my fingers, to take gently hold of Imogen's hand. It felt so soft I could scarcely register the touch on my skin, so warm and light. It was like the paw of a baby dormouse I once found in the garden, but that had been cold, the dormouse dead. My baby daughter was alive! I stroked her hand with my finger – and then put it into her palm. At once she gripped me, so tightly I was startled. And then, looking at her, feeling her minute pink fingers holding so hard to mine, I was hit sideways and bowled over by a great rush of love – the purest, tenderest, most passionately committed love I have ever felt for anyone or anything in my life. I think I will never experience it again, it was as pure as pure oxygen, pure alcohol, fierce, heady, undiluted, strong.

'Oh little one, *live – live!*' I cried to her, silently. She went on gripping my finger. I could have stayed there all night, I was oblivious to everyone, to the room, to my own self, everything in the world, save this tiny girl, and the love I felt for her.

But in the end, we had to leave, and make the crazy, bumpy journey back.

Late that night, I lay and looked out at the night sky. The clouds had cleared, there were stars. I felt quite different, I was having to get used to it. Before I had been shocked and worried, concerned, and I had wanted to find out as much as I could about my baby, but I had also been detached, able to think about her and her situation objectively, to try and work out if she had much chance of survival, and what we would do if she lived, or did not. But now, I had been bowled over by love. All I wanted was for her to live, it was a consuming, desperate feeling, everything about me was committed to it. Imogen was a person, herself and no one else, real to me, not just a premature baby. I had touched her, felt her grip, told her I was there and she had, I was quite sure, heard my voice, responded to me.

Oh please, I said urgently, let her live, oh make her be all right – let her live.

Chapter 12

When she was weighed, on arrival in the hot room of the Special Care Nursery, Imogen was 630 grams – less than 1½ lbs. (Premature babies are not weighed in the delivery room, and no decisions about whether or not they should be resuscitated, or how vigorous the efforts should be to keep them alive, are taken on the basis of weight alone at the time of birth.) She had made some spontaneous breaths, and when they ventilated her, she had responded well. She had been pink – a good sign, and lively – another; a still, pale, flaccid baby gives rise to a great deal more concern.

Antibiotics had been administered to her at once, and when she was four hours old, a brain scan had revealed nothing abnormal.

Those, perhaps, were the positive things. But she had been living in a virulently infected environment for several days – no one could be sure exactly how long – and the infection had inevitably taken a strong grip on her. The worst effect was on her lungs: when she was born, pus had been coming from her nose and mouth, indicating how extensive the infection was.

Poor little scrap – within the first twelve hours of her life she had had so many things done to her that must have been uncomfortable, bewildering, frightening, and painful: needles stuck into her to attach drips and to take fluid from her spine (a lumbar puncture) for testing, a tube had been pushed into her umbilicus so that blood could be drawn off whenever necessary for testing, and the ventilator tube had gone down her throat. So great an invasion of her tiny body, so many people doing things to her – what an introduction to this world!

Because of the complications before and during her birth, I felt great solidarity with her; there we were, attached to our respective machinery – and all for the best possible reasons – and separated only by a room and a couple of corridors but it might have been by a thousand miles. I had touched Imogen's hand, stroked her, felt her grip. What I wanted most of all was to hold her close to me, in my arms, to put her face against mine, whisper to her that I was here, that it was all right – all the instinctive things that mothers do.

On the morning of 28 May, Bank Holiday Monday, I had a succession of visitors. Mark came in – for him it was the usual sort of day off. He had no clinics, no operations, so he could be out of his white coat and suit and into a sweater – but he still had to visit patients, including me, in various hospitals and was, as ever, on call. He seemed to think I was on the mend. He'd been to see Imogen again, and had talked to the paediatricians; things were not good, he felt, but they could be worse – and after all, she was alive, still alive. She'd got this far.

A couple of other doctors came in that morning, Dr Tony Williams to explain about a research project that he was in charge of involving human milk and premature babies. The second, Dr William Tarnow-Mordi, was being funded by Action Research to do work on the ventilation of premature babies. Both of them sat down by my bed and explained, clearly and fully, and as simply as possible, what their work involved and what my part – and Imogen's part – in it could be, if *we chose*. I could have said 'no' and that would have been that.

Of course, I said yes. The John Radcliffe is both a teaching hospital and a major research centre within the University. Important work is being done the whole time on the care and treatment of premature babies, and although neither Imogen nor I were in any sense 'guinea pigs', if we could make a tiny contribution to the general research, I felt that we must.

My third doctor that morning was 'the friendly neighbour-hood anaesthetist', Mike Ward, as jokey and positive as ever. It was his last day on duty before he went off with his family on a week's holiday, but he'd come in to see whether I had had any bad effects from his dural tap. No, I said, none.

'Then the bad news is that you still have to be in a semi-recumbent posture for another twenty-four hours, but the good news is that I'm taking one of the drips out.'

'The fluid one?'

'Yep.'

I cheered. Because of the leakage from the tiny hole in the spinal cord, I had had to be given saline fluid in a drip into my vein, and of course lots of water meant lots of calls for the bedpan – about every half hour. The nurses were probably as delighted to get rid of the drip as I was!

'*And*, today's special offer, you can be propped up a bit on the bed rest. Not too far – but at least you won't have to stare at the ceiling any longer.'

It felt odd, being at something like a normal level again, odd and very good. It also meant that when Stanley brought Jessica in to see me just before lunch, I didn't look quite so strange, and tied down to my bed.

She'd brought me a bunch of flowers, and lots of messages, and she sat as close to me as she could. I'd missed her. She looked fine, if a bit pale, but most of all, she looked huge, a *giant*. I remember glancing down at her hands and thinking how enormous they seemed. And she was still only six!

After a few moments, she began to jiggle from foot to foot, to fiddle with the locker and the bell, to investigate my remaining drip. And then the staff nurse came in. 'I think,' she said, 'that your new sister would like to meet you.'

Jessica's face lit up. Stanley caught my eye and looked anxious – was this a good idea? What was Jessica prepared for – would she be very shocked and frightened? But I knew my daughter better than that. I thought she was well able to cope, that reality is always less frightening than the unknown but imagined; also she had every right to see her sister.

Besides, she was already out of the door and half-way down the corridor, skipping along beside the nurse. Stanley went quickly after them. The door closed. It went very quiet in my room.

I wished I could go, too, but the business of pushing my bed round had been so difficult. I would have to wait until I could go in a more convenient manner.

They came back after just a few minutes. When I looked at Jessica's face, I couldn't tell a great deal from it, but she dashed straight over to me.

'Oh Mummy, she's *sweet*. I love her.'

'You weren't – surprised. She's very small, isn't she?'

'Yes, she's *really* tiny.'

'Did it worry you that she had all the tubes and wires attached to her?'

She looked completely blank. Then she said, 'No . . .', sounding rather surprised. Later, talking to one of the paediatric nurses, I mentioned that Jessica had seemed quite unworried by all the paraphernalia surrounding her sister.

'Yes,' she said, 'it's always like that. Children see the baby, they just never ever seem to notice anything else. It's different with adults – the machinery worries them far more.'

Children, I suppose, home in on the essentials, they see what matters, everything else is not so much ignored as invisible.

I was glad Jessica had been to see Imogen. Her new sister was a reality now, she had a bond with her, the beginning of a relationship. And seeing her, she had loved her – as I had. Now, Imogen really was part of our family.

My lunch came and Stanley took Jessica home. She was going to spend the afternoon with the Lane Foxes so that he could get some sleep – he had spent the previous night on the tiny camp bed on the floor of my room, and had got very little rest. I was so much better, and for the moment Imogen's condition was not causing concern. Tonight, he could sleep in his own bed; he could have a decent meal, too. He had been given a card which allowed him to eat in the hospital canteen, but on Bank Holiday the menu was very restricted, and because of having to stay with me, and see doctors, he had only been able to get across there at odd times when there was even less food available. He had survived mainly on tea and toast and chocolate biscuits, with the occasional plateful of luke-warm baked beans. For a man who likes his food and is such a good cook, this, added to worry, strain, lack of sleep, and having to drive to and fro, was about the final straw.

So I was glad that he would be able to have at least a couple of hours' sound sleep that Monday afternoon, and when they had gone, I felt better about everything than I had done for days. I asked for the prop behind my head to be lowered, and gratefully settled down to sleep myself – and as I had only one drip left, that was considerably easier, too.

Now that my temperature was down, they were coming in to take it and to do the other routine observations only every four hours. With luck, I thought, as I drifted off peacefully, no one would disturb me for a good, long time . . .

'Mrs Wells – Mrs Wells.'

I started from a heavy, dreamless sleep. The midwife was by my bed.

'Mrs Wells, I'm sorry – I have to wake you.'

She helped me up in the bed and raised the back rest. I looked at the clock – I'd been asleep perhaps for forty minutes.

'Dr Rochefort, the paediatric Registrar, is coming in to talk to you – and your husband when he gets here.'

'Stanley?'

'Yes, I'm afraid I had to ring him – he's coming straight in.'

'Oh no, he needs to sleep.' I was almost angry. 'Couldn't it have waited? What's the matter?'

'They're really very worried about Imogen – her condition has deteriorated a lot.'

'But she was fine. They only saw her this morning – they said she wasn't causing them any concern.'

'Well, with such very premature babies, all these things are relative,' she said gently, 'and it can all change very fast.'

It had. Stanley arrived, looking white.

'I wish they'd waited, I wish you could have got a decent sleep.'

'I'd rather be called,' he said, curt with strain and tiredness.

Dr Rochefort came in, young, cool, serious.

'I felt it right to talk to you both now because Imogen's condition is worrying us. She's a very poorly little baby. I'm afraid this so often happens – they survive delivery and they come to us looking pink and lively and perhaps seeming well. Then the problems begin to surface. You have to remember that she is in a totally alien and artificial environment. She was not due to be born for another fifteen weeks or so, everything is too soon – her lungs are immature, all her internal organs, her eyelids are even still fused.'

I remembered the kittens our black cat Polly was always giving birth to, how their eyelids were fused until they were ten days old, and how much more alive they looked when the membrane parted and allowed the eyes to open.

'And added to that, she was born with a serious infection. The lab has just sent back the result of the tests on the swabs we took from her – it was an uncommon infection and it is sensitive only to certain antibiotics. We're giving her those now, but the infection had got a grip on her. We've given her a blood transfusion, and we're afraid now that there has been some bleeding into her brain . . .'

'It doesn't sound as if you give her much of a chance.'

'I'm afraid I don't.'

'No hope at all?'

She paused. 'Well – there's always hope, right until the end of course. But – ' She left it unsaid.

When she had gone, we simply sat in miserable silence.

'Go and see her,' I said after a while.

'Imogen?'

'Please.'

He looked reluctant. 'I don't want to be in the way. They seem so busy, there's so much for them to attend to, and not much room beside her incubator.'

But I knew that wasn't the real reason.

'I want you to go – please. I'd go but I can't, you know I can't.'

Slowly, without speaking, Stanley left the room.

When he came back, he just said, 'They seem to be doing a lot of things to her. She looks awful.' His eyes filled with tears. As he left, he said, 'If there's any change they can call me – and I *must* be called.'

I lay, feeling as bleak as I had ever felt. So Imogen was

going to die then; they seemed to have been preparing us for that. It had all been a failure, hopeless after all. She should not have been born, but she had. She was.

I felt suddenly weary. So much for us all to have gone through, and for nothing. Poor little girl. And as for me – I would have to start all over again. That wasn't in doubt, not even a question – it was a fact. When Mark had come in the previous day, I had said, 'If she doesn't live, I'm going to try again.'

He had looked alarmed. 'Susan, we're not going to have this conversation.'

'I'm just giving you advance notice.'

'Well let's hope it doesn't arise – that you won't have to.'

'Fine.'

Now, it looked as if it would. Imogen was 'a very poorly little baby'. She was going to die.

I looked out of my window. Another grey, wet day with scudding, heavy clouds.

It was no good – the little flame of hope, of confidence, of certainty, refused to go out, it was flickering away there, as bright and steadfast as ever. Imogen was going to die, but I simply could not, did not, would not believe it.

When the midwife came in later, I noticed that she was wearing a cross around her neck.

'Say a prayer for Imogen,' I said suddenly.

She smiled. 'What on earth do you think I've been doing for the last two days?'

One of the hard things about the previous few days had been having to cope with so much all at once. For Stanley, it had been a time of the most appalling strain and anxiety. Since the Wednesday evening, when he had been so abruptly hauled out of his black-tie dinner and summoned to the hospital, he had sustained shock after shock: my membranes had ruptured and I was in imminent danger of giving birth far too early for the baby to survive; I was to stay in hospital for eight weeks and then be delivered; I had gone into labour and later I was hysterical on a ritodrine drip; I had a serious infection; labour with problems – then a very tiny, very sick baby had been born and was in an intensive care incubator fighting for her life against impossible odds; she was ill – she was alive – she was stable – her condition had deteriorated – she would probably die. It was an emotional and physical see-saw that he had been thrust upon. He was lacking in sleep, had spent worried and uncomfortable nights on a small camp bed in the hospital, been awakened at odd times, eaten at odder. In addition, he had to try and work, as well as to buy and cook food, make sure our menagerie of animals was fed and watered; had to look after Jessica, reassure her, love her, give her comfort and security, all at the same time as trying to make arrangements for her to be with friends while he was at the hospital. He maintained his outward calm under the strain; he was, as always, loving, full of concern – but often silent and withdrawn. It was scarcely surprising.

Jessica seemed to be coping well, but I was getting increasingly concerned about her – wondering what was going on inside her head, how worried and bewildered she might be. We did not try to keep her away, or hold anything back from her, and nor did anyone at the hospital. From the very beginning, she had been involved with this baby and I was not going to have her pushed out or away now, even if the reasons might have seemed all the best ones. Nevertheless, it was a tightrope we were walking – it would have been wrong to tell her everything, every risk, every problem and, inevitably, there was much that she could not understand.

She grew up a great deal over those weeks. She was sensible and sensitive – but because she was only six she was also able to let off steam, to switch off from the entire situation when she was with the loving, caring friends who were surrounding us, helping us out.

Looking back on that time, I know that we did the right thing by her, that she did not suffer lasting damage; indeed, she gained what in some strange way one always does gain from suffering and tragedy. She was, always has been, an articulate child, able to ask questions, to talk her feelings and worries out, just as I could, with those who cared for her.

I felt the strain of everything having happened at once, too; I was worrying about Imogen, loving her desperately, afraid for her, at the same time as I was feeling physically awful. Not surprisingly, something snapped – not for very long, or so as to cause any serious harm but, for me, very dramatically and in the most terrifying way.

I had fully expected Imogen to die overnight on that Monday. When I woke on Tuesday morning, I rang the bell at once. A new midwife came in, smiling.

'Please could you find out how my baby is?'

'I already have.' She came round to plump up my pillows and prop up the bed rest – I was now allowed to be at a slightly steeper angle. 'She's still very poorly, but she's holding her own. She had a reasonably stable night.'

I lay back in relief. She was still alive then. But oh, those hospital phrases – 'holding her own', 'reasonably stable'. I wanted to know more, wanted to know what I never *could* know – how she felt about it all, *I wanted to go to her.*

As the midwife helped me to wash, I said, 'When do you think I'll be able to get up?' Apart from needing to see Imogen, I felt stiff and sore, fed up with lying in bed. She said I'd have to wait and see Mr Charnock and an anaesthetist – but possibly in a couple of days. It sounded like forever.

When Mark came in at lunchtime, he was much happier with my condition, at least. I could lose the antibiotic drip, and take the penicillin now in tablet form so that my last encumbrance would be gone. I was allowed to go to the bathroom – and, best of all, I was to be taken back to my room on Level 7. It sounded good, half-way to home. They had looked after me wonderfully in intensive care, it had been the safest place – but leaving it meant I was on the mend: I could do with that – I needed to concentrate on Imogen.

But when the porter finally came, with a midwife from Level 7 to accompany me up in the lift, I didn't want to go. I couldn't have told them, couldn't say anything at all. I joked and chatted brightly on the way, but I realised that I was going much further away from Imogen. Until now, our rooms had been relatively close to each other. I felt she must know that I was abandoning her, would not be able to hear her cry. I wondered if the invisible cord that joined her tightly to me still would stretch that far; but of course, it did – I just *felt* bereaved, I wanted to be going in the opposite direction. She was in the best hands, I knew that, and they were doing everything they could – those were the phrases to use – but they were strangers, they could not love her as I did – she needed *me*.

When I reached my room, the sun was shining for the first time in three days, the sky was blue outside my window, spring had returned.

They pushed my bed into position and put all my belongings in the locker. It was nice to be back, yet I felt – odd, yes – I couldn't put my finger on it quite – just odd. Instead of looking familiar and friendly, everything looked strange and forbidding. For a moment, I wondered where I was. Still, being wheeled around on a hospital bed is pretty disorientating.

I asked if I could get up to go to the loo, and the midwife very carefully helped me. I felt wobbly for a moment.

'Take it steadily.' I did – I was fine.

As I reached the bathroom, the bell rang urgently out at the nursing station.

'I'm on my own,' she said. 'You just stay there – I'll be back. Don't try and get back to bed on your own, you're still not used to walking –'

She dashed out. It was warm in the little bathroom. Quiet. I waited. And then, after a moment, looked around. *Where* was I? What was this room? I didn't recognise it at all. A bathroom, yes. And I seemed to be sitting on a loo. I was puzzled. I realised I had absolutely no idea at all where I was or why. I searched my memory, looked frantically around. No, I simply did not know.

It's very difficult now to convey the fear that this bewilderment caused within me. How could I possibly not know where I was? It's also very difficult to explain what it felt like, but I remember it, my God I remember it, thinking about those moments sends a chill through me. After a little while, the midwife came back.

'All right?'

Who was this?

'Ye-es. I feel – a bit odd – I'm sorry.'

'I'm not surprised, let's get you back to bed.'

'Yes.'

She helped me again into another strange room, up onto a bed. I was glad to be in it, I felt quite exhausted.

'There,' she said, 'I think what you should do is have a sleep. I'll leave you in peace.'

'Thank you,' I said politely. The door closed.

I lay, tired, but not sleeping, for quite a long time. And the longer I lay, the more I worried about where I was and why, so that in the end I rang the bell. I would have to ask her. She came back.

'Not asleep?'

'No. Listen, I'm sorry to bother you – only – please could you tell me where I am? I've been lying here trying to – to remember – or work it out, but I can't. I don't recognise this room at all.'

A spasm of alarm crossed her face. She came close to the bed and said gently, 'You're in your room on Level 7.'

'Level 7?'

'In the John Radcliffe Maternity Hospital.'

It meant nothing.

'What am I doing here?'

'You've had a baby. Imogen. She's downstairs in the Special Care Nursery.'

Yes – yes, that sounded right. I'd heard of Imogen.

'I – I –' I stopped.

'What is it?'

I looked at her in blank, blind panic. Who was this 'I'?

'Who am I?' I said.

I can see her face now, as her mind raced over everything that could be wrong with me, most of it very serious.

'*I don't know who I am,*' I wailed.

I simply did not. It wasn't exactly that I couldn't remember my name – I had no sense of my own identity. I felt myself to be there, a person in a strange bed in a room I did not recognise, but who I was I could not say.

She spoke very quietly. 'You're Mrs Susan Wells.'

Oh. 'Who?'

'Mrs Susan Wells.'

'Where am I?'

'You're in the John Radcliffe Maternity Hospital – you've had a premature baby. She's in the Nursery.'

It meant nothing. I can only describe the experience as being like swimming around in a great blank pool, blindly groping for something that was just out of reach – when I grasped it, I would know who I was, where I was and why, and I would be on firm, safe, dry land again.

'Stay here,' she said, 'I'm just going to telephone Mr Charnock.' She disappeared very quickly indeed. Mr Charnock. I wondered who he was. The name sounded dimly familiar but that was all.

I lay in a sweat of absolute terror, wondering if I would ever regain myself, discover who I was. I knew this was not right, knew I should be able to get hold of who I was, and keep hold. If the mad who lose a sense of their own identity *know* that they have lost it, then it must be hell indeed.

I supposed I must *be* mad.

The midwife came back. 'I'm just going to take your temperature.'

She had, of course, immediately rung my doctor as an emergency, and he had told her to check at once whether or not I was running a high fever, a sign that my infection, or another, had got a grip again and I was seriously ill. At the time, I didn't know this.

'That's fine.' She shook the thermometer down.

Oh. Good. 'Who am I?'

After a while, she left to go to the telephone again and I lay, rigid with fear, wondering what was going to happen to me. When she came back, it was to tell me she had telephoned my husband, and he was coming in at once. That sounded right to me, though I could not picture this person. I asked her if I *was*, perhaps, going mad. She looked nervous.

'No, I think you've been under a lot of strain and, sometimes, having a baby can make women confused.'

'Yes. What will happen to me?'

'You might – go and stay in another hospital for a while, until you feel better.'

I was puzzled. Later, of course, I realised that she meant the unit attached to the Oxford Psychiatric Hospital which treats mothers suffering from post-natal psychosis. This is a rare but very serious – but also very treatable – condition in which

183

women who have just given birth become confused and depressed, and sometimes try to harm themselves and their babies.

In fact, this was not what was happening to me.

The door opened and Stanley came in – and as he did so, everything clicked into place, and I burst into sobs of relief and release. I knew him, knew where I was, what had happened – and most of all, *who* I was again, not as a piece of information taken in by ear and learned by the brain – I felt my own sense of myself restored. It was like getting back into mind and body after having been away and searching, searching desperately for them. I held onto Stanley and cried and he, poor man, bewildered but relieved, too, that I was all right after all, sat patiently waiting for me to calm down.

Of course, Imogen's critical illness was the very worst thing and everything else paled before that, and it still does, but as far as my own condition went, there were two things I would never wish to experience again – the night spent on the ritodrine drip with its awful physical side-effects and, far, far worse, the terror of losing myself for a couple of hours. That has left a scar, deep within me, which will never heal. It has also left me with a much more profound understanding of what it actually can mean to be mentally ill. And I, after all, was myself again very rapidly.

When Mark came in to see me that evening and I told him how I'd felt, his response was very measured.

'I won't say that I was waiting for something like this – but I'm not in the least surprised. If we just look at what has happened these past few days, you were bound to have some sort of emotional and mental reaction, quite apart from a physical one. And it's a very healthy sign – I was a bit worried that you seemed *so* in control.'

That night, after everyone had gone, I had a reaction to my reaction – I cried for a couple of hours, sobbed in exhaustion and shock, and out of love and anxiety for my baby, and as I cried, I felt all the things that had been pent up drain out of me. Then I slept, slept as I don't think I have ever slept before, and woke – I ought to say, feeling refreshed – but, in fact, I felt awful, thick-headed, heavy as if I had been drugged. When I got up to go to the bathroom, I could scarcely walk across the floor. And then, as I bent my head over the basin to clean my teeth, something else happened. It was like an explosion in my brain, or as if someone had cracked me over the head with an iron bar – and was going on doing so, bang – bang – bang – boom – boom – boom. I have never known a headache like it. I crawled back to bed and rang the bell.

For the next day, I was flat on my back again. Every time I sat up, or got up, my head split open. In spite of having been treated with such caution in the hours after Imogen was born, I had nevertheless developed the dreaded consequences of my dural tap during the administration of the epidural anaesthetic. The hole had obviously begun to seal over, but was very fragile and when I had got up, it had opened up again, allowing a leakage of fluid. For days, I was in agony whenever I attempted to make a movement from the prone position. A routine blood test also revealed that I had become extremely anaemic – which was why I had been feeling so pole-axed.

It really was 'one damn thing after another', a terrible chain of bad luck, and awful, though not life-threatening, afflictions.

But so many good things were happening, too. Flowers poured in, vases, baskets, bouquets of them, from family, friends, business colleagues, neighbours, and with the flowers, the cards and letters and messages of concern and love, the offers of help. At home, Stanley and Jessica were overwhelmed by them, supported and greatly helped. People shopped. Angela, our invaluable domestic help, turned herself into a housekeeper, took home all the washing and brought it back, quietly did extra jobs that needed to be done – the place would have fallen apart without her.

It was very good to feel all the care and love surrounding me and my little daughter. Only one or two things were unfortunate; they were no one's fault but because I was in such an extra-sensitive state, they caused me to react badly. It was difficult, especially for people not in close touch, to decide whether it was appropriate to send flowers or not. They did send them and as, after all, I had had a baby, they ordered the kind of flowers and cards that go with such a happy event. Therefore, along with the bouqets and the simple arrangements, I got several nylon-lace cradles and plastic bootees full of pink flowers, tied up in pink ribbon, accompanied by pink Congratulations cards. They made me weep when I saw them. They looked so bright, so normal, too cheerful, for I had not just 'had a baby', I had had Imogen and I should not have done so, and she was so tiny, so ill. I got them to take the nylon baskets out into the corridor. They looked pretty there, for other people to enjoy. Not for me.

In the midst of all this, I felt a million miles away from Imogen. I rang the bell a dozen times a day and asked them to find out about her. I looked at her photograph constantly, sent messages to her, and loved her, loved her.

On the Thursday, in spite of my headache, I could bear it no longer. When Stanley came in, I said I didn't care how they got me there, I was going down to see my daughter. I took two Panadol (which didn't have any effect) and they got me a wheelchair.

Imogen looked quite different, and very, very ill. Over the few days since her birth, she had developed jaundice — common in many babies, and to almost all premature ones, but still never to be taken lightly. She was being treated under the great, bright, flat phototherapy lights above her incubator, and she was a terrible colour, dark yellow, like a little old oriental person; her head looked shrivelled, somehow desiccated. She had electrodes fitted to her scalp, tubes and drips from every orifice, her eyes were bandaged against the light.

I wanted to drag everything away from her, every bit of machinery, to pick her up and hold her to my breast, even if it meant that she died in a few minutes. That would be better than having her suffer this, the pain, fear, noise, bewilderment, being surrounded and handled by strangers. At that moment, I did not see the medical staff as saviours, as people who were caring for my baby and trying to save her life, I saw them as aggressors, tormentors, people who had taken my baby away from me and were doing terrible things to her, who were *keeping* her from me. I was filled with anger and hurt on her behalf.

To a certain extent, I never got over that anger, it has never left me. It was an instinct, deep, irrational, passionate. She was being hurt, and for what? For the best? I wondered. I still do wonder.

If she had become well and had lived, I would not have done so.

I didn't stay very long that morning. The hot room was crowded. The staff were busy both with Imogen and a ward round and conferences over several other babies. Besides I didn't want to stay, I couldn't bear to see her looking so frail, so vulnerable, so ill, and not be able to help her myself at all. This time, I had not even been able to get near enough to the incubator to touch her hand, there were too many people and machines in the way.

Later that day, Imogen had a second blood transfusion. The doctor on duty wrote in her notes, 'No deterioration so far' – perhaps she was surprised.

Back upstairs, I felt wretched and my headache had worsened again. They were polishing the floor of my room that morning – a more serious procedure than it sounds, involving the removal of everything, patient, bed and furniture, into the corridor, and a long wait until the wax dried. I sat in a chair miserably, unable to read, unable to bear the light, unable to do much about any of it, and when I closed my eyes, there was Imogen, tiny, yellow, sick, in her incubator. I didn't honestly know whether I wanted her to live or die – but she *was* going to live, wasn't she? I knew that, underneath it all, I was still confident. So what was going wrong, why was she suffering so many setbacks? I felt so *helpless*. It seemed as if nothing good would ever happen again.

The next day, though, something did. Mark's wife, Margie, had her baby, a fine son. I couldn't go along to her room, two doors from mine, until my headache had gone, and it seemed to split my skull in two every time I sat up, but I sent messages by the midwives, and wrote her a card – it was good to know they were there, safe and well.

The following morning, the anaesthetist came and agreed that I could try sitting up again. If all was well, I could get to my feet that evening. If not – flat on my back again. I moved very, very gingerly to a reclining position in the bed, waited, yes – all did seem to be well. I celebrated by having my lunch sitting fully upright, but I was still unbelievably tired, even eating and drinking seemed to drain me as much as a hard day's work. When the obligatory hours for resting came, between 1.30 and 3.30, I slept like the proverbial newborn baby.

I awoke one afternoon a day or two later to find a stranger standing by my bed. It often happened, various people in white coats were constantly coming to see me for this and that – but this young woman didn't have a white coat, she wore an orange shirt and a swirling black skirt, and dangling gold earrings. I struggled up, puzzled.

'Mrs Wells, sorry to wake you, I've been trying to get up to see you all day but we've been fairly frantic.' She held out her hand. 'My name's Sandy Calvert – I'm the paediatrician in charge of the Special Care Nursery.'

I couldn't get used to so many doctors not looking like doctors, and to those in senior posts often looking so young! But I remembered that the last time one of the paediatricians had paid me a visit was to bring bad news.

'Oh God, what's happened?' I wasn't sure if I could cope with more bad news – but I was half-expecting it, half-prepared all the same.

'Imogen's really doing very well, I'm pleased with her.'

I stared at her. 'But everybody was so worried.'

'I know.' She sat down beside me. 'The thing is – with these tiny babies it can all change so fast, one way or another. Yesterday she was still very poorly. Now, I'm not saying she's fine but suddenly things have started to go right. She's responding to the antibiotics at last – her infection is getting well under control, I think. Her brain waves are normal – we've done another scan, and I don't think there's any problem there. We've dropped her oxygen to 40% and she seems fine. We might drop it again a little tomorrow. And she's even started to be fed a bit of DBM – donated breast milk. Have you given us any milk yet?'

'No – ' I explained about the headache. 'But I want to, just as soon as I can – only – I'm not sure if I'll have any. I can't feel any yet, maybe it's too soon. I mean, she was only 25 weeks – would I *get* any milk?'

'Oh yes, you'll get some – the problem is, you haven't held the baby, and of course she hasn't suckled, so there's been nothing to stimulate your milk. I'll speak to Sister – maybe tomorrow you could try going on the breast pump, let's see.'

'Oh, yes, perhaps even tonight?' I longed to have my own milk to give to Imogen; it was something, the only thing at the moment, that I would be able to do for her, and surely, surely the milk that my body would produce for her would be the best possible thing, would give her something to make her well and strong, as nothing else could.

'Do you really think she's going to be all right?'

Dr Calvert stood up. 'Listen, I don't make predictions, we never do in this game, but I'm telling you that she's turned a corner – and that we're well pleased with the progress she's made last night and today.'

I couldn't sleep any more. I rang Stanley, and told him. He sounded cautiously pleased.

Early that evening, we went to see her, all three of us. Jessica washed her hands first, and was first over to the incubator where the nurse on duty was in the middle of changing her sister's tubes and cleaning her up. When we reached her side, Jessica was standing proudly wiping her sister's arm and tiny hand with a scrap of soaked cotton wool, directed by the nurse. Her movements were so careful, so gentle, her face a picture of tender concern.

'Doesn't she look better?'

She did, oh she looked a different baby. The yellowness had almost faded, she looked a pink colour again, and she was wriggling, squirming, opening and closing her fingers, twitching her toes, where before she had lain very still.

'She's had some milk.' The nurse pointed to her chart. I looked at it – the date, the time, the quantity – 1 ml. *One ml!* I thought of the 5 ml teaspoon in which I gave Jessica cough medicine and tried to imagine one fifth of it – three drops?

Still, it was food being taken into her stomach, not going through a vein. It was a step forward.

She lay, clean, refreshed, alert.

'She's handling well –'

'What do you mean?' Jessica asked, then, as now, an inquisitive child. Every time she visited over the next few weeks, she asked a hundred questions of the medical team, and every time they answered her fully, clearly, cheerfully, simplifying but never patronising, and not trying to hold anything back.

'Just that she doesn't mind when I do things to her.'

'How do you know? You can't say, "Because she doesn't cry," because she *can't* cry. And she can't talk and tell you either.'

'No, but if, for example, something I did was hurting her or making her uncomfortable, she'd clench up her fist, go stiff. I watch all the machines and her heart always goes a little bit faster when we handle her – so would yours, that's quite normal. But if it went really fast, we'd know she wasn't happy. There are lots of little signs they give us.'

Satisfied that her sister was being looked after properly, Jessica stayed for another few minutes but then grew restless; apart from anything else, it was *very* hot in the hot room. I grew acclimatised to it after a few minutes but I was only in a nightdress and cotton robe.

In the corridor outside, there were two boxes containing children's books and toys, and Jessica went off to dig in them while we stayed on. I sat on the high stool and held Imogen's hand, stroking it very gently between my fingers, murmuring to her. She looked so much better, I felt so happy. Now things were going right and she was perhaps past the worst. She just had to grow, mature, get strong. I thought of the photographs on the walls out in the corridor, of the babies being cuddled, fed – and taken home. I dared not think of that. But there was a crib waiting.

And that was a strange coincidence, too. A couple of weeks before Imogen was born, on a cold, wet Saturday, we had gone, together with my aunt who was visiting us, to the Little Clarendon Street Fair in Oxford. It's an annual event, always held in aid of a charity during May or early June. The narrow street is closed to traffic, there are roundabouts, a barrel organ and games, and outside each shop, stacks of things for sale, home-made-cake stalls, and raffles. Young staff dress up as gorillas or walk on stilts, there's a band, there are Morris dancers, you can eat and drink, the place is full of balloons and children and merriment – and a good deal of money is raised every year. It's one of the jolliest events in Oxford, and we try never to miss it.

And this time, it had been in aid of SSNAP – which stands for Support for the Sick New-born and their Parents, the charity that raises money for the John Radcliffe Hospital Special Care Nursery. Barely three weeks ago, and I had known precious little about the Nursery, had scarcely heard of it. I remember standing beside a stall displaying photographs of small babies grown into fine, healthy children, and putting money into a collecting tin, thinking vaguely what good work they obviously did for the unlucky people whose babies needed special care.

At the bottom of the street, near to the roundabout whose horses went merrily up and down all day, was a stall selling children's clothes, toys and baby garments, all in a pile together. I looked idly through the little dresses and romper-suits, but what really delighted my eye was what they were piled into – an Edwardian wicker crib on a stand. It was identical to the one I had borrowed from friends for Jessica, but that had had to be given back, and I had been looking out for one ever since, in second-hand and antique shops everywhere. Now, here it was.

'Is the crib for sale – the one full of clothes?'

The woman looked surprised. 'Oh, I don't really know – I shouldn't think so. Just a minute.'

There was a flurry, someone was sent for, and yes, it was for sale, though they hadn't expected anyone to want it.

Well, I did. Somewhat to his surprise, Stanley found himself carrying a baby's crib down the street to the car, and my aunt allowed herself to be squashed up beside it all the way home. That afternoon, I sanded it, painted it white, and set it out in the sun to dry.

Now, sitting beside Imogen's incubator, I thought of it for a moment, waiting at home for her, one day, one day. And it would be very special, bought at the street fair in aid of this hospital's Nursery I had never expected to have anything to do with.

When I left her that evening, I was quietly contented, grateful that things were going well. My confidence had not been misplaced after all. I had known all along, hadn't I, that she would be all right, it had been promised to me.

Back on Level 7, I went in to see Margie Charnock, lying looking so happy and well, with the baby boy lying beside her. He was asleep, perfect – like Imogen would be one day.

'He's so small,' Margie said. I laughed out loud. To me, he was a giant baby!

Just before nine o'clock that evening, after the hot drinks trolley had gone round, I was sitting up in bed, leafing through a magazine, when I suddenly wanted, overwhelmingly, to go down to the Nursery to say goodnight to Imogen, touch her again just for a moment, let her know I wasn't far away. Could I? Would they let me?

I got out of bed and put on my dressing-gown.

At the nursing station, the Night Sister was writing notes.

'Hello, Mrs Wells, how do you feel now? You're looking much better tonight.'

'Yes, I am, I really am. Do you think I could possibly go down and see the baby, just for a few moments?'

She looked at me thoughtfully, and then said, 'You obviously *want* to.'

'Oh yes, I do.'

'Do you think you can manage it alone – I can't spare anyone just now to come with you.'

'Yes, I'll be fine.'

She smiled. 'Not long though. I'll telephone down and have you back in fifteen minutes!'

It felt very strange indeed going down in the lift by myself. For a moment, when the doors began to close, I felt a surge of panic – what if I passed out now, what would happen? But I realised I'd be found pretty quickly, and I had my plastic identity tag firmly on my wrist – I could hardly have been safer!

Still, my heart was beating fast and my knees were jelly as I crossed the blue-carpet area and went towards the swing doors. The porter looked up from his desk, and nodded. Otherwise, there was no one at all about. Past all the scan-rooms, along the empty corridors – it was ghostly and, for a second, I had a vision of myself, floating through in my white cotton nightie, a ghost myself to anyone coming suddenly upon me!

In the Nursery the atmosphere was different too, but as I got near the hot room, I heard the familiar bleep-bleep-bleep of the machinery, saw the white-gowned nurses, with their charts and their trolleys. Down here, day and night, nothing stopped, babies need the same special care round the clock.

I didn't know any of the night staff, but it didn't matter, they were welcoming, not at all nonplussed by being visited so late in the evening.

A Chinese staff nurse was in charge of Imogen.

'She looks much better.' She smiled. 'We're really pleased with your little girl.'

So was I. I sat on the stool, and put out my hand to touch her, and at once her fingers curled around mine. With my other fingers, I stroked her arm gently.

'See,' she said, 'she knows you – you see her heart-rate increases a bit when you first touch her. Then it goes nice and steady.'

I watched the green digits on the monitor. 'You really do think they know the difference?'

'Listen, we look after her, we care for her, but you're her mother, you love her – that's the difference.'

She went away then to check on another baby, covering for a nurse who had gone out of the room, and I sat on, stroking Imogen's arm. And as I sat, I felt a sensation, at first strange, odd – then suddenly, very familiar – and welcome, so welcome.

'Goodnight, my little love,' I said, and slipped off the stool.

The lift was empty again, but I felt a bit more confident this time. And now, I was in no doubt at all. The Night Sister had left her desk, and was going up the corridor to someone's room. I waited for her to come back. In some of the rooms, lights had gone out, mothers were settling down to sleep, from others came crying. I would have given anything to be going back to my bed with the baby beside me in her cot. I hadn't wanted to leave her downstairs, to wonder where I had gone, why I had stopped caressing her.

The Night Sister was coming back. 'There you are, I was just going to send out a search party! Everything all right?'

'Yes, fine –'

'The baby? I hear she's doing well now.'

'She is, and – my milk has just come in!'

She smiled. 'Now that *is* a good sign.'

I knew it.

'What shall I do?'

'Nothing, not until tomorrow morning. It's far too late to start giving you your first lesson in using the milking machine. Go on – off to bed.'

I did. I almost didn't make the dozen yards up the corridor. I was suddenly overcome by complete and tearful exhaustion.

A few minutes later, the Night Sister came in to take my temperature, check my pulse.

'Hm – ' she said. 'You, my girl, are over-excited.' She put out the light firmly. 'Sleep,' she ordered.

Instantly, I slept.

Chapter 13

Some years before Imogen was born, I remember vividly meeting a couple who had had a premature baby who had spent his first few weeks in a Special Care Nursery. He had done well and was now two years old, but they were telling the dramatic story of his birth and early weeks, and how, at first, he had seemed unlikely to pull through. 'He was so ill one night,' his mother said in a hushed voice, 'that the hospital told us to send for the chaplain and get him baptised – it was as bad as that.'

'And did you?' I asked.

'Of course! Well, you have to, don't you, it was only right – I mean, they did think he was going to die.'

They were not, it seemed, regular or even occasional churchgoers, though they had been married in church, and their religious beliefs were probably as vague and generalised as those of many. Yet when the hospital had suggested their sick baby had better be baptised, they had agreed at once, and had it done with all possible speed.

I was appalled when I heard the story. I am still appalled – and I have heard a similar version of that incident often enough. Partly, I suppose, my repulsion is a reaction to the version of Christianity with which I was force-fed for the first thirteen years or so of my schooling – for non-Catholics and Catholics alike attended the same religious instruction classes and assemblies. I have no idea whether it is still official

Catholic doctrine that babies must be baptised as soon as possible after birth – if necessary, and in an emergency, not even by a priest, but by anyone – to make them proper Christians and Catholics, and that if they die before this can happen, they cannot go to be with God, in heaven, but are banished to a bland-sounding (though, one gathers, pain-free) place called limbo, forever after. Perhaps things have changed, but in those days that is what we were led to believe. It seemed to me at the age of six or so, and has continued to seem, one of the more inhuman and insensitive pieces of Church doctrine – though as it also seemed a laughable one and I could never have believed for one moment in a God who was behind it, it did not make me too angry, I simply brushed it to one side, along with a good deal else.

Which is not to say that I am always and everywhere opposed to Christian baptism. It seems to me a good service, a symbolic way of admitting anyone into the company of those who call themselves Christians – because they are believers in and followers of the essential teachings of Jesus Christ; it sets the child publicly on the side of the forces of light rather than those of darkness, it is a statement of where you want it to stand, wearing 'the whole armour of God'. That is a very much bigger and more important thing than enacting a piece of magic. And in many ways, although never having belonged to the non-conformist churches, it is with them that I side, in preferring baptism to be something delayed until either adult life, or at least 'older childhood' so that the commitment is made with understanding. Because of this, and because I also disliked the 'social occasion' aspect of a christening, Jessica was not baptised as a baby. We intended to let her make the decision about it when she was old enough to understand what it was all about.

Only one nurse in the Nursery had brought up the subject of baptism while Imogen had been struggling through those first few days of her life – we had rebuffed her suggestion, I hope politely, and it had not been mentioned again. I recoiled more passionately than ever from the merest suggestion that we should have the ritual performed 'just in case'.

I had had several visits from the clergy though, and

inevitably they raised the matter. The vicar of our village church was assiduous in coming to see me, and Paul Rimmer, the vicar of St Nicholas, Old Marston which we sometimes attended, came as soon as he got back from holiday, with his usual ebullience and cheerfulness subdued when he recognised how ill Imogen and I both were, but the warmth of his embrace even stronger and more reassuring.

On the Sunday after Imogen's birth, I asked for the hospital chaplain to bring me Communion, and had my first encounter with a man who became an immediate and warm friend. The Reverend John Barton, Anglican chaplain to the Oxford hospitals, is so tall that he has to stoop in the narrow doorways, a gentle giant of a man, calm and steady, one of the best examples I have ever come across of 'a square peg in a square hole'. A hospital chaplain seems to me to have one of the toughest, most demanding jobs in the Church – yet also one of the most rewarding. He is at the sharp end the entire time, he sees people 'in extremes', dying, grieving, in pain, shocked, angry, afraid, bewildered; he is there when all inessential matters and questions are stripped away and only love and truth are relevant. The qualities the job demands are many – tact, honesty, gentleness, steadfastness, faith, reverence, awe, stamina – and the rewards of it must be considerable. In John Barton, I recognised at once an exceptional man.

On one occasion early on, he came down to the Nursery with us to visit Imogen and give her a simple blessing – though not, as I had insisted, to baptise her. He understood my reasons at once and respected them – but the strength I derived from standing beside him while he put one large, gentle hand onto Imogen's tiny one and held mine with the other, was tremendous. He prayed for her in plain, straightforward words, but there was no suggestion of bargaining or begging; he asked for help, strength, healing, comfort and commended her to God's love. That was all, and it seemed to me, at that point at least, to be everything.

After Dr Calvert's visit to me, Imogen continued to do well. Her temperature was stable, her chest X-rays were clear, and so was her brain scan, she was handling well. When I went down to see her, she was always lively, always wriggling, clenching and unclenching her tiny fingers, flexing her little legs. And on one exciting day, when Jessica rushed straight into the hot room and over to her cot, I heard a cry of delight from the corner as I was scrubbing my hands.

'Mummy, come and look, come and look – *quick!*'

I went, looked down at my infant daughter. And she looked gravely back at me. Her eyes had opened, the fusing membrane was gone.

'Just like the kittens!' Jessica said.

Yes. And now, I felt I could look at her and get to know her, meet her eye when I talked to her. Of course, she couldn't focus, I was probably only a blur to her – but until now, she had seemed so closed away in her own world, remote from me, from all of us, almost as remote as when she had been in the womb, even though I could touch her.

And it was now, while she was doing so well, that we decided to have Imogen baptised. I thought about it for the whole of one evening until I was sure. True, we had to make the commitment on her behalf, and that concerned me, but I felt that the statement her baptism would make now was one of hope and a looking forward – and perhaps one of gratefulness, too, that we had come this far. No one would ever make extravagant predictions – but Imogen was not in immediate danger, she was doing better than any of us had dared to dream, and so, perhaps in a defiant mood of optimism, I asked Paul Rimmer to come in the following day.

No one thought anything untoward about Imogen's baptism, except one nurse who came up to me that evening and said, 'I hear Imogen was baptised this morning, is that right?' She spoke in a hushed, almost shocked voice. 'I've just been off duty for a day – I was so surprised.'

I asked her why.

'But I thought she was doing so well – everyone's so pleased with her.'

'That's why we've had her baptised,' I said gently.

She looked baffled.

The ceremony, that morning, had been as simple as possible. Paul had dipped his finger in the water as he spoke the baptismal words, and stroked it very gently onto Imogen's forehead – a drop had trickled down onto her nose, and she had twitched in response.

He had not been able to get over both her smallness and the fact that she was so perfect, so complete. 'Her tiny fingernails – ' he kept marvelling – 'everything here – absolutely perfect but so tiny.' He had never been in the hot room before, never seen babies so small. It moved him enough to mention it in the sermon he preached the following Sunday. After it, when people at the church heard about Imogen, more messages flooded in, more love and thoughts and prayers and offers of help – Imogen's situation touched so many hearts.

The following Monday, 11 June, when she was fifteen days old, I came out of hospital. I felt better in there than out – you get a false sense of security within those safe walls; real activities, the concerns of every day, seem a long way off.

I was much, much better in myself, but the outside world seemed very big and noisy, and very oblivious to the fact that I had just had a baby in somewhat traumatic circumstances. But I'd had this feeling before, even with Jessica, just as I was familiar with the sensation of strangeness at being in my clothes again, after over two weeks of nighties and dressing-gowns.

I was not, though, prepared for the other feeling that overwhelmed me so strongly as I walked slowly beside Stanley across the blue-carpet area to the door and the waiting car. I did not want to go – I was desperate not to go, because I felt as if I were abandoning Imogen. It was the same anguish I had experienced on returning upstairs to my room a couple of days after her birth – but worse, far worse, this time I was leaving the building and going five miles into the country. I was sure she must sense it, would wonder why I did not come so often to sit beside her, hold her hand, talk to her. I felt a physical wrench deep inside my stomach, as the cord that joined us, invisibly but oh so strongly, stretched and pulled tight: but it did not break, it could not. I was leaving her, yes, and I hated it, but the love that bound us together was indissoluble, and stronger than ever.

And after all, I told myself, as I got unsteadily into the car, she was doing well now – she was going to be all right. I had never doubted it, had I, and now I was even more sure that one day, one day, I would be walking out of here with Imogen, bringing her home.

The following morning, Stanley took Jessica to school and then went to do some necessary shopping, and to call into his office and pick up the post. He had scarcely been able to do any serious work since I had been admitted to hospital but he could not have been luckier in having such understanding and sensitive employers. He was in the middle of bringing out a monumental new Oxford edition of the *Complete Works of Shakespeare* – a ten-year task – but the other members of his team willingly shouldered what they could of his work and continued with their own; everyone urged him to make his family the priority – but how long that would have to go on for, none of us knew. At Balliol College, too, he met with more sympathy, support, understanding.

Jessica had gone back after half-term into the loving arms of her other family – the teachers and her fellow pupils at Greycotes School where she was looked after with especial solicitude and tenderness. We knew what a happy, loving and caring atmosphere prevailed there, but until now we had not really had to put it to the test. Everyone was aware of Imogen's situation and what an effect it must be having on her elder sister and every day she came home with stories of some individual kindness. I was happy to see her go off every day, knowing that she was being both well looked after and, also, well diverted. One of the things we learned during this time was that small children, however deeply affected they are by a family tragedy, have a blessed ability to switch off and plunge their whole attention and energy into other things. Neither Stanley nor I could ever get Imogen out of our minds, she was there as we went to sleep and the moment we awoke, it was very hard to concentrate on anything else, but Jessica remembered intermittently, and for the rest of the time, worked and played comparatively normally.

I was feeling, not surprisingly, very tired. The change from hospital to home is always a major one, but I was not unhappy, lying in bed reading the newspaper and drinking a mug of coffee on that sunny June morning of my first day back – missing the company and bustle of hospital life, missing Imogen, but for the moment, unworried.

And then the telephone rang.

'Mrs Wells?'

I could hear the bleep-bleep, bleep-bleep of the hot room machinery in the background, my heart lurched.

'Yes?'

'This is Dr Bernadette Salmon – I'm the Senior House Officer on duty in the Special Care Nursery.'

'What's happened? What's wrong?' I sat up in agitation, and my coffee spilled all over the duvet. I let it.

'I'm afraid Imogen has had a slight setback. Last night, she had one or two episodes of apnoea – that's when she stopped breathing for a moment or two – and then she had some bradycardia – her heart rate became abnormally slow. We weren't quite sure why, but this morning she had a pneumothorax. Do you know what that means?'

I did. Air had got into the pleural cavity, the space between the inner and outer coverings of the lungs, and that had caused the lung to collapse. I asked why they thought it had happened.

'We're not quite sure. Obviously Imogen is a very, very premature baby and all of her internal organs, especially her lungs, are very immature. She had a bad infection at birth, and although that has responded well to the antibiotics and cleared now, it may have weakened a part of her left lung.'

'What do you do now?'

'I've done it. I had to make a surgical incision and drain off the air – a chest drain.'

Poor tiny baby, yet more unpleasant things being done to her, and while I had been lying here cosily in bed, oblivious to any of it. I ought to have been there with her. If I hadn't left hospital, I could have gone down at once, caressed her. I felt hideously guilty, and said so.

'You mustn't. In fact, we couldn't have let you stay while we did it – it's a sterile surgical procedure and besides . . .' She faltered. I wondered what she had been going to say. That

I would not have wanted to watch, because it was frightening, and because Imogen had been in pain?

'There do have to be quite a few of us around the incubator and space is a bit limited in there.'

And she wouldn't have wanted me breathing down her neck – or worse, passing out.

'No – I understand.'

'Please don't feel guilty, but you can come and see her now – as soon as you like. I'm sorry I had to ring you with bad news on your first morning home.'

She really did sound sorry, too, and suddenly I felt sorry for her. I was to gain a lot of insight into the emotional aspect of the job of being a paediatrician over the next weeks, to see what a physical strain the job is, what long – ridiculously long – hours the junior hospital doctors (known as Senior House Officers, or SHOs) work: they do six months at a time in various specialities after completing their general medical training, and qualifying. Most of these SHOs at the John Radcliffe Neonatal Unit were planning careers in paediatrics, or in the related field of obstetrics: they were at the start of a long haul, gaining experience in these half-yearly stints in a variety of different hospitals, before applying for more senior and more permanent posts as registrars – the next rung of the ladder. They are the ones who bear the brunt of the daily medical routine, who go for twenty-four or thirty-six hours at a time without sleep, who are woken up and got out of the bed they may have just fallen into, to attend to a sudden emergency – like Imogen's pneumothorax. They are also very young, relatively inexperienced, perhaps, in the traumas of life – few of them are married or have yet had their own children. But they learn quickly, in a hard school – see parents in extreme states of anxiety, fear, distress, grief, as well as in bewilderment and ignorance. At the other end of the see-saw, they are surrounded by joy and jubilation as a baby survives against all the odds, treatment works dramatically, mothers cuddle the babies they never expected to have and embrace the doctors in outpourings of heartfelt gratitude, weep, laugh – and take their babies home.

It would be easy to understand how and why doctors can

quickly acquire a detached manner. For the most part, it is caused by a mixture of self-defence, and embarrassment.

But although we came across a dozen or more paediatricians in the course of Imogen's time in that Nursery, we never encountered polite detachment, coldness, brusqueness – or anything like that. Every doctor we dealt with might have had Imogen and only Imogen to care for, every one was openly and enthusiastically gunning for her. When things were going well, they rejoiced and were delighted, and showed it. At every setback, they were saddened and downcast. If their will for her to live, combined with their attentiveness and skill, were all that was needed, she would pull through, and have some to spare.

And so, that morning, young Dr Salmon meant what she said – she *was* sorry she had had to phone with bad news: I heard it in her voice.

'What now?' I asked, though I was terrified, really, of being told. 'What will happen to her?'

'Well, again, it's always difficult to make predictions, but hopefully the chest drain will clear everything up and her lung will expand again and there's no reason why it should be more than a temporary setback.'

'It won't happen again?'

'It shouldn't.'

But it did – twice more – over the next few days, her ventilation rate was increased, and she had two more chest drains inserted.

We went in to see her, all of us, and I wanted to weep. She was almost invisible under a barrage of tubes and wires, her colour was bad, her eyes were closed. But she never stopped moving, flexing her limbs, and when I touched her hand her grip around my finger was as firm as ever. And, after sitting with her for an hour or more, I was rewarded by the opening of her eyes, in response to my voice and my stroking, stroking of her arm.

We seemed to be living in a terrible no-man's-land of anxiety, and waiting, dreading every ring of the telephone, tired, having to carry on the routine of everyday life and yet feeling that nothing was important; eating and drinking, and dressing and bathing, were all a huge effort. It's an experience common to anyone who is caring for the sick, or the dying, or waiting for news of someone gravely ill in a hospital. You feel unreal, suspended, permanently tense and exhausted, even though you sleep a deep, heavy sleep.

Something else was exhausting, too. I have said that we were surrounded by loving, caring friends and it was true, no family could have been more supported, and we would not for a moment have had it otherwise – but even that became a strain. Every time one of us went out, there were enquiries; we had to tell the story, each day, of how Imogen was, what changes there had been, to speculate on her chances. In the village, on the telephone, out shopping in Oxford, at the school gates and, for Stanley, at work and at College. People stopped us, wanted to know, were full of concern and care. I'd heard stories of how people were embarrassed by serious illness, and by death, so much so that they would cross the street to avoid having to speak to the bereaved. Never once did that happen to any of us. People crossed onto *our* side of the street and there were times, when I was feeling particularly keyed up or desperate, when I wanted to rush away, to hide myself, to pretend I hadn't seen the well-meaning friend or neighbour.

I don't think I am saying that no one should show concern or make enquiries. Only that, if we were sometimes abrupt or ran away, or took the telephone off the hook, it was forgivable. Perhaps the best friends were those who sent brief notes, or took Jessica out, or baked a cake and left it at the door; or offered, when we had given them the latest news, to ring a few other people and spare us more enquiries. And then there were people like Gillian Morriss Kay (who had lost Toby and now had her Matthew) who, knowing so well what we felt, rarely rang us, but telephoned the hospital direct for information about Imogen.

In the hospital, apart from the medical and nursing team, I had met many other people concerned with Imogen, all willing to help and support us. One day, as I was going into the Neonatal Unit, I met Margaret Norwood who used to be a neighbour in North Oxford.

'What are *you* doing here?' for she was dressed in a tunic and trousers, carried a bleep at her belt, and looked official. I realised suddenly I had never known what her work was.

And she was equally surprised to see me.

'I'm going to see my baby,' I said. 'She was born at 24 weeks – she's in the hot room.'

'Oh, Susan, I'd no *idea* – I haven't seen you since you moved to the country, so I didn't even know you were *having* a baby. I've just been in there actually, treating one of them –'

'She's called Imogen – she's in the far corner, by the window.'

'Oh Imogen,' she said delightedly, 'of course, I know Imogen – she's *lovely*! I give her physiotherapy.'

How on earth . . .? To me, physiotherapy meant either being made to cough after an anaesthetic, or those fearsome, necessary and deeply boring exercises every new mother is put through within half an hour of delivery, to get the tummy muscles back into shape, and the pelvic floor functioning again. I couldn't imagine Imogen being ready for any of that! But Margaret explained that, in order to help her breathing, and her limbs and muscles generally in their gradual development, the physiotherapist spends regular time gently stroking, massaging and flexing the babies as they lie in their incubators.

It was another revelation of the care and time being lavished on Imogen, in the concerted effort to help her survive.

And we as a family were being helped to survive, too, by the patient, ready explanations of all the medical team. Whenever we arrived to visit her, one of the doctors on duty would appear as soon as possible to talk to us, answer our anxious questions, report in detail on her progress.

But as well as doctors and nursing staff, we had Charlotte, who had first appeared beside the incubator in the confused early days, and later, had come up to my room. Charlotte Emery was the social worker attached to the Neonatal Unit. Her role was to liaise between medical staff and parents, to help with particular needs when and where she could. Many families with babies in Special Care have problems with transport – the John Radcliffe Hospital serves a wide region; we were lucky in living only five miles away, but other parents had to visit from as far away as Reading, Northampton, Milton Keynes. Parents may also need help at home with other children, and in some cases financial assistance, and a social worker is there to support them, perhaps for many months, as well as to help with practical problems.

But so far as I was concerned, Charlotte was there to listen. I could talk out my fears and anxieties with her, pour out inner feelings, worry about Jessica, and ask the sort of speculative questions I did not feel able to raise with doctors.

During that week, when Imogen's condition began to give rise to concern, I called on Charlotte a lot, knowing that she was expert and experienced in the situation of babies like Imogen, but also willing to listen as a friend, to advise in an ordinary human way rather than with professional detachment. Bad social workers do a great deal of harm. Good ones, like Charlotte, are more priceless than rubies.

One of the most upsetting things I began to have to cope with, and which I found it terribly hard to talk about, was the reluctance I was feeling about going in and seeing Imogen at all. I found it such a strain, it hurt me so much, to see her weak, in distress and apparently struggling so hard, to so little purpose, going back rather than forwards, I felt helpless, anxious, confused. I also began to feel angry. I had been so sure that she would survive, and it had seemed that she was doing well. Now, one thing after another was going wrong. I wondered bitterly what God thought He was playing at, what was the point of tormenting me, and putting our baby through such suffering.

So I began to make excuses not to visit. It wasn't hard. I was not driving again yet, and Stanley had gone back to work – though of course I could have asked for lifts, and there would have been plenty of willing takers, friends who wanted to feel they could help us out in some small way. I was not feeling well in myself yet, partly because it was such a short time since not just the birth but since all the problems that had gone with it, but also because unusually I was still bleeding quite heavily, and feeling very tired as a result.

And then there was the feeding. The day after my milk had come in, I had begun to use the electric milk pump, a strange, inelegant procedure which made me feel exactly like a cow in a milking parlour. The equipment was a small version of that used by the farmers, a heavy pump on a portable stand, and its rhythmic sound was *exactly* the same as that heard by every dairyman in the land, morning and evening!

My milk was collected into little plastic bottles and frozen, and then taken in to the milk bank in the Nursery when we visited; where it was labelled and became part of Dr Tony Williams's Human Milk Project. At the beginning, some of it had been given to Imogen; now that all feeding by mouth had stopped and she was back on intravenous fluids, it went into the bank of Donated Breast Milk, to be used for other babies.

I went on the pump every four hours, so visits to Imogen had to be fitted in around those times. But I was making excuses – I could have gone much more often than I did. I wish now that I had, that I had stayed with her every minute of the night and day, but I couldn't bear it, I felt so helpless, as if it were all quite futile. While I was away from her, I could be hopeful; when I saw her, I fell into the depths of despair.

It was Pat Gardner who encouraged me to make one particular visit. She drove over from Warwickshire for the day, to be with me, have lunch, talk. We sat in the garden while I told her how well things had been looking, and now how she was suffering so many setbacks.

She said, 'Why don't I drive you over to see her now? That would be all right, wouldn't it?'

I didn't want to go. 'Well, the mornings aren't very good – I mean, they have a ward round, they're always so busy, I don't like getting in the way.' I fell silent.

Pat gave me a sharp look, then stood up. 'I'd like to see my new god-daughter,' she said. 'Come on.'

I agreed for didn't she have a right to see Imogen? I was Harriet's godmother, and now we had asked Pat if she would be our daughter's. I got into the car, first putting the little bottles of milk into my freezer-holdall. 'Just like the drinks for a picnic,' Pat said.

But I couldn't laugh and joke very easily and the nearer we

got to the hospital, the more tense and afraid I grew – afraid of what I was going to find.

I went into the hot room, after showing Pat the way to the observation window in the visitors' corridor, and as I sat down beside the incubator and took hold of Imogen's hand, I looked up and saw Pat's face, tender, astonished at the smallness of her, suffused with concern, and interest, and immediate love.

And, as always, the moment I felt that minute, fragile, soft little hand, and the grip of her fingers, I was glad I had come, wondered why I had ever been away.

'I'm sorry, little one, I'm here now – I shouldn't have left you for so long. It's all right, I'm here now.'

Her blue eyes were wide open, but clouded with – what? Fear? Pain? She seemed calmer though, as soon as I touched her. I went on talking to her above the hum and bleep of the machines, went on stroking her arm.

One of the doctors, Sally Heasman, appeared. 'Hello, Mrs Wells. Nice to see you.'

Was she implying a rebuke? No, I didn't think so. Besides, she needn't tell me what I so well knew, that I shouldn't have stayed away for so many days. It wouldn't happen again. I never wanted to let Imogen go now, never wanted to walk out of this room.

'We've run into a problem.'

'Her chest again?'

'No – but, we've been a little bit worried about her tummy. Can you see?'

I looked. Yes, the tiny belly was slightly swollen and distended, the skin shiny and tight-looking, and darkly coloured as though it were bruised.

'She's had a couple of X-rays. They don't show up anything abnormal, but there's obviously something wrong – perhaps a blockage, or – well, we can't be sure. We're keeping a close eye on it and the surgeons have been to have a look.'

Surgeons?

'Yes, Mr Gough's team. They couldn't find anything abnormal but they agree that her tummy must be swollen for a reason so they'll keep her under review. Meanwhile, she still isn't having any feeds by mouth.'

'What would the surgeons do?'

'We hope they won't have to do anything, that whatever it is will disperse of its own accord.'

'Yes – but if it doesn't?'

'Then they would operate and hope to relieve the obstruction – or do whatever was necessary.'

'Is it sore for her?'

'We think so, yes. The nurses have reported that she seems to be in some pain when they handle her. We've given her diamorphine a couple of times.'

Diamorphine – heroin. It is used as a pain-reliever for small babies in preference to morphine or any other substance because of its powerful pain-relieving effect, without causing some of the side effects in the bowel and abdomen – clearly important factors in Imogen's case.

I looked down at her, as I was listening to all of this. Poor little love. Yet something else to hurt her, make her feel ill, to cause more people to have to probe her, more bodies looking over her cot, unknown voices, strange hands.

'I'm here now,' I said softly, and went on stroking her, touching her. I wanted more than anything else to be able to take her away, nurse her myself, cradle her, rock her, *love* her better. I had never held her to me and I ached to do so, she seemed so alone in there amongst all the wires and drips and tubes and monitors. When the nurses handled her, they did so gently, lovingly, tenderly – but they were nurses. I was her mother. They could not touch her as I did.

'I'm so glad I saw her,' Pat said as we drove away. 'She's so beautiful. I couldn't have imagined how tiny she would be, but she's perfect. She's my god-daughter and I love her.'

I nodded. As always, after visiting, I felt absolutely shattered, drained of every ounce of energy, limp, but anxious, tense, and with yet more to worry about.

After that, I was determined never to leave Imogen for long again, to be at the hospital, beside her incubator, at every possible moment. I got lifts without any difficulty, of course, and it was not true that I 'got in the way' in the Unit – parents are welcome at any time, for as long as they like to stay although, on occasions, if there is a delicate medical procedure being carried out, it is helpful for the medical team to be left alone – there really *isn't* much room. The hot room only has four or five babies in incubators, the equipment taking up a great deal of space. There are larger wards in the other sections of the Unit. If I was asked to leave, I left, to wait in the corridor, sit and drink coffee in the small parents' room, wander about the hospital where I felt so at home.

As I sat there quietly stroking Imogen's hand and murmuring to her whenever I could, I began to absorb the rhythm of life in an Intensive Care Nursery, to sort out the various routines, to recognise when there was a sudden emergency. I got to know the various nursing shifts and to identify individual nurses, to separate the blur of different faces and to put names to them. I looked at the other babies in the hot room, too. One or two were very tiny, and of course very premature, but none so small as Imogen, and most of them seemed to be doing well. Sometimes I walked into the wards off the next corridor. Babies were transferred here when they were well enough to leave the hot room. The babies all looked so much bigger here – as indeed they were. Some were 5 or 6 lbs – and their next move was home.

I worried sometimes about the fact that they were all simply bundled up in their cots and sound asleep. At home, by now, they would be part of the family day, awake and looking around them for some of the time, taken from room to room, stimulated. Here, they were looked after beautifully, fed, changed, washed, loved, but otherwise life was even, quiet, uneventful – monotonous.

(Since then I have visited both the John Radcliffe Neonatal Unit and another at St George's Hospital in South London and found the older, less sick babies propped up in rocking cradles so that they could be awake and be given a more interesting day, or else lying watching mobiles and other cot-toys. As more is recognised about the needs of even very young babies in a hospital situation, more is being done to meet those needs which are not simply medical.)

Life in obstetrics is unpredictable. No maternity unit can be really sure of what each day will bring – X number of mothers may be booked to have their babies during, say, a particular week in September, but of those, some will be late and not appear when scheduled, others will have been delivered any number of weeks early, or have had miscarriages, or be brought into the hospital for rest, perhaps because twins (or even triplets or quads) have been diagnosed. A quiet night can turn into a rush hour, a busy one on paper fail to produce many women in labour after all.

This has a knock-on effect in a large hospital with an Intensive Care Nursery which can move within a few hours from quiet – even half-empty – to a situation the doctors all dread, when they do not have enough cots for the babies needing them. Then, there are emergencies with the babies already admitted, ones who seem to be thriving but who have, like Imogen, a sudden lung-collapse or spells of apnoea, heart-failure, and other serious problems.

I noticed that whenever a nurse in the hot room had to leave the baby she was in charge of, to have her break, to go to the loo, or to fetch supplies from the cupboard in the corridor, she never failed to get a colleague to cover for her. As one of them said to me, 'With these tiny ones, you can't afford to turn your back.'

That's only one reason why the nursing of premature babies is so very demanding. I watched with growing awareness of the skills involved, the stress and tension prevalent in the Nursery, and with growing admiration for the dedication and attentiveness of the nurses. And with even more awareness of the comparatively poor rewards, let alone any extra benefits for special training or privileges of status, accorded to nurses in such a demanding speciality.

There were several dramas while I was sitting there during that week. Once the lights suddenly dipped, and immediately there was a loud siren – the electric power had gone off, and for the few seconds until the unit's own generator took over, nurses rushed to emergency stations, to ventilate babies by hand and observe closely what the machines had a few seconds before been monitoring and recording for them. Then everything had to be re-set.

The noise of the siren was awful – I wondered whether Imogen had been disturbed and frightened by it, whether she was aware of the sudden momentary cessation of the ventilator. How little she must understand, how strange, frightening, noisy, bright this world of hers seemed. I wanted Imogen to be cradled, to be in subdued lighting, to hear only my voice, not to have the constant noise of machines assaulting her ears and the glare of the overhead lights.

But if you are to nurse very premature babies over the desperately dangerous and vulnerable first weeks and months, if you attempt to save the lives of those born as early as 24 weeks, there would seem to be no alternative to this harsh environment. Medically speaking, the lights, the machinery, the noise are unavoidable. That was why I felt now, even more strongly, how important it was for me to be with Imogen when I could, to talk to her quietly – for surely she knew the sound of my voice – and to touch her, to keep her aware of my loving presence so that she associated me with nothing else.

There was also drama on a couple of the early evenings that I was at the hospital. Once, when all was quiet, I went out into the blue-carpet area to stretch my legs and have a change from the hot air of the Unit. I saw an ambulance pull up outside, a routine event, but this one had come speedily up the drive, blue light flashing, and in seconds all the doors were open and a medical team with an accompanying incubator came at a fast pace up the corridor, one running on ahead to open the doors. Bleeps were going off right and left. By the time I got back to the hot room, half a dozen gowned and masked figures were crowded around one corner; I caught a glimpse of the tin foil, the sight of a ventilator tube – and then, briefly, of a tiny, waving foot.

The whole atmosphere of the nursery had changed – from routine calm, to 'full alert' and tension. No one was panicking but neither did they have any spare time or attention, and the urgency of the situation was apparent to me as I sat there, absorbing the drama, wondering about some mother somewhere whose baby had been rushed away by ambulance – feeling for her, remembering Imogen's birth.

I asked her nurse in a whisper what was happening over there.

'A baby from another town – the mother was in a road accident. They had to do an emergency Caesarian – it's very tiny. I don't think they know much about it yet.'

I looked at the backs of all the doctors and the incubator, wondering, hoping.

Stanley came then to take me home.

When I returned the following afternoon, there was a space again in the far corner. I asked tentatively about the emergency baby. The SHO on duty just shook her head.

Later that day, there was another drama when a baby with a heart problem was being prepared for emergency admission to the theatre. I watched again, my heart in my mouth, as the doctors gowned up, took off shoes and put on theatre slippers, covered their hair with those unflattering J-cloth caps, and four of them wheeled the incubator away, out of the hot room towards the operating theatre.

Poor little thing, not knowing what was happening, where it was going, or with whom, or why.

Oh God, please don't let that have to happen to Imogen.

She had her eyes open, they flickered about. Her head looked as frail, as vulnerable as a bird's egg, the skin almost transparent. But her mouth was a tiny rosebud, around the ventilator tube, and her eyebrows were just sketched in, shaped exactly like mine. The longer I stayed with her, the more deeply I loved her, yet I felt I knew nothing about her. She was in many ways so far from me, so closed off in the artificial atmosphere of the hospital world. I longed as I have never longed for anything so badly, to hold her, and when I had held her, to take her home with me – but would I ever? It seemed an impossible fantasy. Other babies went home. Not mine. I had watched them leave once or twice, and had hardly been able to bear the sight, or contain my envy – almost resentment – of their joyful families. I did not believe we could ever be in that position.

The following day, we had been asked to come in and see the Registrar, Mr Cotterill. He, and the nursing officer, Miss Townsend, took us into a small office. He was a serious pale young man, un-smiling. He seemed to find it very difficult to explain Imogen's condition, the reason we had been sent for.

There were awkward silences while he looked desperately at his hands. We found ourselves encouraging him, helping him out with the words. So did Miss Townsend, acting quietly as a sort of interpreter. Some doctors, we were discovering, had the blessed knack of being able to communicate with parents, were easy and relaxed but for others, it was difficult, they might be excellent doctors, but they found talking to us embarrassing or upsetting, they were shy, tongue-tied, ill at ease.

But about Dr Cotterill's concern for Imogen we were in no doubt.

She had, he said, been seen by the surgeons again. Her abdomen was still distended and sore, though the X-rays still showed up no abnormalities. Nevertheless, it was getting worse, not better. Her bowel might be obstructed – they simply didn't know. If things were no better by the next day, they had decided to operate.

Curiously, I felt almost relieved. At least something was going to be done. I didn't like the idea of her being in pain and of her getting worse, though the idea of an operation on her filled me with dread.

'You realise,' he said, hesitated, looked down despairingly at his hands again and then away across to the other side of the room – 'You know – just how serious this is – what the risks are?'

'Perhaps you could tell us,' Stanley suggested.

The doctor shot him an anguished look. 'There is – an operation on a baby of this size carries far more risk than – ' Another silence. 'There is more than a chance that she won't come through it at all. On the other hand – well – the risks of *not* operating – her tummy isn't getting better, that's for sure. There isn't really a choice – but if you – you have to consent, of course.'

'We'll be guided by you – naturally.'

'I don't want you to go away from here with the wrong idea – not realising how serious things are.'

We did not. We went away in silence, and in the car held on to one another for a moment, still not speaking, not needing to.

The following day lasted for a hundred years. By now, I had become used to the strange distortions of time, the way hours, days blurred, shrank, expanded crazily. I telephoned in the morning to be told that the surgeons had seen Imogen and had decided it was essential now to perform a laparotomy, an incision into the abdomen to examine the situation and see if a clearer diagnosis could be made of the cause of her stomach swelling. They could not give me an exact time when she would go into theatre – probably not until the evening.

So, all we could do was wait. I told Jessica as carefully as I could what was going to happen, and felt I had to prepare her, just a little, for the worst.

Her blue eyes widened. 'She won't die will she? I thought they were going to make her better. Mama, why are they doing it if it might make her die?'

'Because if they don't, well, then she really will be very ill – and it's hurting her now. They want to stop that, don't they?'

'I don't want her to die.'

No. Oh, no.

'She won't,' I said firmly. And half believed it. For still, somewhere, was the thread of my optimism, the assurance I believed I had been given at the very beginning, that all was going to be well.

The previous day I had met Sue Clayton, the Sister who had looked after me in Observation Area during the days after Imogen's birth.

'I keep in touch,' she said, 'I pop into the Nursery every so often to see her – and I'm praying for her all the time.'

So were so many others. If ever a tide of prayer could have power to heal, it must surely be the one on which we all rode now.

I don't remember much about the day, except for the feeling I had like a hot, burning knot in the pit of my stomach. Neither of us could eat or concentrate on anything, only fiddled about with routine jobs.

I remember suddenly thinking in the middle of the afternoon that I would rather she died now, today, than drag on for more agonising weeks, even that perhaps I would rather she died peacefully and quietly before she got to the operating table. I could not bear to think of her there, I wanted desperately to go with her, to tell her I was there, stop them from doing anything to hurt her, reassure her that it was all right. What must she think of this mother to whom she had been as close as breath, and from whom she had been forcibly separated by a traumatic birth, and who then came close – but oh, never close enough – to her now and then, only to vanish just as abruptly? I *knew* that Imogen felt safe, felt better when I was near her, that the sound of my voice, and my touch meant everything to her, meant love and safety. Could I prove it? Yes – every time I touched her, she relaxed and the monitors showed it; her heart-rate settled, her limbs were calmer, her eyes searched less frantically about. And her tiny fingers always, always gripped mine.

Now I was consigning her to more strangers, with their gowns and bright lights and scalpels. All the time now, as well as feeling anxious, afraid, and in an agony of love for Imogen, I felt guilty.

Just after six o'clock, Jessica was in the bath and I was sitting on the floor, watching her play an elaborate, obscure game with her water-toys. My stomach was churning. I imagined how Imogen would now be being got ready for the theatre, saw the scene as clearly as if I were there, the green gowns, the masks, the caps, the figures all round the incubator. I wanted to get away from my own thoughts, the pictures filling my head but, except in the deepest sleep, that was one thing I could never do.

Downstairs the telephone rang. Stanley was cooking lamb chops which we were not going to want to eat. I heard him answer, heard his voice sounding slightly surprised. 'Oh – hello.' Then nothing, then, 'Yes – yes. I see – yes. Right.'

I stopped listening and started to talk to Jessica, assuming the call was to do with work.

A few moments later, he came bounding up the stairs, and into the bathroom.

'She's all right!'

I spun round.

'She's all right – they've done the operation and she's back in the ward. She came through it very well, he was astonished

216

and delighted how well – they all were. She did have a bowel obstruction and they've had to cut away a length of it and give her a temporary ileostomy' (in which a portion of the lower intestine is brought through an opening in the abdomen, so that the waste matter can be got rid of this way, and the rest allowed to heal).

'She didn't die, you see, I knew she wouldn't,' Jessica said, and blew a great mass of bubbles out of her water-toy. She didn't die. No. But I realised I had been expecting her to. But I should have gone on trusting that she would be all right; so many people were praying for her, she was going to be healed – it was quite clear now. Why had I had so little faith?

Well, not any more.

We all hugged one another in delight.

'I'm hungry,' Stanley said, and went off downstairs again, from where soon came the delicious aroma of roasting lamb and rosemary. We all ate like the starving. It was the first meal I had enjoyed, tasted even, for days.

There was wine, too. We raised our glasses to our little daughter. Perhaps she had turned the corner at last.

Chapter 14

On Tuesday 26 June, we went to the Retiring Fellows' Dinner at Balliol. It was a warm, balmy, beautiful evening, the gardens of the College were richly green, the herbaceous borders high and full, the great court shady with all the chestnut trees. We stood about with drinks, watching the bees drone gently in and out of the snapdragons, and the college tortoise amble across the grass. It was a black tie dinner with all the wives in long dresses; it was the end of the summer term, the beginning of the vacation; everyone was relaxed, full of chat.

And Stanley and I stood, nodding, smiling, responding to a stream of kind and sensitive enquiries. Yes, Imogen had had an operation – no, we hadn't really been given any idea of her chances. Yes, she had done well so far, the news had been better, but she had had a setback or two the previous weekend; we agreed that all we could do was wait and hope.

'Live from day to day,' someone said.

'Minute to minute,' I felt like replying. Except that, in the old phrase, 'time had no meaning any more'. I had long since lost track of the days, of anything, indeed, in any regular order. We were like zombies, going through the motions of normal, everyday life, but in reality with our minds, our hearts, all our thoughts and emotions, elsewhere, beside the incubator in that crowded hot room.

The day after her operation, Imogen had been apparently much better and her wound had been clean and healthy. But the following night, she had had a sudden deterioration, her blood pressure had fallen, her circulation was poor, and she had had to be resuscitated twice.

Every day we had talked to a different houseman and had received a different report. Every nurse who came on duty had a new set of circumstances to deal with, every half-hour, Imogen was 'more stable', 'less stable', 'very poorly', 'showing a little improvement'. We felt as if we were living on a switchback, not knowing what to feel, whether to hope, to be relieved, to rejoice at what sounded like better news, how to put it into proper perspective, what the real, underlying state of things might be. It was no one's fault. The condition of a very sick premature baby does change every half-hour, no one could give more than a short view of things.

But that night on the college lawn, we felt confused and battered, we simply did not know how to react. When anyone said, 'I hear your baby is doing well, that she's much better', we had to counter their optimism at once, for fear they thought she was now out of the wood and about to come home. But to those with grim faces who said how sorry they were, our instinct was to express optimism, to explain what a fighter she was, how many dangers and crises she had already come through, say that all was certainly not lost.

It was an exhausting evening, and I remember very little of the eating and drinking, the speeches, the friendly chat.

As soon as we decently could, we caught one another's eye and slipped away. No one was offended.

In the car we said very little – each knowing how the other felt, tired beyond belief, and yet too keyed up and strained to think of going to bed.

As we went along the Link Road, we saw the lights of the hospital on the hill ahead.

'I wonder how she is,' Stanley said.

A pause. Instead of turning the car left, onto the country road, he drove straight on, without needing to suggest it. We both knew we wanted to go and see.

Another quiet night in the hospital, another walk along the blue carpet. No one about at all, past the porter at his desk. He nodded, knowing us well enough by now. I looked at

Stanley, in his black velvet dinner jacket, remembering the last time he had come in here straight from a college dinner.

As soon as we walked into the hot room, I saw that something was different. Up until now, Imogen had been nursed in an open incubator – rather like a flat perspex tray on which she lay, on her fleece, attached to all the machinery, but accessible, being only covered in the bubble-polythene sheeting.

Now she had been moved into one of the large, closed incubators, with portholes for access. The lid was over her and the portholes closed. I felt the most dreadful sense of separation from her, the plastic dome made her visible, but set her far apart. I hated it.

'We had to move her – to try and keep her stable,' the nurse said. 'She was losing so much body fluid in the open incubator and her temperature has been fluctuating a lot.'

I sat on the high, uncomfortable stool, opened the porthole and reached my hand in – touched Imogen, took her hand in mine. She did not respond. In the twenty-four hours since I had last seen her, she had changed, she looked even tinier, and shrivelled, a bad, dark colour, her eyes were closed, her limbs still, on her tummy, huge bandages and bindings.

Dr Heasman, the SHO on duty, appeared quietly at our sides.

'Her tummy is pretty bad,' she said gently. 'It's very swollen and the wound has got infected – we think she has septicaemia. She's very sensitive at being handled. We have to be very careful. She's on full 100% oxygen now . . .'

Her eyes were steady on mine. I read in them what she wanted me to know, what she could not put into words.

'We're giving her pain relief – diamorphine – all the time, and antibiotics, of course.'

'Yes.'

'I'm sorry – things don't look too good at the moment.'

'No.'

We stayed a little longer. But for the very first time, I felt that Imogen was unaware of me, wrapped up in her own daze of pain and narcotic and illness. She had never, never failed to open her eyes, to stir, or to return the pressure of my finger in her hand. Not until tonight.

On the way home through the dark, woody lanes, we wept. In bed, we lay in each other's arms, still weeping, saying nothing at all.

The following morning, we went in to see Dr David Baum, the Senior Paediatrician, and Sandy Calvert, acting head of Neonatal Unit (the permanent head, Dr Andrew Wilkinson, was in the United States for six months).

As much as anything, we wanted an overall view, a considered prediction of Imogen's chances. We said that we had felt confused by the daily reports, did not know whether to be hopeful or prepare for the worst.

From David Baum we got exactly what we wanted, a clear concise appraisal, no lies, no waffle, a statement of the case as he saw it.

'I think we operated at just the right time. We couldn't have left it any longer, hoping it would right itself, but it was best not to jump in too soon. Any operation on a tiny baby is a very risky business – and things often *do* get better of their own accord. But her chances of succumbing to infection were always going to be high.'

'Is there anything going for her at all?'

He hesitated. 'The fact that she's a girl – they always do better than boys – and that she has battled and come through so much so far against all possible odds. She's a fighter – '

I knew it. Oh God – let her have some fight left, give her more strength to get over this, just this, then things will be all right.

They *would* be all right, I knew it, I was sure, wasn't I? Wouldn't they?

'Can you say what her chance is?' Stanley asked abruptly.

David Baum met our gaze straight on, across his desk.

'One in five,' he said, and added, 'That's four to one against.'

We left his office.

'Shall we go and see her?' I said.

I saw Stanley's face.

'Just a few minutes then. I don't like to get in their way.'

He didn't want to, couldn't bear to see her any more.

Imogen looked worse, her abdomen swollen like a little drum under the bandages. The nurse who had been with her for much of the time had asked to be moved to a different baby. She hadn't been able to cope with handling Imogen, knowing that she was in such pain.

Briefly, I put my hand into the porthole of the incubator, stroked her arm, again and again. I minded the fact that she could not hear me now as I murmured to her, the lid shut out my voice. I put my finger onto her palm. Very weakly, she curled her own towards it, but there was no strength there.

The following morning, the Registrar telephoned. Would we please go in and talk to him.

Dr Cotterill looked even more desperate at having to communicate with us. The same room in which he had told us about Imogen's need for an operation, same chairs, same everything, only now he looked not just serious, but grave. He sat with his knees apart, looking down at his own clasped hands. Miss Townsend sat quietly at his side.

'Imogen had a very bad night. She had to be resuscitated twice. We're very worried that her abdomen may burst – it's tense and distended. She's obviously in pain – she –'

He halted. The room was silent. Then I realised that he was fighting furiously with his tears, unsuccessfully.

'This isn't going to come right,' he said in an odd, choked voice. 'Not now – there's no point in saying any more. It's not going to come right.'

At that moment, his bleep went off and he left the room at once, mumbling his excuses, wiping the back of his hand across his eyes.

We sat on with Miss Townsend who, after a moment or two, began to speak to us gently, quietly, about how they would try to keep Imogen out of pain now but not do any more tests, give up 'aggressive nursing', fight at all costs to keep her going, make her respond.

I hardly heard her. I wonder at what point I took in the fact that Imogen was going to die and that this was what they had all been trying to tell us for the past week?

In one way, I never did – or at least, not until the last hour or so of her life. I continued to believe, defiantly, hopelessly, in what I had been told, always known – that somehow all would be well, a miracle would occur, she would be healed, made whole, come through. I could not, *dared* not abandon that faith now, however irrational, however foolish, however blind to all the evidence before my eyes. That flicker of trust and hope and true belief in the idea that she would live was as obstinate, as vital, as unquenchable as Imogen's own fighting spirit, her determination, her will to live.

Yet another part of me must have been hearing what they were saying, taking it in, in a way, I was prepared.

In a way.

Watching someone die of a grave, long illness, someone who is old but who has had some good life, is hard, of course it is, but there is an element of acceptance in the onlookers as well, perhaps, as in the dying person themselves. My mother had known she was dying, and had given in to it. I had waited for it, been prepared, accepted that it was the right, the best and only thing.

But a child, a baby, whose time is not ripe, who has had no life yet to speak of, who has all hope, all potential, everything to come – it is impossible to accept, one's instinct is to hope against hope, to do battle, to fight for its survival no matter what. So in a sense, I did not ever 'accept' Imogen's dying.

The next few days were among the worst of my life. How could they have been anything else?

Friends, realising what was likely to happen, were rallying round us closely again, taking Jessica out, offering whatever we needed. We went to her school Open Day, but arrived late from the hospital; the last place we wanted to be was in a building full of mothers and fathers and teachers and children, chattering and laughing, eating cream cakes for tea. But when we arrived, we felt embraced in everybody's loving concern. Jessica had been given a Governor to look after until we arrived and was full of seriousness and importance at showing her around the school, but when I saw her, I realised how pale and wide-eyed she had grown these past few days, felt her cling onto my hand tightly.

We took our tea and sat, slightly apart from everyone, at a table in the shade. People smiled, a few asked how things were, we felt the familiar warmth and caring surrounding us, shielding us from the rest of the unknowing, unfeeling world.

When we visited Imogen now, it was a case of enduring things with her, trying desperately to let her know we were there, full of love and tenderness, urging her on, willing her to take anything she needed from us, strength, life, health, hope, comfort. They were nursing her as tenderly as possible, disturbing her as little as they could. She was unresponsive but obviously, when handled, in considerable pain.

It was agreed that I would stay at the hospital as much as I could. I sat there hour after hour, all through the long day of Friday 29 June in a sort of trance, stroking her arm, talking to her gently. She never opened her eyes now. I tried to remember how it had been when she had looked up at me so gravely, puzzled, curious, bewildered. I had felt able to reassure her then. But now? There seemed to be nothing I could do.

Stanley and Jessica came in. But Jessica was upset to see her, and they left quickly. Later, Stanley came back alone.

'Jessica cried in the car,' he said. 'She'd better not see her sister again.' He went to get a glass of water – it was hot outside so that the temperature in the Unit had soared even higher. I was wearing only a thin cotton dress, and had to keep going out for what fresh air there was. Stanley had brought my bag with night things. I was having a bed upstairs on Level 7 so that they could call me whenever I was needed. Imogen's colour was poor, her body still, her eyes closed.

'Mrs Wells.' It was the houseman on duty, Dr Robert Yuen, from Hong Kong. 'Have you held Imogen at all?'

'*Held* her? No, of course – I couldn't – because of the ventilator and everything – '

'Would you like to now?'

Would I? But surely –

'It's all right, we can manage. Sister and I can hold the tubes – don't worry. I'm sure it'd be a good thing for you both.'

Oh, but too late, I thought, she's past this now, the time to have held her was at the beginning, when she was responsive, doing well. It might have given her the strength she needed to keep going.

I sat on the stool while they took a very long, careful time to wrap her in shawls with infinite tenderness, and take her, wires and tubes and all, out of the incubator. Then someone brought a screen, someone else a more comfortable, low chair. And at last, at last, as Stanley watched anxiously Imogen was lowered infinitely gently, into my waiting arms. And as she was settled there, Dr Yuen produced the Polaroid camera and took a couple of pictures. I have one here, on my desk in front of me now. There is my red-and-white flowered dress, slightly blurred, my hair falling forward; there is Dr Yuen's hand on the ventilator; Stanley in the background in his shirt sleeves. And there, just visible above the white blankets and soft towels, is Imogen, her tiny head covered in a white knitted cap, mouth open for the ventilator tube – you can scarcely see her face. And yet, looking at it now brings her exactly, clearly into focus, I can feel myself back there, smell the hospital smell, hear the bleep of the monitors.

Holding her in my arms was the most miraculous, most wonderful thing. And as I held her, I felt her tense, taut little body relax and, for a moment, suddenly, her face twitched, twitched again – and then she opened her eyes, and I saw that brilliant blue, clouded, perhaps unseeing – but there.

'She likes that – look.'

What? I glanced up. One of the Sisters on duty was smiling, pointing to the monitor.

'She likes that, she knows it's you. Look.'

And sure enough, her heart rate was almost normal, all the monitors were steady. Oh, but I knew that she liked it, that she knew me because I had felt it. I sat, talking to her quietly, bending my head close to kiss her fragile head, completely happy, wrapped in a cocoon of love with her, oblivious to anything else in the world.

If I had been able to do this, all day and every day, from the time she had been born, perhaps, perhaps . . .

It had not been possible. Older premature babies, less sick, less tiny ones, those not on ventilators, can be held, and mothers are encouraged to handle them, even walk about the hospital with the babies strapped up to their breasts. It had been out of the question with Imogen, but I knew that night, absolutely, the power of love, the reality of its strength between mother and baby, saw, felt for myself its healing effect.

I stayed in the Unit until very late. I had had to relinquish my hold on her in the end, though everyone had stood very patiently, no one had wanted to hurry us. But the houseman had been called into the next nursery, and the Sister was overdue for her break, so that at last, reluctantly, I had handed her over, to be laid back in the incubator. But I did not let go of her hand, went on talking to her, murmuring and, for the whole time, the monitors were steady and calm.

No one had expected Imogen to live through that day, and now I was warned that I would most likely be woken in the night, that in all probability she would deteriorate again quite soon. I almost decided to stay with her, but as she was more peaceful since I had held her, they were not, for the time being, too worried.

Stanley was offered a bed in the hospital but had to get back to Jessica.

'Get some sleep while you can,' the Sister said to me. I went gladly enough, shattered by tension and by emotion, but feeling more fulfilled, more calm than I had done since her birth, knowing for sure that as I held her at last, she had been aware that I was really there, that her being in my arms had helped her in her struggle. She knew that I was there and that I loved her, for the first time she had *felt* that love all through her body.

I could go to sleep with a less heavy heart, I was no longer fretful. *I no longer felt guilty.*

Up in the lift to Level 7. All was quiet. Most of the lights off behind individual doors. It felt odd being up here again – as though I didn't really belong.

The Night Sister asked me if I'd like a cup of tea – but suddenly, I was so tired, I could barely stand, I felt dizzy and weak.

'No thank you – I'd better just get to sleep straight away. They'll probably ring for me before long.'

'We'll wake you at once if they do.'

I lay down, and immediately Imogen in her incubator was before my closed eyes. I felt far away from her again, separated by more than a few floors. I wanted to be back with her, holding her again.

'I *will* come back, little girl, but I've got to go to sleep for a while now,' I whispered.

Then I slept heavily as though I had been drugged, and without dreaming at all. When I woke, it was light, a dull morning. For a few seconds, I was unsure where I was. How long had I slept? Then the door opened – Sister, bringing me some tea.

'All right, Mrs Wells? Have you got a chit for your breakfast? You can go across to the canteen any time. I'm just off duty in a few minutes.'

'Off duty? But whatever time is it?'

'Nearly eight. You've had a good long sleep – you'll be all the better for it.'

'And they didn't ring from the Nursery?'

'Not a word. All quiet. Why don't you ring down now, while you're having your tea, and find out how she is?'

I did. I could not understand it – surely they wouldn't have simply failed to call me, forgotten I was here at all?

They hadn't. But there had been no need to send for me. Imogen had had a quiet, calm night, and this morning was showing some improvement. Her blood gases and heart rate, all the monitors, were much better – she herself seemed more comfortable.

It seemed impossible to believe. Except that *I* knew why, knew that since I had held her, things had begun to go right again. Oh, maybe, maybe – *could* she?

I dressed, and went straight down. Yes, the nurse said, things were better, relatively speaking anyway. She had had a quiet night, seemed in less discomfort. Just then all the doctors were busy, they had had a couple of new babies admitted during the night. I went off to eat breakfast, to stretch my legs in the hospital grounds, buy a paper, feeling extraordinarily elated. Imogen was going to get well. I began to believe it again, all my hopes had revived. I telephoned Stanley and told him.

'Do they hold out any hope?'

I said I hadn't asked. 'But I do,' I said. He didn't reply.

Before returning to the hot room, I went on another walk across to the main hospital. I wanted to go and sit in the chapel for a few minutes – to do what? Pray, I suppose. To ask for Imogen to be well, to ask for last night's improvement to be a real turning-point.

The corridor of the John Radcliffe General Hospital was quieter than on a weekday but there were still plenty of people about. In the chapel, there was nobody. I sat down on the lightly-coloured wooden pew in the small, modern room, and tried to stop my mind from darting about, to be quiet, to concentrate. I began to say things in my head but it didn't work, I couldn't begin, no words would come. I gave up after a while, confused, and simply sat. And as I sat, I had a message. I don't believe in 'hearing voices' in any literal sense, but a phrase came into my head and was repeated several times, a message from my own subconscious, prompting me. 'Go to Imogen now,' it said. 'Go to Imogen.'

I went.

There had been no dramatic change in her condition. In the corridor, I met Bernadette Salmon, the SHO on duty. She stopped to talk to me.

'I'm very sorry Imogen is so poorly now.'

'Oh, but she's so much better this morning,' I said. 'She had a good night, her monitors show a real improvement.'

She looked at me for a while without speaking. Then, she said, 'Mrs Wells – Imogen is very gravely ill. You must realise that. Her condition is very serious indeed.'

'Yes. Oh I know that. But – '

I tailed off. She shook her head. After a moment, there seemed nothing more to say, and I went slowly to wash my hands, and sit beside my baby daughter.

She was dying. I knew that now. I could see it, quite clearly. She was far, far away from me, still, quiet, flaccid, unresponsive. Her colour was poor.

The rest of that day was one of waiting, and it seemed to go on forever. I sat beside her, stroking her all the time, talking to her, once or twice she half-opened her eyes, but it was as

228

though the light hurt, and she closed them again at once. After a while, I found a piece of towelling, and laid it over the top of the incubator, to shield her from the glare. Otherwise, I could do little. They were nursing her but handling her as little as possible now, but they gave me a piece of damp cotton wool with which to bathe her limbs gently, wipe her face. They tried not to disturb her wound which was now, they said, completely black and moribund, and excruciatingly painful if touched. She was given diamorphine throughout the day.

Doctors came and went, the nursing shifts changed. I sat on. Stanley came in several times during the course of that day, in between keeping things going at home. He would look down in distress at his daughter in her incubator, glancing up every so often at the monitors. Afterwards he said that he had willed her to live, wished all his own life and strength upon her, to help her in her struggle.

We did not talk to one another very much – what was there to say? Each of us knew how the other felt, we shared our vigil quietly.

I had occasionally watched other parents in the Unit, sitting beside their respective cots; in fact, we didn't any of us overlap on visits a great deal. Though most of them were happier people than we, with every prospect of taking their baby home sooner or later, they too had sat together for the most part in silence, supporting one another, as we did, but without words.

'It's different for a man,' I heard people say, and they even implied that because the father had not physically given birth, he must inevitably feel less deeply, suffer less keenly when his baby is sick. I could not believe that when I saw my husband's overwhelming grief and fear, and the force of his love for Imogen. He felt what I felt, all of it, there was no difference between us.

Jessica came with Stanley on one of his visits. She looked at Imogen briefly, held her hand, went away quickly. She was going off to a friend's birthday party. I was glad. It wasn't right for her to linger here now.

John and Pam Edmonds-Seal came – Pam who had driven me in the night I went into labour, five weeks ago, Pam who

229

had prayed for us constantly, and looked after Jessica when we had called for help, tall and calm and unable, now, to find many words.

Several times I went out for a walk, or a drink, for a break from the tension, the awful, dreadful waiting and watching. I didn't eat anything. When I was there, I went on stroking my baby, murmuring to her but, as the day wore on, she slipped farther and farther from me.

Gradually, remorselessly, the monitor showed the slowing of her heart-rate, the decrease in all her functioning. Her kidneys had been affected by the septicaemia now, she had not passed water for twenty-four hours, her whole system was poisoned.

Sister Di Davidson, who had looked after Imogen so expertly and tenderly for so much of her life, had changed her duty in order to be with her now. Bernadette, the SHO, was still there, together with the Senior Registrar in charge for the evening, William Tarnow-Mordi. He it was who had come in to see me to explain his ventilation project, that first day of Imogen's life. Now he was regularly in the Nursery, and kept coming in to look at Imogen, speak to me briefly, put a comforting hand on my shoulder now and then.

The day slipped into evening. Dr Mary Ray, the beautiful Indian paediatrician with a long dark plait of hair that Jessica so admired, came on duty and suggested I might like some screens around Imogen's incubator to shelter us in our corner from any visitors, any other parents in the hot room or the corridors, but no one came. It was a quiet evening in the Nursery. And every time I glanced up at the green digits flashing on the heart-rate monitor, they were lower – below the 100, the 70s – the 50s. They fluctuated a little, but all day, all evening, they drifted downwards.

At half past seven, I went out again, to collect something from my bag on Level 7. I was prepared to stay overnight again – only I realised now that it probably would not be necessary.

The Sister on duty was at her desk, and all was quiet – there weren't many mothers in. She offered me a cup of coffee – the kettle had just boiled. I stayed and talked about nothing in particular, glad of the break from my vigil. But suddenly, as I was drinking the coffee, I heard the inner voice again, the same message –

'Go to Imogen.'

I went at once, leaving the coffee undrunk. As I walked into the hot room, Sister Davidson looked up, relief on her face.

'Mrs Wells, thank goodness. I didn't know where you were – her heart-rate has dropped right down now.'

I looked at the monitor. 30 – 28 – 26 – 29 – 30 – 25 . . .

Dr Tarnow-Mordi came into the room. Together we looked down at Imogen.

'She looks very old,' he said. I knew what he meant. She had gone smaller, looked wizened. Rather wise, but peaceful. And far, far away, miles beyond my reach now.

'Please can I hold her?' I said, and suddenly I knew it was urgent, and I longed to be as close to her as I could again, not so that I could do anything more for her now, but to ease her passing, have her go from me finally while she was in my arms, not lying in her impersonal, perspex box.

Quickly, expertly, Dr Tarnow-Mordi and the nurses took her from the incubator, wrapped her and gave her to me. Dr Mary Ray came in, and held the ventilator tube. I looked at the monitor for a moment – 20 – 17 – 11 – 11 – 4 . . . 9 – 12 – 8 – 8 . . .

I bent down and held her fragile, minute body to me, kissed her head, her cheek, spoke to her, words I can't remember – but she could not hear. I stroked her cheek with my finger – the skin was so soft, it felt like nothing, as if it were not there at all.

'Mrs Wells – ' The voice seemed to come from somewhere far away. 'Mrs Wells – it's gone right down now.'

What? I glanced up. There was no reading on the monitor, and the line had gone flat – there was just a pulse, a bleep –

'It's gone down, Mrs Wells. Do you understand?'

I looked at Imogen. Her skin was very pale, but when I kissed her again, it felt just the same. Soft. Warm.

'Mrs Wells – ' Sister Di was holding my hand, bending beside me. I looked into her eyes. They were full of tears.

'That's only the ventilator you see now on the monitor. There isn't anything else. Imogen's heart has stopped.'

I sat for a long time, holding her. She looked no different. Just even further away from me – quite out of reach.

That quiet time immediately after she had died might have been seconds, minutes, hours. There was no time. After a death, when you are close to it, have witnessed it, the world seems to be suspended, time ceases to have any meaning at all, nothing beyond this room, this momentous event, exists.

Death seemed such a simple thing to me then, so easy, so . . . I cannot express or explain. It was the most important, the most significant thing in life, I felt in awe of it and yet quite peaceful, as though I were in the company of a familiar friend. Imogen was here, death was here, too – yet I did not really know what that meant. I was not afraid, I did not recoil, and I wanted this time to last forever, to hold on to it. Because here, now, I felt as if I were within reach of understanding the secret of the universe. I was 'at the still point of the turning world'.

All those things I thought and felt and knew, as I sat on, holding my dead infant and no one hurried me, they gave me all the space I wanted and needed. It was over now, there was no urgency about anything. Is it always like that at a death bed? I hope so.

But, in the end, I had to give her back to Dr Mary Ray and Sister Di. That was when I saw that they were both crying. I wasn't. Not yet. I just felt completely drained, unable to think or feel anything any more.

'I must go and tell Stanley,' I said.

Sister Di took me out to the doctor's room. In the corridor, the night staff were coming on duty, and as they came in, they were being told about Imogen. People put their arms round me, held my hand briefly. In the doctor's room, somebody brought me a cup of tea. Dr Bernadette Salmon came in. She had been on the other side of the Unit. She was crying, too. Everyone cried, everyone except me. But I was glad that they could. That there was no feeling of shame or letting the professional mask slip, or embarrassment. Doctors and nurses have emotions. They ought to feel free to show them to patients – it isn't a sign of weakness, people aren't made to feel insecure, or fear that the doctor has lost control. It's a sign of solidarity, a real comfort, that there has been real human emotion shared as well as medical expertise shown. They had loved Imogen, I realised that now. For five weeks, they had been gunning for her, desperate for her to make it, so much hope and skill had been invested in that little person, and her last days had made everyone greatly distressed.

'You're stronger than any of us,' said Bernadette, wiping her eyes again. I smiled. At the moment, yes. Inside, I was hollow. Hollow – and very, very angry, with a silent, cold anger.

They left me alone while I telephoned. It was just my luck at that moment to get one of the jolly operators on the hospital switchboard.

'*Thank* you,' he said, when I gave him the number, 'and where are you calling from, may I ask?'

'The Special Care Nursery.'

'Ah – ha, the Nursery. And may I enquire if this is a private or a hospital call.'

My mind went blank. I didn't know.

'Heads or tails,' he said.

'Hospital. Sorry.'

'On your own conscience be it.'

'Yes.'

'I'm dialling for you now.'

'Yes. Thank you.'

'Cheer up, love – it may never happen.'

It just has, I wanted to say, shut up, you stupid man, don't you understand? *My baby has just died.*

But I didn't say anything. He wasn't to know, so why upset and embarrass him? I daresay a lot of people were glad of a 'life and soul of the party' telephone operator at night in the hospital.

Stanley answered at once. He had been waiting for the call. I told him, briefly, about Imogen's dying.

'What shall I do?' he asked. 'Jessica is in her nightie – but she's not in bed.'

'Bring her with you. Put her dressing-gown on and bring her.'

Afterwards, I asked him how it had been when the telephone call which he had been dreading finally came.

'I was cooking our supper,' he said, 'steak – we had to eat. When I finished talking to you, I put the phone down and looked at her. "Jessica," I said, "you know what I've got to tell you, don't you?" Then she cried, and I cried too. We wept together.'

I went to wait for them in the parents' room, away in the next corridor. Walking out of the Unit for the last time felt strange, nurses were still coming over to me, saying they were sorry – the whole atmosphere was subdued, quiet.

I sat, looking at a magazine, not taking it in. I made myself a cup of coffee and my hand shook, I couldn't drink it. On the notice board, advertisements for special premature baby-size clothes. On the table, the book full of success stories, photographs, newspaper cuttings, about John Radcliffe babies who had made it against many odds, gone home – the number of 'little miracles' was high. I closed the book quickly. But still, I couldn't cry.

Stanley appeared, looking grey and tired and serious, with Jessica in her red dressing-gown. She was not seven for another two weeks, yet she now looked enormous to me.

Sister Di came through. 'Would you like to see Imogen now? We've taken her out of the incubator – I can bring her to you.'

Stanley hesitated, gestured towards Jessica.

'Yes,' I said. 'It's fine – yes, please.'

In a few moments she returned, carrying Imogen in the crook of her arm, cradled like any baby. She wore a fresh white bonnet, was wrapped in a soft white shawl. I sat in the chair, and Sister Di handed her to me again. She weighed nothing, it was like holding a butterfly in a blanket. Her mouth was open still, where the ventilator tube had been, it would not relax and close yet. She looked the same as in life, but still, eyes closed. Her skin was smooth, she seemed curiously thoughtful. I kissed her. She was cooler now. All that, I thought, all that struggle, all that care, all that love – for this, for nothing.

No, not nothing. Whoever could say that this whole, complete little daughter was nothing?

I gave her to Stanley and he looked tenderly down at her – touched her gently with his finger. I realised he had not held her, as I had, when the breath of life was still in her.

'Poor little battle-scarred head,' he said, for there were bruises and marks from wires and needles. 'We wanted you so much.'

He made to hand her back to Sister Di, but she turned to Jessica. 'You'd like to hold your sister, wouldn't you?'

Jessica nodded, quite sure straight away. So was I. Imogen was her sister, she should share in this farewell. And I wanted her to look death in the face now, and to see that there was nothing to fear, know the reality of it. People are too much separated from it – they think they are protecting children, shielding them from the unpleasant, by hiding death and the dead, away. I knew on that evening, as Jessica sat solemnly in the chair, very still and proud, and her dead baby sister was put into her arms, that we were doing absolutely the right thing. Her face softened as she looked down, with love, pride, interest – but with no trace of fear or anxiety.

'She's lovely – ' she said. 'She's lovely, Mama.'

'Yes,' I said.

Oh yes.

And then Sister Di took her away.

Chapter 15

I lay in bed at home that night exhausted yet wide, wide, awake. As soon as I closed my eyes, I was back there, in that hot room, watching Imogen, holding her, talking to her. I went over and over every minute of the past hours – or rather, I didn't do anything, the events went through my head like a reel of film. I saw, heard, smelled every detail. And I wanted to be back there, to be with her again, wherever they had taken her. The old feeling of having abandoned her to strangers swept over me again and again so that I almost got dressed, and said, 'We must go to her.' *Where* had they taken her, what had they done to her and with her?

I knew those questions of old. When David died, and my mother and father, I had asked the questions then, wondered endlessly what exactly was being done to their physical body, in what sort of place they lay? In a mortuary? Yes, I supposed. So – what was that like? Who had touched them? What would happen next?

I think it is all perfectly normal. At one time those questions would not have been asked, there was no need – people died at home, or their bodies were brought back there, and at home they lay in their own beds and, later, in their coffins. They were washed and dressed for the grave by the family, or by the local woman whose job it was, and there was nothing hidden about any of it. People came in to see, too, to 'pay their last respects', and the dead member of the family spent those last days in the midst of the ordinary life of the household. If it could still be that way, how much better it would be, how much less morbid and frightening. I would have given anything to have had Imogen with us at home like that.

But I couldn't and we didn't and so I could only picture her, in her brief life, and in her dying and, now, in death.

As soon as we got home, I had telephoned Mark, but he had already been told by the Nursery. There was not much for us to say to one another that night. He was gentle, subdued, sad – all his efforts for her, for us both, had come to nothing. He had been in to see her so often, however busy his day, had wanted her to make it every bit as much as we had. We had asked him to be her godfather, so he had been even closer to her.

I went in to look at Jessica, fast asleep again, hunched up under her duvet. I wondered what she was dreaming – nothing perhaps. I envied her the child's ability to shut everything out in sleep. But I was absolutely sure that we had done the right, the only thing, in letting her see her dead baby sister, hold her, say goodbye to her. I did not want her ever to be afraid to look in the face of death.

I went back to bed and lay beside Stanley – put out my hand to him. He turned over to me. But there was nothing, really, we needed to say.

I suppose we slept, on and off, but it was one of those hot, airless, restless nights of tossing and turning, and getting up, and having odd half-awake dreams. It was a relief when the dawn came. I felt as limp as a rag, thick-headed, but strung-up.

Stanley brought me a mug of coffee. 'What would you like to do this morning?'

Because, suddenly, it was all over, there was nothing particular *to* do. Jessica was being taken off for a picnic with friends.

'Go to the hospital,' I said. It was the only place I felt I belonged, everywhere else was strange, I was pulled back there, I wanted to be inside the doors, among the familiar smells and sounds, and all the people who knew and understood, who would shelter me from – but I didn't know what.

And I needed to be with Imogen. I could not let her go.

We telephoned, and spoke to Miss Townsend. Yes, of course we could go in, she would arrange for us to see Imogen again – ten o'clock? It seemed strange to have to have an appointment.

But when we got outside the doors of the Unit, we weren't sure what to do – we had been part of it, had belonged there for five weeks. Now? It was different. We rang the bell.

They didn't take us down the familiar corridor towards the hot room and the nurseries. We went into the offices instead. That felt odd, too. They were empty, it was Sunday. We sat on hard chairs, among the typewriters and the filing cabinets. This wasn't where I wanted to be, this wasn't right.

Miss Townsend came and talked to us about arrangements – I can hardly remember, I wasn't concentrating, I wanted to be with Imogen. I thought, if I get up now, quickly, and go into the hot room, to her corner, she'll still be there, it will be like it was, she'll open her eyes and grip my finger – I recalled a line from Shakespeare's *Richard II*, which had haunted me in the past.

'Oh call back yesterday, bid time return.'

It seemed to sum up everything.

'Would you like to come with me?' Miss Townsend said. Oh, at last, now it would somehow be all right, now we would see her.

She wasn't in the Unit itself, we went away from there and down the corridor. Miss Townsend opened the door into one of the radiography rooms. I remembered lying on the couch here, having ultrasound scans, when Imogen had been alive and moving inside me.

Now, she lay in a crib, the same sort they use for newborn babies, not an incubator. She was dressed in the long white shawl and little bonnet.

'I'd just better warn you,' Miss Townsend said. 'Do hold her if you'd like to, of course – lift her out, just as you want, but you will notice that she's very cold.'

But I didn't want to lift her out. Last night, when I had held her, she had looked the same as in life. Now – death had taken her, removed her far away. Her face had shrunken, sunk in, her flesh had gone dull and waxen. This wasn't Imogen.

'She looks – not the same,' I said.

'No. They do change, of course. Would you like me to lift her up for you?'

'No,' I said quickly. I didn't even want to touch her. I had my memory of her from the previous night, how she had felt in my arms, how she had looked. I didn't want to disturb that.

I turned away.

'Thank you for letting us see her.'

'You can come again, you're welcome to see her any time – just give us a warning call.'

'No,' I said. 'I won't want that.'

We walked away slowly down the corridor, and as we went, I felt the final breaking of the cord that had bound me to her, and I remembered the Bible's words.

' . . . or ever the silver cord be loosed or the golden bowl
be broken . . . then shall the dust return to the earth as
it was: and the spirit shall return to God who gave it.'

Going out of those doors, driving away slowly down the hospital drive, I felt as lost, as bleak and bereft and homeless as I have ever felt in my life. I didn't belong there any longer, that was over. Imogen was dead and out of reach, the baby I had never really known, but had loved more than life – she had gone. The little creature in the cot this morning had not been her. Her struggle, mine, everybody's, had been as futile as any battle in any war – the end result only pain and loss and emptiness.

At home, then, I began to cry. I had not really done so until now: I cried for her, for myself, for us all, for the waste and the anguish, her pain and bewilderment, my guilt at causing it, cried out of misery and desolation and bereavement and rage. And as I cried, milk poured out of my breasts, another kind of weeping.

Stanley came and lay beside me and, after a time, I was quieter. I was thinking – deep, deep down inside me, as well as the hurt and the grief, there was anger: I had been betrayed, let down, my rage against God was a bitter, passionate thing.

But there was something else, too, a small fierce spark, that had always been there, had not gone out, though I had not

239

been able to pay it much attention over the past few weeks – perhaps hoping that I would not need to. Now, I felt it spurt up again. I was very silent, becoming more and more aware of it.

Stanley said, 'Are you thinking that you want to try again?'

We have often been telepathic like that with one another.

'Yes,' I said, and sat up, 'oh, yes I am. I've *got to*, I've got to do it.'

'I thought so, but – not yet. We need a rest – this has shattered all of us. Wait a bit.'

'Of course.'

Yes, I knew I wasn't ready physically or mentally to think of conceiving again yet, and that was right. I must not. But I was as sure as breath that I would, that I must, that I would get there, succeed in having a full-term, healthy, living baby, if it was the last thing I ever did. My determination had never wavered.

'Whatever it takes,' I thought. But was I right?

Oh, but then, it was Imogen I wanted. I didn't want to replace her with another baby – I couldn't *imagine* another baby; *she* should have lived. *She* was the only one I wanted, the one I should have brought home, to put in that waiting cradle at the other side of our bedroom. Jessica's sister.

And so I cried again, and I went on crying, healthy, necessary tears, and I raged too, raged bitterly inside myself, against God – if He was there. After all, who had broken all His promises, led me so cleverly up the garden path, deceived me, cheated, made Imogen suffer and done nothing about it, allowed her to die? When I was alone in the house, I walked about like a wild, mad woman, like Ophelia, or the demented mother in Britten's opera *Curlew River*; I cried out her name over and over again, and I beat on the walls and into the pillows with my fists, and sometimes screamed so loudly, in such rage and pain, that I made my throat sore.

If anyone had heard me, I think I would have frightened them. They would perhaps have been seriously concerned for me, but in fact I knew instinctively, at the time and even more now, how right and healthy it all was. Letting out grief and all the pent-up strain, by crying and shouting, expressing and releasing anger, are good and healthy things to do. They are *right*. In countries and cultures where they keen and wail in their ritual mourning, bereavement and all the distress that accompanies a death are treated in the natural and proper way, they do not become a long-term problem. But we have grown used to bottling things up, trying not to show distress, except in the most genteel, publicly acceptable way – a few widow's tears into a white handkerchief at the funeral. We have perhaps become afraid of letting go, not so much of the grief as of the anger, but it's the anger that needs above all to be released.

The next few days were taken up with arranging Imogen's funeral. Although I was bitterly angry with God – and for much of the time now had simply ceased to believe in Him at all – I never doubted that a funeral was what we wanted and needed. My old friend and mentor Canon Joseph Poole, formerly Precentor of Coventry Cathedral, once said to me, 'Death is a mess, there is nothing we can properly say in the face of it, but a good funeral can make sense of everything.'

I was certain he was right. I'd attended a good many of his special, carefully composed funeral services. They are 'rites of passage', they have tremendous symbolic significance.

Imogen's death started me questioning every aspect of my once apparently sure and certain Christian belief. I questioned the Bible, the person and teachings of Christ, the very foundations of religious faith, the existence of God, the point of life – and of death, the nature of suffering, and the role and relevance of the Church. And I went on questioning, and thinking, wondering, stumbling, reading, for the next four years – indeed I am still doing so. I began by assuming that this must be a bad, a negative thing. Now I am not so sure.

So, it was in a strange, bewildered, raw, angry, mixed-up state that we began thinking about Imogen's funeral on that first Sunday afternoon. Paul Rimmer, the vicar of St Nicholas, Old Marston, came to see us. He had talked about Imogen in the family service that morning, he said; he had confessed to those who had been praying for her, and for us, that he could not pretend to make sense of any of it – and that he

241

would not offer glib words of explanation. There had been tears, open tears, and many messages for us. He would be glad to conduct the funeral service, and to have Imogen buried in his churchyard. That was very important to me, too.

I know and understand all the rational, practical arguments for cremation: I have friends – of all religious faiths and none – who feel passionately that it is the only good, clean, final way to end a life and who also find the idea of burial abhorrent. I respect that. But I cannot agree. I have an equally passionate revulsion from the idea and the process of cremation. I cannot bear funeral services at those terrible places. The idea of burial is to me natural and right and, above all, I care about a grave – not in any morbid way, of needing to visit and re-visit it, but a grave as a focus of grief and of remembrance. I have always felt happy and contented in churchyards, I find them good places to be.

Like many churches, St Nicholas has more or less outgrown its graveyard, and now uses a field a few hundred yards away, on the opposite side of the road.

'But I think,' Paul said, 'that I could find a place for Imogen behind the church itself – there are a few spaces, and there is certainly room for such a small grave, up against the old wall – if you'd like that.'

Oh yes – that was *exactly* right.

'Yes, please.'

'So far as the service itself is concerned,' Paul said, 'really, it's up to you – I'll be in your hands. Do you want to think about it and write down any ideas over the next day or two?'

What I wanted to do even more was consult the one person who I knew would help us get it exactly right – Joseph Poole. When I telephoned he was away for a day and a night, but I spoke to Judith, his wife, and explained what I would like him to do. She rang me back a few hours later, having talked to Joseph on the telephone. Not long before, he said, he had composed a service for the funeral of a baby who had died – a cot-death – the daughter of some parishioners of the Cathedral at St. Albans. He thought that we would be able to use anything of that as a basis for our funeral, and then add our own personal readings, prayers, and so on. 'You should make it *your* service, for *your* child – ' he said, 'it should bear your mark upon it.'

We spent a couple of evenings working on the order of service, selecting Bible passages, talking about what sort of readings we would have. We enjoyed doing it, it was a positive, satisfying, thing to do. As Joseph had said, it would have our mark upon it, and it would help to pull the formless mess, the destructive negativeness of death together, begin to give it some sort of pattern and meaning.

I've heard and read many sad stories about the aftermath of infant deaths: how the baby has been 'taken away' by the hospital to be disposed of in a mass grave, how no one has felt able to ask for a normal, proper funeral. The parents have been left, feeling stranded, things haven't been brought to their proper conclusion, and for years afterwards, they have lived with this, had no grave to visit, nothing to remember. A funeral of some sort is as important as a photograph of the baby, and as it is to see and touch and hold it, before and after death. There *have* to be these comforts, these rituals. I have never ever dreamed about Imogen since she was buried. I think that is probably because everything was resolved and properly dealt with, that we were so well guided through it all. There is no unfinished business left to do with her in the recesses of my being, no loose ends to be tidied and tied, for dreams are often only a frantic attempt to complete what is incomplete in a relationship or an experience.

On that Monday, we had appointments with two people. The undertaker, helpful, courteous, slightly lugubrious, with the professionally subdued manner they all acquire, and the usual jargon of the trade which struck just the right Dickensian note to amuse us, in spite of our misery.

And Mrs Ashfield, who labours under the slightly off-putting title of Bereavement Officer at the John Radcliffe Hospital. Stanley had encountered her when he had had to see to arrangements after the death of my father. He had found it enormously helpful to have someone guide him through all the dreary business with registrars that attends on a death. She had been kind, efficient, attentive.

On the Monday morning after Imogen's death, when we both went to her small office in the main hospital, I was feeling tired, shaken, battered, and as confused as anyone in the same situation feels, as everyone Mrs Ashfield encounters five days a week feels. But when I met her, it was as though I were the first, the only, grieving person she had ever met, so closely did she listen, so specially, individually, did she treat me.

If ever there was the right person in the right job, it was she – warm-hearted, Irish, uninhibited in the way she opened her arms and embraced me – a complete stranger – and without a trace of falseness or awkwardness, genuinely sharing our grief by telling us of the death of her own young daughter; she combined practical help with personal caring; for anyone who found it difficult to talk about death, to begin to cry, to express their own shock or anger, for those without a sympathetic listener and a welcoming shoulder to cry on, for people who had no one in the world who would give them an embrace full of real feeling, real understanding, here was the woman they needed.

We had each other, we were a close, united family, able to talk and cry together, surrounded by helpers, friends, the medical professionals – if we were comforted and supported by visiting her, made to feel a little stronger, more able to cope and face the immediate future, how much more would other, far less fortunate, visitors to Mrs Ashfield's office.

Recently I read a sneering reference in a newspaper column to 'the professional carers, paid to have a finger in all the private crises of human life'. I daresay they were referring, among social workers and probation officers, to the bereavement officers of major hospitals. They can never have had occasion to need help from a Mrs Ashfield.

The strength we got from all the people who surrounded us was reinforced during that week a hundredfold, as letters, cards, flowers, messages began to reach us. And how essential those were, how much it meant. I understand those who ask 'no letters please' but I could not do it. The letters people wrote to us about Imogen's life and death were a source of inexpressible comfort and joy, as love and concern and fellow-feeling poured out of them. They came from friends who lived locally and from those further away, from neighbours, Stanley's colleagues, Jessica's school. I welcomed all of them, and I've been told by other people who have lost a child by death – as well as those bereaved in some different way – how vital those letters were. It wasn't what they said, really – just the fact that they meant, 'We feel with you, we're thinking of you, we're so sorry.' And flowers, as always, carried their own special message. The landlady of our local pub put a tiny posy of freshly picked flowers in a small jug on the doorstep with a simple note; elderly people from the other side of the village whom we barely knew walked slowly round one evening with some roses, just taken from their garden, and left them for us.

And most of all, I was moved and helped by those people who had lost children themselves. I learned that there is a great, half-secret army of them; everywhere I turned, I found someone who, perhaps many many years before, had had a child die – and now confessed to it. John Barton, the hospital chaplain, told me about his son, Nicholas, still remembered on his birthday, thirty years later; Mr Busby, who sometimes helped me in the garden, stuck his spade in the earth, and came over to me, wiping his earthy hand on his shirt, before shaking mine. 'Not many words to say, but the feelings are there. We lost a little one.'

Gillian and Angela and Emily, who had all lost babies, wrote, sent flowers, shared their own renewed grief with mine and, in remembering Imogen, remembered Toby and Jed and Will.

And Benedikte Wilders, a friend from Oxford, whose only daughter Catherine, bright, beautiful, full of life and promise, was killed on a Norwegian mountain at the age of eighteen. Benedikte appeared one glorious afternoon, with flowers from her garden already arranged in a vase full of water, most carefully carried from home. 'So you don't have to do anything else but enjoy them.' She sat in the sun with me and told me, then, the full story of Catherine's accident, which I had never properly heard.

'And have a grave,' she said, 'a grave is very important.'

I felt so surrounded by all these people, and was able to be myself with them, talk, relax, as with no one else, simply because they knew *exactly* how it was, they had been there.

During the last couple of weeks of Imogen's brief life, summer had come, only we had scarcely noticed. Now, it blazed up in glory, the week after her death was hot and sunny, with constant blue skies. The day of her funeral was a perfect one, the gardens full of all the flowers of midsummer in their glory, roses, delphiniums, sweet peas, lupins, phlox, the air smelled sweet and droned with bees. It was good to have it so, good that the usual rain and greyness of funerals did not come, good to be able to stand outside the church porch in the sunshine and feel the warmth of it on our faces, as we waited.

And so many people came, and that helped; I had never realised before how important it is to go to funerals, not for the sake of the dead, but for the comfort of the living. We were carried through it just because there were so many friends: Pat Gardner, Joan Tranter, Jessica's headmistress; Gillian Morriss Kay, and Pam and John Edmonds-Seal, so close to us during Imogen's short life; Sister Di from the Nursery and her colleague Carol Aldridge who had both been with me at the end, our friend Kate Lea, on her own behalf and 'for', she said, 'all your friends in the village'.

And then it was eleven o'clock, and there was the undertaker's car with, on the back seat, the very small coffin. When he had visited us, Mr Bromley had asked if we would like 'the traditional casket for a baby, lined in white'. But we had not expected the outside to be white, too, an amazing, quilted satin; Stanley and I exchanged one glance of horror, tempered by a flicker of amusement.

But Jessica was impressed. 'Oh,' she breathed. 'Oh Mama, look! Isn't it *beautiful*?'

We walked down to the car, and the undertaker laid the coffin across Stanley's arms, and I put my hand on it and held Jessica's hand in my other, and so we went slowly, carefully, into the church.

We did not want hymns, or a great deal of noise, but we did

want some music, the organ playing quietly at the beginning – obvious, perhaps, but complete silence would have been unbearably oppressive.

We reached the chancel steps behind Paul Rimmer, and the coffin was set down on a table. As we took our places, Paul said, 'The lamb who is at the throne will be their shepherd, and will lead them to springs of living water; and God will wipe all tears from their eyes.'

And then he spoke, not for very long, or in great detail, not pompously or pretentiously, but simply, and with feeling, saying only what we all felt, what everyone there felt, that he did not pretend to understand Imogen's life and death, or to have any answers, that it was a fact, that he simply had to believe that sense could be made of it, some time, somehow. And he told of what he had learned from seeing her, and of the love he knew she had drawn out of so many people.

All the right things, well and briefly said. Some, at least, of what we were feeling.

'Receive, O Lord Jesus Christ, into the arms of your loving care your child Imogen, and keep her close to your presence, where she will forever be protected from any evil, and may grow into that perfection which is your will for her.'

Then, Pat, as Imogen's godmother, read a poem, the poem from which we took the inscription on her grave, a poem by Ben Jonson. We had hunted through anthology after anthology for just the right one, coming close, but never hitting it exactly, until Stanley had thought to ring his old colleague, the English scholar Elsie Duncan-Jones, now retired and living in Cambridge, a walking treasury of quotations from English literature. She directed us at once to the perfect poem –

> It is not growing like a tree
> In bulk, doth make men better be;
> Or standing long as oak, three hundred year,
> To fall at last, dry, bald and sere:
> > A lily of a day
> > Is fairer far in May.
> Although it fall and die that night

It was the plant and flower of light.
In small proportion we just beauty see;
And in short measure, life may perfect be.

It expressed, better than anything else I can imagine, what I felt about Imogen: how, looking at her, I had looked on perfect and complete innocence, which had no time to be spoiled.

We then all said, together, Psalm 23, 'The Lord is my Shepherd', after which we sat to hear Jessica read the lesson from St Mark:

> They brought children for him to touch. The disciples rebuked them but when Jesus saw this he was indignant, and said to them, 'Let the children come to me; do not try to stop them, for the Kingdom of God belongs to such as these. I tell you, whosoever does not accept the Kingdom of God like a child will never enter it.' And he put his arms round them, laid his hands upon them, and blessed them.

She did it so clearly and with great and serious composure. Stanley was serious, too, but a little less composed, nearer to tears, as he read a passage from *The Magic Apple Tree*, the book I had written three years previously about our country home and the family life into which we had hoped to welcome Imogen. The passage included a quotation from one of the pieces of English prose which has meant a great deal to me over the years, taken from the sixteenth-century writer Thomas Traherne, and which ends:

> Is it not strange that an infant should be heir of the world, and see those mysteries which the books of the learned never unfold?

There were prayers of thanks, including those 'for all the gracious ministries of human affection, especially for those who so tenderly cared for Imogen'.

And the prayer of John Donne which I read, which has always seemed to me perhaps the most beautiful ever written in English:

Bring us, O Lord, at our last awakening, into the house and gate of heaven, to enter into that gate and dwell in that house where there shall be no darkness nor dazzling, but one equal light: no noise nor silence, but one equal music: no fears nor hopes, but one equal possession: no ends nor beginnings, but one equal eternity in the habitation of thy glory and dominion, world without end.

Then the Lord's Prayer and, before the final blessing, one that Paul had composed especially, which included the phrase – 'Help us through the mystery of Imogen's life and death, to discover truths which are now hard to discern.'

We walked out of the church, again carrying Imogen's coffin, and around the grass path, to bury her there underneath the stone wall in the sunshine. The churchyard was full of flowers and birds and friends, and of sadness and of love, and when we drove slowly home through the lanes, we felt, all of us, better. Joseph had been right, a good funeral had been a balm poured over many raw and angry wounds.

A few days later, I wrote a letter to Richard and Maggie Turner, the parents of the baby for whose funeral Joseph Poole had written the order of service we had shared. Somehow I wanted to say thank you, to reach out to yet another family who had suffered the death of their child, and with whom we had a bond, made stronger by the fact that her name, Susanna, had been Imogen's second name. They replied, warmly.

It was the right thing to have done.

Chapter 16

I read an article not long ago about death and dying, written by a doctor. In the course of giving a lot of extremely valuable advice to the bereaved, he said one thing with which I disagreed totally. When parents of a child who had died went to him saying that they wanted to set up some sort of trust fund in that child's memory – perhaps for research into the disease it had died of, or in some way to help parents in a position similar to their own – he said he always advised them to think again, or at least to go away and only come back to the idea some time later if they were still really sure it was what they wanted to do. For working to set up such a fund might, he advised, do a lot for other people but wouldn't do much for them, and that they would be better employed in putting all their energies into finishing the business of grieving, rather than into 'such displacement activities'.

I think he profoundly misunderstood an absolutely instinctive and healthy need in many people who have lost a child (or, indeed, sometimes have been bereaved in another way). Many, many times I have heard, or known, of various funds and trusts established by parents which have given them some positive reason for going into the future, and made them feel they can do something to help make sense of and bring positive, living good out of an essentially negative experience. The instinct is so strong, so common, that I'm certain it must be right to heed it, and sure, too, that it need not in any way displace or cut short the proper business of grieving.

Certainly we felt, at once and very strongly, that we wanted to *do* something after Imogen's death – to help those who had helped her, and us, to put back into a system, expensive and always short of funds, a little to compensate for what we had taken out, to say thank you, to help express all our feelings, and also be a permanent remembrance of our daughter.

If anyone had advised us against it, had blocked our strong desire to give, I think we would have suffered a serious deprivation, one outlet for all the restless energy would have been dammed up, and where, then, would it all have gone? Back inside, I suspect, to turn into seething frustration.

But the original impulse for a gift of some kind to the hospital had come, as such things usually do, in response to the question about flowers for Imogen's funeral. A flowerless funeral is depressing, but we knew there would be flowers in abundance growing in the churchyard all around her, and that we could take some from our own garden to lay on her coffin. There was no need for sheaves and wreaths and posies from the florist.

But some people wanted to give something, in lieu of sending flowers, so that when we composed the death announcement for the newspapers – one national, and the local ones in Oxford and Stratford – we felt it necessary to add an indication of where money could be sent. It read: 'Donations would be most welcome to the Imogen Wells Fund, for the Special Care Baby Unit of the John Radcliffe Hospital, in whose tender care she lived and died.'

I suppose we had it in mind that perhaps a hundred pounds or so might be sent, with which we would purchase a small piece of equipment.

When Imogen was born, we had also put in an announcement in the Births column, indicating that she was very small, very premature, and fighting for survival. That had alerted very many people, friends and strangers too, to her existence, and those who were not able to discover about her progress in any other way, apparently scanned the columns anxiously during the next few weeks, wondering if she was doing well, hoping they would not read the notice that did eventually appear. The response to it was, as they say, overwhelming.

251

We had letters and cheques, not only from very many people we knew, including many long-lost friends, and from colleagues and various business firms with and for whom I had worked, but also from innumerable readers of my books, all unknown to me, and from others who had lost children, or who had been touched by the death announcement, or who, as Stanley put it, seemed to be 'looking out for a charity to which to give money'.

There was a donation from a collection made by the staff in the branch of the building society we use, and a penny collection from the village playgroup, and another from the parents of Jessica's school. One friend, who has very little money to be free with, pushed five pounds into my pocket when we met in the street. Another gave me that week's child benefit. And at the other end of the scale, we were given cheques from private and business accounts, for amounts of several hundred pounds, as well as a gift from a charitable foundation, of which we had never heard, for £1,000.

We rapidly realised that we would either be able to buy a much larger piece of equipment than we had anticipated or several smaller ones, or do something rather different. When we talked about it together and with the paediatricians and nurses at the hospital, we decided we wanted to do something that would be continuous – a living, on-going memorial to Imogen, and we felt strongly that it should be of benefit to the nurses, both present and future. For it is the nursing staff who bear the burden of day to day, hour to hour care of premature babies, they who observe them, monitor them, tend them, get to know them. Besides, there are already established sources of funding for doctors – but nothing comparable for the nurses who were grotesquely badly paid, with little extra money at all given for special training skills and responsibilities, as in neonatal nursing. We couldn't augment their salaries but we decided we could use the income from the fund (which in the end reached over £4,000 and has had various additional donations over the years) to make it possible for any who wanted to go on courses, to conferences and on visits to other centres, for all of which they would normally have to find expenses in full out of their own pockets. In addition, any

252

nurse with some special and extraordinary need could be helped from the fund from time to time. We wanted to keep it very simple and entirely flexible, and so it has been.

To date, over two dozen nurses have used the fund which we hope will continue to be available for many years to come. We want it to be used, and to be useful. It was set up out of the generosity of many, and the business of establishing it gave us, then and now, great satisfaction but it didn't divert any of our energies from our grieving – however could it? It was in no way, to use that dreadful jargon, 'a displacement activity'.

The rest of that summer, July and August, passed wearily enough.

'You need a holiday,' everyone said. 'Why don't you get right away somewhere?'

That's another thing people are supposed to want to do after a death, and perhaps, for some, it is the right thing, but the tiredness of bereavement is not a normal tiredness that can be cured by a few good nights of sleep and a decent rest away from everyday demands and duties. We thought about taking a holiday, for Jessica's sake as much as for our own, even got brochures and went through them. But, in the end, we went nowhere. We knew we needed to be together, at home.

And I still felt that real life, and everything that mattered, was at the hospital, and it remained the focus of my attention and energy. But the Intensive Care Nursery was full of other people's babies now. We had no place there – and I found that hard to bear.

I did return, a couple of weeks after Imogen died, to spend a miserable night after a minor haemorrhage, and to trail down to the scan-room, opposite the Special Care Nursery, to be investigated. It was very hard. I had a quick operation to remove some fragments of retained placenta and cure the problem, and this made me feel physically better and so, at last, slightly more able to cope with empty days.

Most of all, I felt suspended by not being pregnant, and not able to be so yet. Wanting the baby I had lost, feeling guilty about craving another – totally confused. It was limbo time, I cried a lot, could not concentrate on anything at all, not even a magazine, thought about Imogen, was angry.

But beneath it all, I was kept going by a single-minded, bloody-minded determination. In the end, I would get there. I would do it.

It was still absolutely the only thing that mattered.

But whether or not I was right to allow myself to have this obsession with giving birth to another child was a different matter. I was incapable of assessing the right and wrong, the very *sense* of it, because it consumed me, and distorted all reason. It was like insane, passionate love, or religious mania; all I wanted, my whole reason for being, everything else, my family, friends, work, my own health – everything, paled beside it. They either had to take care of themselves, or be carried along by it too – or, I suppose, go under.

Looking back, I see that it was very dangerous and could have been deeply destructive – and very selfish, too. Yet I could exist in no other way, and I could not help myself.

But I was already forty-two, and supposing it all happened again? No one knew why Imogen was born early – there was no detectable reason for the rupture of the membranes and, therefore, no real possibility of ensuring that it would not happen another time. The risks of something, anything, going wrong, were increasing every year. Already I had had early miscarriages, a premature baby, and had put my own health in jeopardy, all because I seemed more than usually prone to have things go wrong post-natally. Was I right to risk the life of another baby, risk having some other tiny innocent creature suffering pain and sickness and bewilderment, tied up to machines in an Intensive Care Nursery, and, finally, death? Was I right to neglect my family emotionally and in lots of other ways, to make their happiness subservient to my own desperate need? What was I trying to *prove*?

But I could not have *asked* those questions, let alone answered them dispassionately. Perhaps no one will fully understand who has not been taken over in a similar way. Perhaps I was, indeed, to blame.

If it had not all come right, how much guilt would I have had to shoulder? What damage would I have done?

I don't know. I just don't know.

I had wanted Imogen to live more desperately than anything I had ever wanted, loved her in a way I do not think I could ever love again.

Still eaten up by that longing, that wanting, I stumbled on through that summer and the golden days of September.

I was grieving, and that was good; otherwise I was waiting, simply marking time before setting off on another of those perilous, necessary journeys.

Part IV

Clemency

Chapter 17

I had been told very firmly not to allow myself to become pregnant again until at least six months after Imogen's death – which took me to November.

I then conceived at once.

Neither of us found it possible to rejoice when I did so. Stanley's reaction to the news had been muted – unsurprisingly. He faced the prospect of standing beside me, standing beside all of us, through more weeks and months of anxiety, wondering what disaster was going to strike us this time around. And how could he bear the idea of losing another child, after he had loved Imogen so desperately, staked so much on her life?

He had felt as I had felt during the five weeks of her existence, but he could not possibly feel my passionate desire to succeed in having another child, was not driven as I was by the intense physical, biological need to bear a baby. He could only stand by, heart in his mouth, fearing, worrying.

Yes, he would like to have another child, if things went well, and yes, he was entirely supportive and generous in the strength and love and care he gave. But I have little doubt that it was harder for him than for me to allow a new pregnancy to go ahead.

There were several differences this time. Always before, I had felt confident, supremely so with Jessica, when of course there had been no reason to feel otherwise, but all those other times, too, confident in a foolish, semi-superstitious way, believing sentimentally that I was somehow being specially protected, that it was all sure to be right because it was 'meant to be'.

There was none of that now. I had no confidence at all, no trust, nothing but pessimism and a dull sense of doom. Whatever could go wrong before had done so, why should this time be any different?

As Mark once put it, my blood pressure level was excellent throughout but my anxiety level was off the machine.

So when the usual bleeding began during the early weeks, I was not surprised, not startled, not, perhaps, even very concerned. 'Here we go again' more or less summed up my attitude, as I told Stanley, telephoned Mark, packed my bag for the hospital one day immediately after Christmas.

The ward was still covered in tinsel and paper Santas, the crib was in its place by the lift doors, and the Christmas Day babies still in residence.

I lay in bed reading, went for a scan – expecting the worst. The old routine, same scan-room, same misery, as I went past the Special Care Nursery.

But it was all right. There was a heart-beat, there was an eight-week fetus.

'Looks good,' the radiographer said.

But I couldn't raise my spirits, or my hopes.

'Don't worry about the bleeding – that'll settle down.'

'Yes.'

Would it? If it didn't, I thought, there was bound to be something else.

I spent another night in, just to be safe. I ate a lot of biscuits and watched Agatha Christie on the television. And made a friend, sent to her by one of the nurses.

'Go and talk to Jane; that'll cheer you up.'

I did and it did. Jane Bellhouse had been in residence since the previous August, awaiting the birth of her third child. A placenta praevia had been detected and, because of the risk of haemorrhage, she had to remain here until her baby was born by Caesarian – at the end of January. But she was expansive, optimistic, friendly, welcoming and she took my mind off my own gloom. I promised to call in from time to time and see her when I went to have my HCG injections twice a week – back on that routine again. It was good to have made yet another friend, experience the old solidarity among pregnant women with problems again.

The other new experience of this pregnancy was to be a cervical stitch.

Although no one knew, or would ever know, why my membranes ruptured, there is a theory that sometimes the cause is a weakness in the cervix – the neck of the womb – which opens far too early, as soon as the baby reaches a certain size, allowing labour to begin prematurely. Sometimes, if a woman has had a previous forceps delivery – I had – and one or more dilations of the neck of the womb – I had – a weakness may have resulted.

Treatment is to put a stitch, rather like the sort that ties up a dolly-bag purse, around the cervix and draw it up tight. For safety's sake, Mark said, it was a stitch for me.

'We can't be sure there was a weakness but I think we act on the principle of "let's do anything and everything, in case something helps."'

I didn't like the idea of having a general anaesthetic when pregnant. I knew the procedure carried a few more risks than usual, but I didn't want to go into labour at 25 weeks again, 'for want of a nail'.

So in February, I was back in the John Radcliffe. Mark came to see me that evening.

'There's a patient of mine across the corridor – she's just had her second son and she had a cervical stitch each time. She'd had lots of miscarriages, spent the whole of her last pregnancy in hospital. No problems this time but perhaps she'll be able to tell you what it's like better than I can. She's had one, I only put them in!'

Another new friend, Clare Preston, another half-hour of swopping experiences. She had just had a Caesarian which wasn't, she said, much fun. But the stitch had been fine, no problems at all.

I felt happier. And then went along to see Jane for a moment. Jane who, after all the weary months of lying in bed, now had another son, Freddie. But she was feeling very battered, and I only stayed a few seconds.

'Don't have a Caesarian, that's all,' she groaned. 'Nature's way is best.'

I came out of hospital two days later, all sewn up, without any mishaps – just with a healthy dread of Caesarian sections. At all costs, I must avoid one of those. But I thought the chances of my needing one were pretty remote. I had had two babies in the normal way, and the procedure after a cervical stitch would be that at 38 weeks of pregnancy, I would be admitted and the stitch snipped out – no anaesthetic would be necessary – which in itself would probably be sufficient to induce a speedy labour.

If, that was, I ever got that far. I couldn't really believe it, could not see that far ahead, *dared* not. Another couple of weeks of HCG injections, but otherwise I lived a quiet, restful, thoroughly pessimistic life.

We had told Jessica quite early on in my pregnancy with Imogen that we were having another baby. Now, we had kept quiet – I could not bear her to suffer more anxiety and disappointment, would say nothing until I couldn't conceal things any longer (though that looked as if it would be quite soon since I grew much larger much earlier this time around).

But I had underestimated my daughter. She came to visit me, the day after I had had my stitch – quite cheerful, having been told that I was not ill, just in (yet again) for a small operation; she was used to all this.

She marched up to the bed and looked down at me.

'Hello.'

'Mama,' she said firmly, '*why* are you in the *maternity* hospital?'

I caved in and told her, wondering how, after Imogen, she would react, expecting her to cry or show fear.

Her face lit up. 'Another baby? Are we going to have one?'

'Yes,' I said decisively, but then I had to add, 'I hope so. It's very early yet, Jessica – you remember – '

'Yes, I know, I know.' She shut me up.

I didn't press things. Then the nurse came in with the monitor.

'Hello, Jessica. I'm just going to listen to your Mummy's baby – would you like to hear?'

She oiled my tummy, put the sensor on me. Bump-bump-bump-bump-bump came loud and clearly magnified through the room.

'That's your baby's heart beating.'

But, oh, I was afraid to listen. Suddenly, I realised it was all real, all true, I had a baby in there, and I was desperately afraid for it.

And so, it continued. Every day I awoke, I was quite sure that disaster – either a familiar one, or some new horror – would strike. I was afraid to go anywhere far from home or the hospital – and so I simply didn't. I read a lot, sewed elaborate needlepoint, rested – and grew larger.

As the 24th week loomed ahead, I became almost hysterical with anxiety, telephoned Mark and other doctor friends repeatedly for reassurance. Did lightning ever strike twice in the same place, obstetrically speaking? No one could ever tell me with complete confidence that it did not.

The week before, I happened to switch on the radio and tuned in to a medical programme which casually stated that although the maternal mortality rate had declined dramatically in the past fifty years, nevertheless a proportion of women did still die in pregnancy and childbirth every year of causes directly related to their condition, and many of these deaths were at present unpreventable.

I rang my friend Gillian Morriss Kay in a state of terror. She, rational, clear-headed and yet entirely sympathetic to my anxiety, tried to help me put things in perspective, and said, 'You *know* there are risks, you've accepted them, but keep them in proportion. They're really very small.'

I could not be so level-headed. I expected to die – of a brain haemorrhage perhaps or a sudden thrombosis. Each new day brought a new fear, and I scarcely dared to open newspapers and magazines for fear of reading some news item or comment which would add to my worries.

Week 24 arrived. I felt numb and hardly dared to leave the house. Suddenly, one afternoon, I began to have quite strong contractions. All pregnant women do have these – they are

263

called Braxton Hicks contractions, they become noticeable from about the 20th week and with each successive pregnancy they seem to become more pronounced. (I scarcely felt them at all with Jessica.) They are painless, but definite, a hardening and tightening of the whole uterus which lasts for anything up to a minute and a half.

I let them continue on and off for a few hours, tried to ignore them, but by the time Stanley came home I was in a total state of panic. I knew that because of having a cervical stitch in place, I would need to be in hospital at once – if my labour really was under way.

'I'm a bit worried,' I said. 'I'm having contractions.'

Calmly, Stanley suggested that we eat our supper and then, at the end of it, he said to Jessica cheerfully, 'Well, we're off to the hospital now – come on. We're just going to make sure that Mummy and the baby are all right.'

Her eyes widened in alarm at once. 'Is it going to be born tonight?'

'No,' Stanley said firmly.

Meanwhile, I was ringing Delivery Suite at the John Radcliffe, and explaining who I was and what was happening.

'You'd better come in and join us, Mrs Wells,' said the young Sister on duty, in a welcoming voice which made me feel calmer as soon as I heard it.

So we did. Up the long drive, in through those familiar doors. The moment they closed behind us, I relaxed, felt much safer, and the contractions ceased when I was put on the monitor. The Sister and then the Senior Registrar on duty examined me. All was quiet.

'We'll keep you in overnight for luck,' the Sister said, 'but I'm quite certain nothing will happen.'

And, of course, it didn't nor on the other two occasions when I had a similar false alarm. Everyone joked about my hypersensitivity and tried to keep my anxiety level down, but no one ever refused to take me seriously either, and I was never made to feel foolish or neurotic.

I tried hard not to think too much about Imogen; it was so upsetting and, as time went on, my predominant feeling about her was one of guilt. Often at night I would lie awake and a picture of her would flash onto the screen of my mind; in her incubators, in my arms, in death, I would see her tiny, frail body, her perfect fingers, her bewildered eyes, and weep for her all over again. And I often visited her grave, to sit for a few moments beside the small simple Welsh-slate gravestone. 'A lily of a day'.

I could not, of course, have ignored my increasing size or the vigorous movements of the baby, but I could not bring myself to relate to it, to try and imagine it. When I thought of real babies, I pictured Imogen. But I enjoyed the feel of those tiny limbs flailing about inside me, the turnings and shiftings that made me so uncomfortable in the night – and increasingly so by day, too.

When I reached 32 weeks, I permitted myself a small celebration – after this, I knew that the baby would have every chance of surviving and doing well in the Special Care Nursery if it had to be born early and provided that nothing else was wrong with it. Ah, but then, there was that anxiety, too. As with the last pregnancy, I had not had any amniocentesis or other tests, and the risks of the child being handicapped, now I was forty-three, were even higher. But my thinking on that subject had not changed – if anything, we both felt even more definite – so it had not been an issue. Besides, if the odds were now 50-1 that was still 49-1 against – you'd think those were pretty long odds on the racecourse.

I began the course of ante-natal classes at the hospital – which I had so resisted with Jessica. This time, I hoped to be able to have a good, normal delivery, and if I could manage without an epidural, so much the better. After the last time, I thought I'd rather avoid those.

The classes were very good, positive and helpful. And many of us were elderly, several mothers over forty like me, and most over thirty – I no longer felt the freak I had, eight years previously.

May came. The 27th. Imogen's birthday. During the next weeks I thought about her a lot, sadly, guiltily, but there is no doubt that the anniversary was not so poignant and painful as it would have been if I had not been pregnant. It was a year ago and it felt much, much longer.

June was hot and I was very tired, bone-tired, I could hardly lumber up the garden steps. I became forgetful, muddled, 'slightly deranged' as Stanley put it – all normal symptoms of pregnancy, but exaggerated. At night, I lay with the window wide open and the bedclothes thrown back and felt the baby moving, a shoulder here, a foot – or a hand – there. Who are you? I thought. What are you? Shall I ever know you? I wanted a girl, that was all I could be sure of, we all did.

But all the time, my disbelief in this pregnancy continued, the apprehension, the dread, the anxiety, the refusal to believe all the good signs. When I went to see Mark, all was well, all was normal – if it had not been for my nervous state, this would have been the most straightforward, unremarkable pregnancy in history.

At 37 weeks, I was longing for it to be over, thinking of the following week when I would be going for my last check. I couldn't get away from the certainty that there was something wrong, something specific. It wasn't only my general sense of unease and doom – I didn't *feel* right.

I lumbered slowly up the stairs to the consulting-room and heaved myself onto the couch. Mark took my blood pressure, and listened to the heartbeat. Fine.

'Now, we'll just feel if the baby is the right sort of size and length and whether it's settled nicely down yet. It all seems fine.'

He shot his cuffs and gently put a hand on either end of the bulge. Paused. Looked slightly worried. Felt again.

'Have you been feeling anything different – a bit more uncomfortable than usual?'

'Yes.'

'Yes. That's because the baby is still upside down – here's the head, up here under your ribs – with the feet tap-dancing about down below.'

'A breech baby?'

'At the moment, yes.' He went to the sink to wash his hands. 'When you're dressed, come and sit down, will you?'

Leaden hearted, as well as footed, I did so.

'Now this does just introduce a new factor,' Mark began. 'Of course, it's only 37 weeks – we have to remember.' I'm

266

going to induce you next week, at 38, but normally you'd have three more weeks to go – and in that time the baby could well turn and settle down into position.'

'But I thought they didn't usually do that so late.'

'Well, they don't, no, not usually – but it's possible.'

'Can you turn it?'

'We can, but that isn't entirely without risk – and the trouble is, so often baby simply turns back again. I think we at least have to face the possibility that this baby is breech and likely to remain so. In which case –'

I looked him in the eye.

'I know,' I said. 'A Caesarian section.'

'Yes. I'm never happy about delivering breech babies vaginally but in a case like yours – with your previous history and such a precious baby –'

'No, I understand. Oh God, I knew something awful was going to happen – I *knew* it.'

Just for a moment, my world crashed around my ears. I *had* known – and the one thing in the world I dreaded was a Caesarian. I'd never been under the surgeon's knife and I didn't want to start now. I wanted a good, uneventful, normal delivery.

Mark tried to make reassuring noises – it really might not be necessary, the baby could turn during the week, and even if it didn't, a Caesarian was surely not such an ordeal to have to face, it . . .

I wasn't listening. I was making plans, preparing already for what I knew was bound to happen.

Curiously enough, a few weeks before I had sent for one or two pamphlets from the National Childbirth Trust. Going down the list of what was available, I had, on the spur of the moment, ticked the one about Caesarians. Why? Who knows?

I went home and dug it out.

I also settled down that evening and made two telephone calls, one to Emily Richard whose second baby had been born by Caesarian and who had had an epidural anaesthetic, so as to be awake throughout; the other to Gillian Morriss Kay whose son, Matthew, had been delivered by Caesarian under a general anaesthetic.

I told them what was probably going to happen, and I asked them to tell me everything, absolutely *everything* they could. By the time they had finished, I was a good deal better informed, not only in general but in all the tiny details and snippets of personal advice that can only ever come from another person who has had a similar experience.

I also rang the local National Childbirth Trust helpline and spoke to someone else who had had two Caesarians. By the time everyone had finished talking to me, I was feeling better – much less unhappy.

The next day I went to the bookshop, too, and bought a couple of useful paperbacks about Caesarian birth. Over-informed? Over-prepared? All I can say is that it was my way of dealing with the situation and it worked. I was still afraid but no longer ignorant, no longer terrified. I thought I could go through with it – just as well, really, since I had no choice!

The only decision left was whether I would be awake or asleep, have an epidural or a general. Everyone I asked had different advice. I veered towards being awake but first I needed to talk to a consultant anaesthetist and ask a few searching questions.

By the time I had left Dr Len Carrie's office, I was entirely confident. He saw absolutely no reason, he said, why he should not give me an epidural for my Caesarian without the slightest problem and never mind my previous experience.

'But why decide now?' he said. 'Why not wait until the morning you're due for delivery? It makes no difference to me either way. Wait until you wake up, and then do as you feel. For now, just put it out of your mind.'

I did so. For the rest of the week, I got ready, sorted things out at home, welcomed Louisa Lane Fox's niece, Rachel, who was coming to help us for a month, packed my bag. On Friday, 19 July, in pouring summer rain, we drove to the hospital. In through the doors again, across the blue carpet, into the lift. I ought to have been feeling excited, delighted – I'd almost made it, after all. This time tomorrow –

But I couldn't feel anything except panic and apprehension. It was a pity – I could have been enjoying tonight, looking forward to having my stitch out and giving birth in the way I knew about. Instead I had that sick, leaden feeling of dread at what was, in spite of all my homework, still essentially 'the unknown'.

And this pregnancy had really been so smooth, there had been no recurrence of any of my earlier problems. I had not miscarried, my baby had not been born too early, I had got to the end – it all seemed too good to be true. In one sense, I seemed to have been pregnant for ever, there had been so many weary days of anxiety, so many hurdles to overcome, so much to dread. Yet in another, it had all passed in a sort of dream. It was as though I had been somehow suspended. I realised tonight that I had never truly believed in any of it, never been able to accept the pregnancy – dared not.

Tomorrow then I would have a baby. So they told me. Yet I could not imagine that either, I felt so fatalistic about myself and my ability to bear another child, so superstitious. The idea that it would all go smoothly could not be admitted, it was tempting fate. I was detached, waiting, waiting for the inevitable blow.

Stanley and Jessica went. The evening stretched ahead. Mark came. Dr Carrie came. I had my last meal, feeling like the condemned man. The midwife came and took away my water jug in case I absentmindedly drank a sip in the night. Oh God, it all seemed very real, very imminent. I remembered Jane and Clare again: 'Nature's way is best.' 'I don't recommend a Caesarian.'

Various people came and asked me various questions, wrote notes, went again. I stood at the window, looking down. I was in Room 19, the nicest one, the one Gillian had had, overlooking the green.

The rain had cleared now, and there was a cricket match in progress; long shadows across the grass, the nostalgic thwack of leather on willow, sound of my Yorkshire summers in childhood when I had lain awake through the long light evenings, and heard them playing, the cries of 'Howzzat' on the ground that was opposite our house.

The sound carried me back, and then I began to remember other things from the past, other scenes, and understood my reasons for being here now. I remembered Aunty Matron, and the comfort of being a small child in her kitchen, and the sight of a baby in its crib beside the range; remembered the Dybdale nursery in the evening, curtains drawn, lamp on and, half in the shadows, the rows of cots, the babies. Yes, those babies were my reason for pushing myself this far.

I thought of Aunty Matron herself, and wondered what she would have to say to me at this moment – something brisk and commonsensical, I knew. But there would be understanding too, and gentleness beneath the efficient exterior.

My mother would have been more apprehensive for me, re-living the details of her own confinement through me. I was glad that she had not had to face these past four years of my struggle to have this child, yet I wished she could have known the joy her grandchildren would surely have brought her. And I wanted her to have seen that I had managed to do what she never expected – to marry happily and have children.

I stood for a long time, listening to the sound of the cricket, watching the shadows grow longer on the grass, remembering, tracing out a pattern from past to present, fitting things together, making sense of it all.

The baby was heavy inside me now, and it was very uncomfortable having a head pushed hard up into my lungs and liver. I cupped my hand around it gently. This time tomorrow. Oh, it had to be all right – meaning, let it be all right.

But I could not pray now, had not been able to do so in any way since Imogen's last days when I had asked and asked and had met only with silence. Now, I knew I was on my own.

I got into bed. Lay for the last time with that weight on my stomach, 'great with child'. The light was fading, the cricketers had gone home.

A tap on the door. John Barton, the hospital chaplain.

'I've come to give you a blessing, to send you on your way.'

How did he know I was here?

He sat on my bed.

'I feel pretty – apprehensive,' I managed to say.

'I'm not surprised.'

He put his hand on mine firmly. Gently said a few words, committing us both 'into the caring hands of God'.

'Tomorrow,' he said, 'I will be saying a prayer of thanksgiving. But now – off you go to sleep. All's well.'

The door closed softly. I turned over, feeling, for the first time in the whole of the previous nine months, totally calm, entirely confident, quite relaxed, all fear, all apprehension gone.

I slept.

Chapter 18

I woke at dawn and lay looking at the sky, and at the swallows sweeping and soaring beyond the windows. Saturday, 20 July.

I put my hand on my stomach. A faint stir, then quiet. Now I savoured the feeling of heaviness, traced out the lump of the baby's body, talked to it again. I knew that if things went well – or perhaps even if they did not – I would never experience any of this in my life again, that for all of these common, everyday, simple, astonishing things, it was 'the last time', that I would never again be so intimately close to, so physically bound up with this baby, or any other. And I remembered the other mornings, the beginning of labour with Jessica, in excitement and delight; and with Imogen, too early, in distress, in dread.

Now again, I felt curiously detached, as though I were an onlooker. It was partly that I was waiting for other people to take this birth out of our hands – the date, the time of it, and even the way had been decided, and now events would follow, things would be *done* to us, nothing was spontaneous. I wasn't sure how I felt about that, whether I minded. I just wanted it to be safe and smooth and over with.

I was still going under the knife.

Dr Carrie had suggested that I wait until this morning to choose whether I would be awake or asleep for the birth – to see how I felt. The previous night, I really had not known, I swung one way and then the other –

Now I heaved myself out of bed, and stood at the window.

A few people on bicycles coming up the long drive, an ambulance – the hospital day was beginning. And the sun shone.

'Come on,' I thought, 'you know what you want – *courage, mon brave!*' It was what we used to say to one another as students, going into the examination room.

The door swung open, and the Sister appeared. 'Good morning Mrs Wells. Today's the day – I've come to get you ready.'

After that, things moved very quickly as I underwent all the usual, routine preparations. People put their heads around the door to wish me luck – night staff going off duty, day staff coming on; the housekeeper tormenting me with other people's trays of tea and breakfast. I didn't know when I'd get food and drink next. And then it was time for the porter to wheel my bed down – and we were on the way to the lift. For a second, I wondered if this was what it felt like going to one's execution.

In the anaesthetics room, there stood Dr Carrie, green gowned, green capped.

'Well, now – which is it to be?'

'Epidural,' I said, firmly. 'I want to be awake.'

There, it was out. No going back.

'Fine. Good girl.'

The tedious business began of having the epidural anaesthetic inserted. In the course of it, while I felt my lower limbs begin to fizz and tingle and then go numb, Mark arrived, came across to say hello and then went off to get scrubbed. I was shivering, with apprehension? No, apparently that was the anaesthetic.

And then another green-gowned, capped and masked figure appeared.

'Hello.' The blue eyes of my husband over the top of the mask! He had been up early to take Jessica to Louisa's where she would wait for the news – though she had been told not to expect anything until lunchtime. Stanley, like me, had no idea how long the operation was likely to take.

'Action Man Surgeon!' I said. He looked quite pleased with himself, I thought. 'You're definitely coming in to watch then?'

'Certainly I am.'

Brave man. Having things done to me was one thing – and

my stomach was full of butterflies as well as the baby – but I thought that watching it done to someone else would be quite another. But he had seen his two other children born, he didn't want to miss this.

And then, Dr Carrie was saying, 'Right, tell Mr Charnock we're ready – and in we go.'

The theatre door opened. I saw bright bright lights. Tiled walls, a sink, more green figures.

Then I remembered what Emily had said. 'There was only one moment when I wanted to run away – just as we went into the theatre and I thought, "Let me out of this!"'

Oh, yes! Oh, yes! But there was no getting out, no going back.

'Are you sure I won't feel anything? Are you *quite* sure it's had time to take effect – are you *quite* sure I'm completely frozen?'

Obstetric anaesthetists must hear that every day, but really it isn't surprising. When you are so near to having someone cut you open with a sharp knife, and you are still wide awake, you *do* want them to be absolutely sure.

'Quite, quite sure. Can you feel this? or this?'

'What?'

'You see?'

'Hello, Susan – remember me?'

Another pair of eyes over a mask – then, just for a second, she slipped it down.

'Sue?'

It was Sue Clayton, the midwife who had admitted me the night I had gone in with Imogen, and also had delivered her, the following Sunday.

'I want to see you through,' she said. 'After all that happened last year, I wanted to be able to rejoice with you now.'

Rejoice? Oh, yes – oh, please.

Then Stanley was standing by my head, with Dr Carrie on the other side. They had put a metal bar across in front of me at chest level and draped it with green cloths so that all I could see were the ceiling lights, Stanley's face upside down, and the top of Mark's head. I could see the Registrar and Sue, when they peered at me over the top, but I could hear their voices, quite clearly.

My tummy had been painted with disinfectant, above and below it draped in more cloths.

'How are you?' asked Dr Carrie.

'Fine.'

I was. I didn't know, because I deliberately had not asked, how long it would take from the incision to the moment when the baby was lifted out. Half an hour? I resigned myself to waiting.

Some minutes passed. I felt someone trace a thumbnail lightly across my stomach. I wondered why. Then, subdued voices. Some odd sucking noises, just like at the dentist. Then, the most extraordinary sensation, as though I were a drawer and someone was rummaging in me looking for something.

'Susan, we're nearly there – we're just sucking out the liquor – and here's a baby – I've got my hands around a bottom – well and *truly* upside down.'

So soon? I didn't know that he'd even picked up the knife. And I'd felt nothing.

'In a second, you'll feel me lift the baby out. Here we are – *there!*'

I did – they had found what they were looking for in the drawer and now it was gone, leaving the drawer feeling strangely light and empty. I realised I had not been able to breathe easily for some weeks because of the way the baby had been lying. Now, all at once, and miraculously, I could. I took deep, deep breaths.

'And it's a little lady,' Mark was saying, 'a girl – and she looks absolutely perfect.'

Then the room was full of relief and laughter and everyone saying 'Congratulations!' and in the midst of it all, a cry – that first, amazing cry, of life, and outrage and bewilderment, the sound like no other sound in creation.

Within minutes, her mouth had been sucked out to clear any mucus, the cord was cut, the paediatrician had given her the first rapid check – she scored ten out of ten – and then Sue came around the other side of my screen.

'Here you are – one daughter.'

She settled her carefully in the crook of my arm and stood close, in case she slipped since I was still lying flat.

'Don't let the blanket fall off her head, she needs to be kept warm.'

I looked down in wonder. She had a lot of very dark hair. Eyes open in a peeping face which was haloed in the white blanket.

'Hello,' I said. 'Hello, little one.' (For this time, we did not yet have a name.)

She was very still, looking, listening intently, wondering. My perfect daughter. And this time, love flowed out of me immediately, overwhelming, passionate love and relief. I looked up at Stanley and saw it on his face, too. Love – love and triumph.

We had made it.

There is not, really, a great deal to say about all the rest and, in any case, it is a blur, a blur of things being done to me, voices, Stanley's tears, being tidied up and wheeled out of the theatre and away down the familiar corridors into Observation Area. And as we went, the sun came slanting through the windows straight into my face, and in front of me went Sue wheeling the cot. A blur of Stanley telling me about the phone call to Jessica, and later, of Jessica arriving with flowers and apprehension still on her face until she saw, saw for herself, that all was as well as could be.

'Mama, she's beautiful!' I remembered how she had said it the last time, how different things were, but how she had meant it just as fervently.

A blur of flowers arriving and messages, and then a haze of dopeyness and tiredness. I had a pain in my stomach as the day wore on and the anaesthetic wore off, but never once was it a pain I could not cope with, never as agonising as I had been led to fear – and I am not good about pain.

A couple of times I thought I was going to explode and would have preferred to die – the first time I got out of bed, the time I sneezed suddenly and violently – and then there were all the usual minor physical discomforts and indignities. But the whole experience, of birth and its aftermath, of being wide awake to feel and hear my daughter born, and now, of having a clear head to enjoy her, rather than one clouded by the hangover from a general anaesthetic – all of it was good and positive and on the whole, exciting, momentous, and enjoyable. I would recommend it to anyone.

The rest of my stay in hospital is a blur, too, as the days merged into one another. The room filled up with flowers, every day the delivery van brought in more, they overflowed into the corridor; there were presents and cards and visitors, nurses from the Special Care Nursery who popped in to share the joy, old friends from radiography and physiotherapy, even nurses who had left the hospital and were calling back to see old friends among the staff, came to my door.

'We've heard! We've just heard the news!'

And through it all, my baby daughter lay sleeping peacefully. She was the sleepiest of the three – her hair dark upon the sheet, her mouth the exact shape of her elder sister's and when I sat up with her snuffling and suckling at my breast, I could not, truly, believe in her.

'You must have felt *so* full of joy,' someone said.

Yes, but then again, no, not joy, apart from one piercing moment of it at the second of her birth. Joy came later, crept upon me gradually; what I felt at first was simply relief. It was all right, she was and so was I, nothing had gone wrong, she was here, safely born, sound and whole and perfect. We had made it.

At the moment immediately after the birth, I had been flooded with relief, the relief that absolutely every woman who has just given birth wants to feel at being told that all is well. Because whether she is at particular risk or not, at the back of her mind throughout pregnancy is always that question – will my baby be all right? Will it be in some way flawed, damaged, handicapped?

What you want to hear first is the sex of the child, but immediately after that, you need to be told that it is all right. And I had been very anxious about it, of course I had, however rationally and calmly I had accepted the risks. Only the previous week I had talked to Mark about facing the possibility that the child could be born with a handicap. But she was not. She was 'a little lady and absolutely perfect'.

I had done it – shown them – proved myself – all of that. Relief and love – oh certainly love – and pleasure at seeing Jessica's delight and Stanley's tenderness with his new daughter. And it was all such fun, too, we were like Royalty, receiving all those flowers and gifts and friends and good wishes, seeing everyone else's delight. The whole week was *fun*.

And in the middle of it all, we chose her names – Clemency Isabella Grace – and sent cards, and announced her in the papers, and took photographs – all the usual, everyday, routine and uniquely exciting business of having a new-born baby.

I was in no hurry to go home. I wanted to feel fully fit, but more than that, I wanted to linger in this happy time that I knew would not come back, and to bask in all the love and relief and happiness. I don't think anyone can ever have had such a good time in a hospital!

But we had to go in the end, of course, and the last day and night were like all last days, at school, at college, in a particular house, at home, before marriage; a mixture of sadness, regret, and a sense of the ending of things, merged with looking forward to the new life to come.

I've never found anyone who has fully understood my attachment to the maternity hospital, the way I felt – still feel – about it as a place in which I belonged, and where I was, eventually, so very happy. When I return now, perhaps to visit a friend with a new baby, or to see to some business about the trust fund, I feel at home the moment I walk in the doors; the smell of the entrance brings a thousand memories swirling around me. When I see it across the hill, even the lights of it in winter or at night as I drive by, it comforts me, makes me long to rush there, go in, belong again. For I do not belong now, I never shall belong properly again, I am a visitor, an outsider. It feels like a bereavement.

So that the morning I left, with Stanley carrying my bag, and Jessica bobbing along in front and the nurse carrying Clemency, I was near to tears, confused because although I knew we could not stay for ever and although I wanted to be home – yet I did not, *did* not, want to leave.

We said all our goodbyes, waved, and waved. The car turned down the drive. I could not bear to look back.

But the moment I stepped out into the lane beside our cottage, and smelled the sweet fresh smell of the country air after a shower of rain, the moist earth and the damp leaves, it was all right. I knew I was where I should be. I stood for a moment at the top of the seven stone steps that lead down into the garden, looking out over the sloping meadows, to Otmoor below. Tinker the dog came up, wagging his tail, making little yelps of greeting, and then the cats, weaving around my legs.

'Look, look!' called Jessica and pointed, and I saw that in the little pond, they had installed a fountain that rose up just far enough, and cascaded gently over itself and down into the water, a pretty thing, and the soft sound filled the garden.

'It's a welcome home present.'

Home, home, yes. I carried Clemency into the house, and upstairs. Everything looked the way it always does when you return from being away, slightly strange, very slightly different from how you thought it was, but at the same time, safe, right, totally familiar.

I laid Clemency down in the white wicker cradle and, just for a second, I thought, 'But you shouldn't be there – it wasn't bought for you.'

She was asleep, still, beautiful. I touched her cheek with my finger, and she stirred slightly, like a leaf in a faint breeze, then settled back again.

No, it was all right. She belonged here, my third child, not a replacement, not a consolation or a substitute, not a way of forgetting. Just herself, complete. Another person, taking her place.

'We're home,' I said.

Part V

Into Perspective

Chapter 19

Eighteen months after Clemency was born, when I was beginning to feel far enough away from that whole period of my life during which I was trying to have another baby, I was asked to write an article about it, for *Good Housekeeping*, a magazine for which I had worked as a book reviewer for the previous six years, and to which I feel an especial loyalty and closeness.

At first I was unsure, but from the comments I had received from a few other women who had had various traumas and tragedies over pregnancy and childbirth, I felt that perhaps it might fulfil a real need. 'You should write about it,' was the gist of what they said. 'There isn't anything much for women in that situation, apart from the medical books.'

Because of that, and because I wanted to put a shape on it all, for my own benefit, and to say some of the many things that were in both my heart and my head, I did write. The piece was called *Another Beginning*, and it told, in brief, the story of this book.

When it appeared, I was *overwhelmed* by a deluge of letters; I had never expected or imagined such a response. They were heart-rending letters in which woman after woman poured out her own story and, in doing so, her own feelings which had in many cases been pent-up for years; they were stories of miscarriages, infertility, stillbirth, premature birth, and death, and cot-deaths; they were stories of frustration, despair, pain, humiliation, loss of hope, stories of medical negligence and insensitivity, stories of human courage and endurance and stoicism; there were, thankfully, some stories with happy endings. They were cries for help, cries of despair, cries to say 'Now I know you've done it, tell me I can go on and do it too.'

Through the letters, I learned so much I had only previously glimpsed and guessed at, about women in their role as child-bearers. I made friends, I wrote letters of encouragement and shared my own experiences with them and, in some cases, I have continued to hear from those women – and many of their stories have had happy endings, too.

Sometimes, it was as though I were reading a re-run of my own story. One woman had a son at the age of thirty-five, waited five years to conceive again, miscarried, waited again, but all this time (and here her story differed from mine), received no moral support or words of comfort from anyone in the medical profession. 'No one even said they were sorry when I miscarried, just that it was a very common event. True, but not comforting.'

Another lost a baby in utero at 16 weeks when her first son was three, then miscarried twice more. 'All that time to become pregnant,' she said, 'all that – just to lose them.'

Both these women went on to have babies successfully. Others were not so lucky. I had sad letters telling of a succession of miscarriages and fading hopes, as well as grieving ones for babies who had been premature and who died after a few days of life.

There were also astonishing letters of determination and courage in the face of united opposition from doctors and family. One woman, having had a healthy daughter, was 18 weeks pregnant with her second child when the membranes ruptured and she was admitted to hospital, classified as an 'inevitable abortion'. Against the doctors' advice and predictions, she resisted all attempts to have the pregnancy terminated, in spite of several episodes of serious bleeding. But because scans always showed a heartbeat, she was determined to save her child and opted to stay in bed for the rest of her pregnancy. In spite of several bouts of contractions as the weeks progressed, she finally made it to 32 weeks, when her small but fit and healthy second daughter was born.

It's extraordinary how many women have problems after having given birth once without any trouble at all. One of the saddest letters came from a mother who had a fine boy, now aged five, but who then suffered a cot-death, the death at two days of a very premature baby, and three early miscarriages.

Experiences like that set my own into perspective.

When one of the women who contacted me suggested I wrote a whole book, going into much more detail than was possible in the article, I hesitated again for a long time, not least because a couple of people I knew expressed themselves very vehemently on the subject when I raised it to test their reactions.

'I don't think you should write it – I don't think you should even have written the article. I think it's wrong to expose your intimate self in that way. And those stories are always sentimental, it would be a self-indulgence. There are far too many of those soul-baring, personal books – there isn't enough reticence.'

Was all that true? I agonised for a long time before deciding I must write the book.

In a way it has been, if not self-indulgent exactly, certainly done for *myself*. I needed to make sense of everything that had happened, to sift through a great, messy, amorphous mass of experience, to try and make a pattern out of it, to pull it together, as a way of learning from and understanding feelings, happenings, thoughts, consequences.

It has been an interesting voyage of discovery, a painful, cathartic, revelatory thing for me to have gone through all over again, of great personal value. I do not feel ashamed of declaring that.

When I asked Stanley how he would feel about having our experiences so publicly exposed to view, he said, 'But you *must* write it – people need it.'

Yes. In the end, that has been my best justification; the book has been for all those women who wrote to me, and for the many, many who did not but who might have done, simply to say, 'I was there. This happened to me, this is how it was and how I felt.' So that in this book, they may find something which echoes their own feelings and experiences, and makes them realise they haven't been alone.

In the end, I hope the message is a positive one. I had my third child. She is there, three now, swinging on her swing in the garden, sturdy, dark-haired, dark-eyed, funny, naughty, stubborn, loved and loving; the usual, normal, happy mixture that is any child, any human being.

'But should you have gone on with it? Can you look at her and recall the cost and say it was truly worth it? That you did right?'

Ah, how can I say? How can I possibly say? My youngest daughter, like my eldest daughter, like any loved and wanted child, was, is, worth anything and everything, is more precious than rubies. There is no way you can make up a balance sheet, weigh this against that on some scale.

For my own part, I learned a great deal about myself, and the experience was more than worthwhile. I learned about the strengths of my own feminine and female needs, about the passionate desire to bear a child and how it can overcome any obstacles and dominate your life and every waking thought, and take over your reason. It is a force for which I now have the utmost respect.

I learned that I cared passionately about the right to life, and the wrong, so far as I was concerned, of doing anything to harm or take away the unborn child.

I learned about the strength of my love for my husband and his for me, the underlying sureness and solidity of our marriage, for it endured a great deal and was strengthened even further by what happened. I learned about Jessica's depths of tenderness and reserves of strength, as well as her vulnerability. And about the love of friends and the value of friendship and the solidarity amongst women.

I learned more about grief and loss and death. I learned that I had inner resources to draw on and a basic toughness and physical health.

I would have no regrets.

Were it not for Imogen.

A year or so ago, after one of the multiple births in this country which make the headlines for a while, I overheard two women discussing them in the street.

'But they're not babies at all, are they?' one said. 'They're like little rats. You can't call them people at that age, can you, they're not *human beings*. They shouldn't try to keep them alive.'

I wanted to turn on her and cry out in anger and grief and

protectiveness, 'Of *course* they are babies, of *course* you must call them human beings. How can you possibly know? You can't ever have had one; if you had, you wouldn't say that.'

I thought of Imogen, only 25 weeks old, 630 grams. A rat? No, a loved and wanted baby, a child, a human being, unique, my daughter. Any mother of a premature baby would say the same. When it's born, when you see it, touch it, you learn at that moment if you did not learn before, a profound reverence and respect for human life, and the precious individuality of every child.

But while I have been writing this book, there have been headlines, reports from a conference on medical ethics. Professor Alexander Campbell, head of the Department of Child Health at the University of Aberdeen, said:

'There must be limits to intensive care, if it is not to become a new and potentially cruel form of child abuse. The decision that an infant would be better off dead is an awesome one but one that sometimes must be taken.'

In many cases, he said, there were high risks of serious brain damage, if premature babies survived. 'In my view, 750 grams' weight is a flexible level below which medical intervention should not be continued.'

Babies would, of course, be given water, so as not to die dehydrated, and in some cases, food – and otherwise kept warm and loved, be held by the parents. But strenuous efforts to ventilate, treat, resuscitate at all costs, would not be made.

Clearly there are some cases where there is, or should be, little argument. If Imogen had been born with a severe handicap, or if she had been badly damaged at birth, if she had been any younger, or weighed 100 grams or so less, if the first scans had revealed extensive and irreversible brain damage, then probably we would have agreed that there should be no rigorous, aggressive attempts to keep her alive. We were in the hands of the experts, the paediatricians, if they had advised us, at the hour of her birth, that she had no chance of life, that they could do nothing for her, we would have accepted it, however much it would have grieved us, and we would have hoped simply that she would be made as comfortable as possible and would die peacefully and painlessly.

But that was not so. Imogen was, I think, a genuine borderline case by today's definitions, though her birth weight was below Professor Campbell's 'flexible level' of 750 grams. If I read him aright, then if the clinical decision had been his, he would not have tried to keep her alive.

Was it right that the doctors at the John Radcliffe did? Oh, how to answer that? It is always easy to talk with hindsight. Imogen suffered, of that I have no doubt, suffered pain and distress – through no one's fault but simply by the nature of her physical condition and the way it progressed. During the first week or so, she was probably as comfortable as she could be, and doing comparatively well – but after that –

The hardest thing to bear was watching that suffering, and worst of all, feeling, instinctively, that she was lost, bewildered, as well as in pain, that she merely suffered this strange incubator, these bright lights, noises, probing instruments, assaults on her tiny body, a succession of strange hands and voices, as an animal might suffer, not knowing why, not knowing any different, not understanding. But there was a contrast. She had known the life inside the womb, the warmth, closeness, safety, intimacy with her mother's body. And she knew me when I held her, of that I have no doubt, because I had objective proof; she felt right, at home in my arms, safe.

And then, I was gone again.

Trying to look upon it now, I believe that it was wrong, that Imogen should not have been ventilated at birth, that she was on the wrong side of that borderline, that she should have been given to me to hold, and then nursed tenderly but non-invasively until she died.

Ah – yes. That is hindsight speaking, that is the voice of the one detached by time.

But supposing Imogen had made it? She almost did, at one point, she was doing so well. We might have been lucky. A few days before she was born, another baby arrived, at 24 weeks' gestation, and weighing 570 grams (60 grams and 1 week less than Imogen); she was nursed in the Intensive Care Nursery of a large London hospital and she survived. She is now a fine, healthy four-year-old. That might have been Imogen. How could we have told?

Yet Imogen might have grown up with some handicap, trace-able to her early weeks, which might have come to light much later: she might have been scarred to the depths of her being by all the frightening and painful events of her weeks in intensive care, and emerged a nervous, disturbed, unhappy child, an adult with deep, psychological wounds that would never have healed. Who knows, who knows?

I only know that at the time, I wanted her to live, and could not have told the medical team to allow her to die at any point once the struggle for her life had begun. But if the decision had not been ours but theirs and been taken at the very start, I think I could have borne it more easily than I bore what did happen to her. And she, oh, she would have borne it a lot more easily.

That may sound like blame *but I blame no one*. I had and have nothing but respect for the medical team who cared for her. We supported their decision fully at the time and I do not withdraw that support now. I am simply coming down on one side rather than another because of what I have since learned, how my thoughts and feelings have developed and crystallised. But most of all because, in writing this book, in going over Imogen's birth and brief life and her death, re-treading every step, I have gained a new insight, a fresh perspective, seen from a distance.

But at the time, we were close, too close.

A friend who had herself lost a baby son many years before, wrote to me after Imogen's death.

'You will never ever forget her or stop loving her,' she said. 'You will think of her every single day without fail, for the rest of your life. Take comfort from that.'

I have. I do.

Postscript

Chapter 20

A breeze blew up suddenly, riffling the leaves of the apple tree again. It felt chill. There would be a mist later tonight, it would come creeping stealthily up from Otmoor, to hang about the edges of the garden until dawn.

In her crib, sensing perhaps the change in the air, the baby stirred, whimpered. I stood up, and looked down at her.

Already she was changing, opening out from the sleeping cocoon of early infancy, waking to the world. Soon she would smile, then laugh, roll, struggle to sit up, soon this tiny-baby stage would be over.

I would miss her – miss the *physicalness* of an infant, just as I had missed being pregnant. Still do. Already, there was a gap in my life and it was widening every day, distancing me from those years of child-bearing. I minded, I was so conscious of the preciousness of the time that was passing, the time now, now, in this autumn garden, that would not come again, I could feel it slipping through my fingers, even as I lived in it, tried to hold onto it.

Yet here we were, we had arrived, she and I.

'The journey, not the arrival matters.'

But both mattered to me, on that journey I had gone to the depths and the heights of grief and love.

Looking at Clemency, I thought of those other babies of mine who had scarcely been, tiny flickers of life like candles that die out almost as soon as they are lit. But they had *been* lit, they were lives, and sometimes, when lighting a candle, I remember them, and wonder: Who were you? Who would you have become?

And Imogen. Oh, I remembered Imogen, I looked round for her in the garden, for she was always there, somewhere just out of reach, out of sight, always with me. She was who she was, entirely herself, for that brief time, though who knows what she, too, would have become? In her, I saw perfect, holy innocence.

And now, Clemency. With her, the story was all over, and just beginning.

I lifted her up out of the white crib and she opened her eyes and looked at me thoughtfully before sinking back into those close, secret realms of sleep.

The dog Tinker, sensing that the day was at an end, trotted on ahead of us across the garden, towards the house.

I followed him, and went inside, and closed the door.